Good Ole Boys
SHOOTING
DECOYS

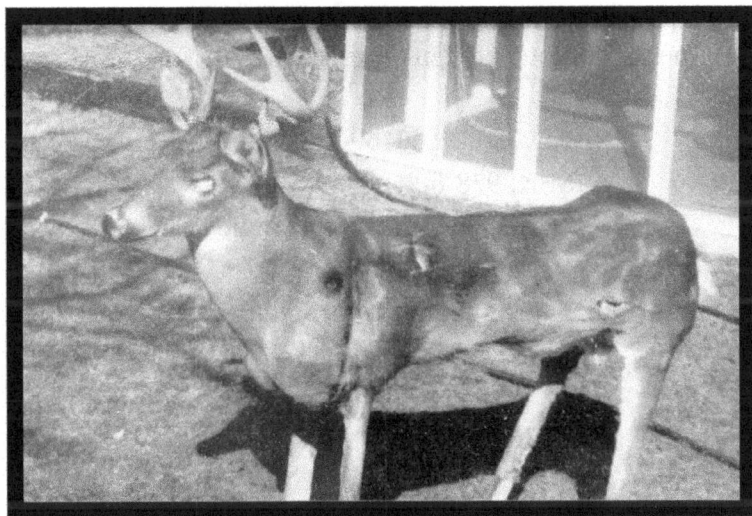

Joel D. Glover

Good Ole Boys Shooting Decoys

Copyright © 2021 Joel D. Glover

ISBN: 978-0-9600469-4-2 (Paperback)
ISBN: 978-0-9600469-5-9 (ePub)
Also available for Kindle

Book design and layout: Lighthouse24

Dedication

Believe me when I tell you I have encountered many good ole boys during my career. Some of them truly were good ole boys and some were really bad boys. The development of the wildlife decoy provided a great way to differentiate between the two. Sure, there were some basically good folks who made a bad quick decision. However, the decoy standing in the field often revealed folks' true intentions.

One of my mentors, Conservation Enforcement Officer (CEO) Byron Smith was the creator of the decoy in Alabama. He would eventually establish Conservation Decoy Company and provide wildlife decoys to officers in almost every state in the country.

As you will read in this book several times, one of the results of using the deer decoy that many people did not comprehend was the untold number of animals it saved. Just knowing that a deer or turkey might be a fake kept many folks from pulling the trigger on a live animal.

Law-abiding sportsmen across the country owe CEO Byron Smith a debt of gratitude. I owe him more than that. He instilled in me the desire to go the extra mile in making a case and provided volumes of valuable advice through the years. I dedicate this book to him.

As always, I thank my wife for being such a rock for me. Thank you, my sweet angel baby.

Contents

Introduction

IMAGINE YOU'VE BEEN LOOKING FOR A DEER all season long with no luck. Then, all of a sudden, you spot a buck standing on the back side of a field along the wood line. You roll on past and reach for your rifle. You turn around and ease back down the road. The deer is still there and you stop in the road and stick your rifle out the window. The deer turns and looks at you and you know he's about to run. You settle the crosshairs on his neck and squeeze the trigger. You can't believe you missed him but you must have since he's still standing there looking at you. You bolt another round into the chamber and try to line up another shot and then it dawns on you. Deer don't just stand around after being shot at. You look in your mirror and see blue lights coming up fast and you realize you have just taken a ride on the game warden's roller coaster.

Seeing the buck was what you had hoped for. The fact that it stood there long enough for you to get a good shot seemed too good to be true. And now you know it was. Realizing you have just shot the game warden's decoy has left you so low a snake could crawl under you while wearing a hat! I helped a lot of folks take that ride. The reactions were many and varied. Many totally denied it even though we had just watched them do it. Others simply stepped out and raised their hands, knowing they had messed up.

I watched this scenario and others like it play out many times during my career. The deer decoy was probably the greatest advancement in wildlife law enforcement in our lifetime. It was and continues to be a tremendous tool. Working alongside the game warden that created wildlife decoys was a blessing. Not only did he teach me how to utilize the decoy, he also inspired me to put in the extra effort needed to make cases that would stand up to scrutiny. The deer decoy became a staple for game wardens in Alabama and across the country.

Although they were sometimes humorous, violations involving the deer decoy presented plenty of danger. While we definitely dealt with some bad people, several who would just as soon shoot you as look at you, most of the folks were just good ole boys. While some folks figured out the deer wasn't real and did not shoot at it, others would empty their gun and try to reload. I had as many as three shooters standing in the road at one time trying to shoot the stuffed wonder. The decoy worked well both day and night. The first few decoys could not hold up to the barrage of gunfire directed at them. I remember one of our first ones had forty-three holes in it when we had to replace it. Initially, shooters did not hesitate to fire at the decoy. Today, most violators think twice before shooting. This hesitation is probably the greatest asset of the decoy. From the beginning and still today I have folks stop me and tell me they recently saw my deer decoy. Over 95 percent of the time we haven't used the deer where they say they saw it. Obviously, they saw a live deer, and because of the existence of the deer decoy those deer are still alive. There is no way to know how many deer were saved by the advent of the decoy. It was my good fortune to be there and see it happen.

Disclaimer

THE STORIES IN THIS BOOK ARE TRUE to the best of my knowledge and recollection. Many names have been changed. Some of the things you will read you may find hard to believe. I found a lot of them hard to believe and I was there! Everybody makes mistakes and some bad choices. It is not my intention to embarrass or malign anyone. If one of the fictitious names I selected matches yours, I apologize. You could always have your name changed if it proves to be a problem.

Decoy Guru, Byron Smith

MANY TIMES, I HAVE MENTIONED I was very fortune to begin my career when the deer decoy was still a fairly new tool in the game warden toolbox. Working the decoy was often some of the most exciting times I can remember. I never have tried to add up how many cases the usage of the stuffed deer led to, but suffice it to say it was a tremendous amount. The decoy placed the violator, their quarry, and the officer all at the same place at the same time. When a game warden is tasked with covering literally hundreds of square miles, the decoy levels the playing a field, at least a little bit.

When the decoy first came on the scene in the early 1980s, it was wildly effective. People who had hunted illegally on a regular basis had no qualms shooting a deer standing in a field and/or alongside the road both day and night. During the early years and still today, many folks do not suspect the deer they illegally shoot at isn't real but is in fact a fake the game warden has placed there. Once the existence of the decoy became widely known, it significantly changed how violators practiced their criminal craft.

While the use of the decoy prompts several questions, there are two that I have been asked more than others. The most frequent question is "How is the use of the deer decoy not entrapment?" The second is "How can someone be charged with

5

an offense involving a deer when it isn't really a deer?" Those are good questions. Although I am very far from an attorney, I will attempt to explain what I understand about it.

When someone asks how can they be charged with killing a deer when it was in fact a decoy, it is evident they likely do not understand what they are charged with. The charges of hunting from a public road, hunting at night, hunting by the aid of a vehicle, and/or hunting without permission are charges brought in response to "hunting" illegally. They aren't being charged with killing anything. While their intent is normally to kill something, they did not necessarily do so. If someone does actually kill a deer at night, they can be charged with a separate charge of taking deer at night.

Various court cases have defined entrapment as implanting in an innocent person's mind the disposition to commit a crime and then inducing that person to commit the crime so they can be prosecuted. Inducement requires persuasion or coercion. If I were to place my decoy in old man Johnson's field and go down the road to Bubba's hunting club and tell the members I had seen a good buck in old man Johnson's field and a member decided to go and see if he could spot the deer and shoot it, an argument could be made that I entrapped him. If I haven't been by the club, and a member decides to drive down the road and see if he can find a deer to shoot and shoots mine, it's on him. Merely giving a person an opportunity to commit a crime is not entrapment.

Think about how many times you have driven down the road and spotted a deer standing in a field. Did you shoot it? If you are like me, you have seen a lot of deer from the road; however, I have yet to shoot one of them. While several people asked me if the decoy was entrapment or told me they thought it was, I never had anyone attempt to use that as a defense in court.

Today, folks are much more hesitant about shooting a deer from the road than they used to be. Coincidentally, deer decoys have come a long way from the early prototypes. Fortunately, Byron Smith, the creator of the Alabama deer decoy, was assigned to Elmore County, which is immediately south of Coosa County, where I was assigned. Byron was a good mentor and remains a cherished friend. I asked him to share with me the origin of the decoy in Alabama. How can you title a book *Good Ole Boys Shooting Decoys* without talking about decoys?

I'm sure you have heard the saying "Necessity is the mother of invention." That adage is once again proven true in the case of the deer decoy. Game wardens spend untold hours hidden on the side of the road, often in the middle of nowhere, in response to complaints of people shooting deer from the road and on property where they have no authority to do so. Many of the hours expended are fruitless. While you may have vehicles pass by your location, if there are no deer present, your chances of catching a poacher are severely diminished. Being able to have a deer on the scene definitely increases your chances of apprehending someone.

To satisfy this need, Byron decided to create a deer decoy. The prototype was nothing to write home about from a cosmetic point of view. It was a traditional wall mount of a buck bolted to a wooden sawhorse. The body was constructed of chicken wire wrapped around the sawhorse. The wire "body" was stuffed with newspaper and covered with a layer of cardboard. The tail was a white paper towel painted brown on top. The idea was the paper towel would be blown around by any breeze, making it appear more lifelike. For nighttime work, a piece of reflective tape was placed on the eyes of the deer.

Byron and his partner set out on the virgin voyage with the decoy. The site chosen to employ the Rube Goldberg contraption was across from a church in rural Macon County. Just in case you aren't old enough to know who Rube Goldberg is, let me explain. Mr. Goldberg was an award-winning cartoonist best known for drawing cartoons that featured highly complicated contraptions used to complete simple tasks. He gained popularity in the 1920s. To the best of my knowledge, I had never heard of Rube Goldberg until I was sitting in a graduate school class at Mississippi State University with my major professor, Dr. Dale Arner. During his lecture, Dr. Arner referred to a device an early wildlife researcher had used as a Rube Goldberg contraption. I was feverishly taking notes and recorded Mr. Goldberg's name and placed a star by it so I would remember to look it up and see what his invention was. Only later when I looked it up did I learn it was just a way of referring to a thrown-together device. Although I doubt many of my classmates knew who it was either, I was glad I did not raise my hand and ask about it. I digress.

Back to the first decoy deployment. At approximately 4:00 a.m., a vehicle slowed to a stop with their headlights illuminating the makeshift deer. Quickly, a shot split the night. Immediately after the shot, the vehicle moved forward about twenty yards and a second shot shattered the darkness. With the deer still standing, the driver turned his headlights off and took off. Byron was quickly behind the vehicle with his blue light flashing. Fortunately, the driver quickly pulled to the side of the road. Both occupants exited the truck. While this is normally a tense time for an officer, in this instance the intensity was somewhat diminished when Byron realized both of the men were laughing uncontrollably! As he safely approached, the first thing the driver said was, "Now that's a good one." He then said when he saw the confetti fly out, he knew he had been had.

It was evident that the carboard body wasn't going to hold up to shotgun and/or rifle blasts. Therefore, Byron decided to use a deer hide to help hold the deer together, look more realistic, and cut down on the amount of the confetti flying after a shot.

During this time, the procedure for reporting cases was that every Sunday morning, every officer in the district would call his lieutenant on the radio and report the cases he had made during the week. I'm not sure why this was done the way it was; however, it did provide each officer, and everyone else listening to the radio, the opportunity to hear how many or how few cases the officer had made. After one such Sunday, the lieutenant called Byron and told him he needed to meet with him to discuss the number of cases he was reporting. He told him he would like to meet him at the café the next afternoon.

The two met and the supervisor got right to the point. He told the young officer he was reporting two to three times as many cases as his "seasoned" officers, who had been working for a lot longer than he had. He said the high number of cases led him to believe he was doing something that was either illegal, immoral, or unethical and wanted to know which one it was. Byron answered that he did not believe it was any of the above. "Then how are you doing it," was his exasperated response. Byron told him to come out to his truck and he would show him.

Under the plywood bed cover on his pickup was the pitiful looking decoy. He said the lieutenant looked at the ragged deerlike contraption and announced that no one would shoot something that looked like that. Byron responded with, "Well how do you think it got all of those holes in it?" The lieutenant stared at the deer for a minute and then said, "I think you need to make cases the 'normal' way." Byron replied he thought this was much more effective. After a little silence, Byron decided to take a chance and told the supervisor he felt certain he could make a case with the deer before the supervisor could make one the traditional way. The elder officer contemplated it and told him he would take that bet. It was decided the officer who made the first case would be treated to supper by the other officer.

Both officers left the café on the hunt for a game law violator. Byron drove five miles to a soybean field on Macon County Road

2. He positioned the decoy in the field and pulled into a hiding spot across the road from it. He took out his camouflage parachute and covered his truck and then poured a cup of coffee. Before the cup reached his lips, a shot rang out. He quickly slurped down some coffee while removing the truck covering. A second shot sounded. When he pulled out into the road, he was face-to-face with three individuals in a pickup truck. The driver had a rifle in hand with the barrel out the window and was wearing a confused look on his face. The passenger made eye contact with the officer and mouthed the words "Oh #&!%." Byron got the trio out of the truck and the driver looked at the deer and then looked at the officer and said, "That just ain't right."

During this time, we were using a radio system that used repeaters set up across the state. This meant that depending on the repeater you hit, you could be heard for a long way. Knowing this, officers had developed a system of letting each other know when they had had some success. The clandestine code was fairly simple. When an officer made a significant arrest, such as a road hunter or night hunter, they would pick up the radio microphone and say, "Bingo." Byron keyed the mic and said, "Bingo." The lieutenant immediately keyed his mic and responded, "No way."

Byron returned to his hiding spot and poured another cup of coffee. Ten minutes later, another vehicle rolled to a stop and put another new hole in the ragged decoy. Byron pulled out and apprehended the two Georgia residents. With the paperwork completed, he returned to his hiding spot, picked up the microphone, and said, "Bingo, Bingo." The lieutenant immediately answered and said for the officer to meet him at the café.

The lieutenant could not believe that within forty-five minutes of them parting, on a Monday afternoon, Byron had made three arrests. He told the officer that this tool was too good for him to keep to himself. He said he would like to show it to another veteran officer and get his opinion on it. He asked if Byron could meet him in Russell County that night. The time and place were set. During this time, officers often worked basically nonstop for days at a time.

A few hours later, Byron traveled to Russell County and met the officers. He showed the ragged decoy to the old veteran, who eyed it for a minute and then said, "Let's put it out and see what happens." "Mac," as the old guy was called, suggested they put it up along the Uchee Road. At 9:00 p.m., they had the deer set up in a field alongside the road. Twenty minutes later the officers heard the telltale sound of mudder tires on the highway. The tires roared, making a *WA-WA-WA* sound coming down the road. As they neared the decoy the sound changed to a *wa-wa-wa* until it stopped. Then the still night was shattered by a rifle blast. When the deer didn't go down, the shooter realized something wasn't right and took off. The lieutenant said he would get him and took off in pursuit. He chased the vehicle out of hearing and was gone for a rather long time. When he returned, he had some interesting news. He announced to the others that the shooters were two young guys they had been trying to catch for at least five years. The officers explained to Byron that the two they apprehended were the sons of two veteran night hunters from Georgia who had a camp in Alabama and hunted more at night than in the daytime. The fact that these seasoned night hunters shot the deer so quickly sold the two officers on how well it worked.

The lieutenant and the Russell County officer said they had to be out early the next morning, so they decided to take it in. Byron told them he thought he would try his luck in another area before heading for home. He moved to a likely looking spot and placed the decoy in a field alongside the road. It wasn't long until he heard a vehicle approaching at a high rate of speed. I can never write a line like that without remembering what my longtime partner, Hershel Patterson, would always say when I would comment that a vehicle was going too fast to be hunting. He would dryly say, "They've got brakes."

Byron said the vehicle flew past the decoy; however, he did notice a rapid deceleration. He said it was only a minute until the vehicle slowly came back toward the deer. The vehicle came to a stop and another hole was quickly added to the Swiss cheese body of the decoy. Byron pulled out of his hiding spot and turned his lights on, which revealed a red Corvette with T-tops and a man standing in the passenger seat with a rifle in his hand. Fortunately, the driver did not try to take off. Byron had the two men to get out of the car. Noticing they were very well dressed, he asked where they had been and they replied they had been to a club in Columbus, Georgia, and were headed back to their camp when they saw the deer. Byron realized he had failed to get the court information for the county, so he took down the men's information and told them he would be in touch with them. He returned home at 3:00 a.m.

Three hours later he was back at work. He later called the lieutenant and told him he had caught two more night hunters after they had parted. He told him he would meet him later in the morning with the information. After checking a couple of baited areas, he met the lieutenant and gave him the violators' information. He noticed the supervisor was staring at the tickets with a look of disbelief on his face. The lieutenant uttered that he could not believe it. Byron reminded him that he had told him the decoy was effective. The lieutenant looked at him and said, "You don't understand." He then asked, "Do you know who this is?" Byron replied, "Nope." The lieutenant told him these were the fathers of the boys they had caught earlier last night. He reiterated they had been trying to catch them for five years! To say the lieutenant was sold on the decoy was an understatement. He told Byron he wanted him to bring the deer to the next district meeting.

Byron said the reaction at the meeting was mixed. Several of the old officers howled with laughter and said no one would shoot such a thing. Some said they didn't think it would be fair to use a fake deer, while others thought it was a great idea and wanted to know how they could get one. This was the beginning of the Alabama decoy revolution. Of course, this meant a set of guidelines would soon come out stating how and where the deer could be used, what size it could be, and several other stipulations.

One of the rules was the deer could not be used on major roadways except in the wee hours of the morning. This made good sense in many areas since you did not want the fake deer causing a traffic problem. It was not unusual for some folks to lock up their brakes upon seeing the decoy standing in a field. The rules stated the decoy could only be used from midnight to 5:00 a.m. on what was considered major roads. This was important since many of these roads received a lot of night hunting pressure in many areas.

Bullock County Conservation Enforcement Officer (CEO) Richard Hartzog contacted Byron and told him the night hunters were wearing him out on Highway 82 and asked if he could bring the decoy and see if they couldn't put a dent in the illegal activity. It just so happened the request came just after Byron had added a couple of new features to the now "robotic" deer. He felt sure the addition of a movable head and tail would be a game changer. He was right.

Officer Hartzog, Officer Mike Pollard, and Byron set up on Highway 82 in Bullock County. Byron positioned the deer under some huge oak trees on the Midway Plantation property. To stay within the policy, the deer was set up at 12:30 a.m. None of the three had any idea what was about to occur.

The site was on the Barbour and Bullock County line only a few miles from Barbour Wildlife Management Area (WMA). The Barbour WMA was a favorite hunting spot for hunters from all across Alabama. Back in the day, it was not unusual to have thousands of hunters to attend a hunt on the area. Therefore, the officers surmised they would get a significant amount of traffic as it got closer to daylight. Since the policy dictated the operation would have to end at 5:00 a.m., they hoped they would have traffic before then. That turned out not to be a problem.

With the decoy in place, the officers took their positions. Five minutes later, the first vehicle approached their location. Although the car was moving at a pretty good pace, which made it unlikely they were hunting, Byron activated the remote control, which turned the deer's head. The driver never touched the brake; however, the passenger hung out the window and shot the deer. The chase vehicle ran the car down and wrote the two violators citations. The officer had just got back in his hiding spot when the next vehicle stopped and shot the manikin. The vehicle was stopped and the two occupants cited. This exact scenario repeated itself another eleven times!

The violators were coming so quickly the officers could not keep up with the volume. As a matter of fact, at one point CEO Pollard had a vehicle stopped (blue light flashing) three hundred yards from the decoy when another poacher stopped and shot the deer! By 4:30 a.m., twenty-six people had been charged with hunting at night. It was a night which, to the best of Byron's knowledge, was never duplicated.

The next morning, Byron counted an amazing fifty-five holes in the decoy! While shots from rifles normally pierced neat holes in the decoy, shotguns loaded with slugs and buckshot would quickly destroy the deer. A single load of 00 buckshot holds nine pellets. While that would wreak havoc on the mounted deer, it usually wasn't as bad as a hit from a slug. When a slug hit the mounted deer, it usually created a hole you could easily see through. Repairs were often necessary after a good night of using the decoy.

As you might imagine, it did not take very long for the news of this ticket writing marathon to get out. The CEO in Barbour County called Byron and told him he would like to use the deer in his county on the night before the next WMA hunt. The WMA hunts were normally two weeks apart, so Byron had time to make necessary repairs to the beleaguered decoy.

The officer had identified a good spot in a peanut field on Spring Hill Road to deploy the secret weapon. Byron met the officer and they set the deer up at 11:00 p.m. It wasn't long before the action started. It was another incredible night. Amazingly, eleven out of twelve vehicles that passed the decoy shot it! Only the number nine vehicle did not shoot. He passed the deer and, like many, went down the road about three hundred yards and turned around presumably to come back and shoot it. As he was turning around, vehicle number ten stopped and shot the deer. The CEO pulled out and stopped the shooter. Seeing the stop, the driver of number nine decided to again turn around and go on his way. The CEO wrote up the pair of guys in number ten and then returned to his hiding spot. Two more vehicles passed and each one stopped and shot. When the officer returned from writing up number twelve, Byron noticed he appeared extremely distraught. So much so the man literally threw up.

After he regained his composure, he explained to Byron he had thought he had been a good game warden and had the violations in his county under control. He said the decoy had proven he was wrong and it literally made him sick. They loaded up and headed for home.

As you might imagine the popularity of the decoy among officers grew exponentially. This spurred Byron to continue to improve on the product. He quickly came a long way from a mounted head with a cardboard body. It wasn't long until Conservation Decoy Company was established. During the next few years, the company sent decoys to almost every state in the country. The product was not limited to deer. The needs were different across the country. Elk, mule deer, antelope, black-tailed deer, turkey, pheasants, red-tailed hawk, coyotes, bears, groundhogs, and more. I could continue to write stories about the use of the decoy and there are many more stories in this book. However, I would like to tell you about an aspect of the decoy that many folks never think about. Obviously, the decoy was and continues to be a tremendous tool for game wardens to employ. While decoys are great tools for apprehending violators, I'm certain many folks don't realize the total impact of the device.

Early on and until this day I have folks stop me and tell me they recently saw my decoy. They often go on to tell me the deer didn't look all that real and they are surprised anyone would shoot at it. If they don't volunteer the info, I will ask where they saw it. They normally are always willing to answer questions, seeing how they think they have in effect caught me trying to catch them. However, the truth is that 95 percent of the time we have not used the deer where they say they spotted it. Therefore, they have in fact observed a live deer that they did not shoot because they thought it was a decoy. I'm just guessing that you can multiply that number by thousands for the ones who hesitated to shoot a deer thinking it might be a decoy and then had the deer run away. Most folks aren't as quick to admit that, although I feel certain that is often the case.

Think about it. In one night, 92 percent of the vehicles that passed the deer shot it! It would have been 100 percent if there had been a couple of minutes between two of the vehicles. I understand that was a different time and many things have changed since then. However, that statistic gives you an idea what was happening at the time. There is no doubt the development of the decoy shined a three-million-candlepower spotlight on what was taking place.

While I received many complaints of night hunting and shooting from the road during the past season, it is a very small fraction of what it used to be. I'm sure this is due to several things. When I started my career thirty-five years ago, the fine for a first offense of hunting at night was $250 plus the $65 court costs. Today, the minimum fine for a first offense is $2,000 and the court costs are $350! I can't help but believe that what the decoy revealed played a major role in that change.

Is the decoy still effective? Yes. As I mentioned earlier, I had people during the past deer season tell me they had spotted the stuffed wonder. Is the decoy still effective? You could ask the seventy-six-year-old man who shot my decoy in the daytime, from the public road, in an area where he did not have a permit and during the closed season. Yes, seventy-six years old. I have a lot of folks who think it's just "kids" who shoot from the road and at night. Believe me when I tell you it runs the gamut.

As I interviewed Byron for this story, I continually was remembering how he had served as a mentor to me and had assisted me with decoy repair and advice even during the past season. Even though he has been retired for twenty-one years, listening to the stories puts me right there with him and I love it. While I owe Byron a tremendous amount for his mentorship and friendship, everyone who appreciates wildlife needs to understand the contribution to conservation that he provided. As I mentioned earlier, he shipped decoys to almost every state in the country. Many of these are still in use today. I have four of them.

Few folks can say they changed the landscape of their vocation forever. It's quite an accomplishment. I was blessed to observe it.

I cherish my friendship with Byron and his wife, Trish. I thank him for his contribution to the conservation law enforcement profession, America's, wildlife and my life. I appreciate him allowing me to tell this story and many others and I thank him that he was the driving force that allowed good ole boys to shoot decoys!

Out of Gas and Luck

THESE GUYS WEREN'T THE SHARPEST knives in the drawer. As a matter of fact, they were so dull calling them a knife at all was quite a stretch!

Although many arrests are the result of long hours of work, some fall in your lap. However, you either must be out there or willing to get out there to catch any of them. During my career, I did my best to respond to each call I received. If you didn't respond when called, you soon quit receiving calls. This was often difficult, especially after our department got serious about us not working over forty hours a week. The hours restriction made the job of conservation enforcement officer (CEO) much more difficult. That was especially true for me since I basically worked forty hours on the wildlife management area and the enforcement work was on top of that. Prior to the crackdown, it was not at all uncommon to work sixty to seventy hours or more per week during the deer season. Although this took its toll on officers and families, the multitude of violations demanded it and it did allow the officer to have a much better handle on what was going on.

I don't think I'll ever forget the district meeting in which the captain laid down the law about not working over forty hours a week. This was following the conclusion of a lawsuit brought by

Good Ole Boys SHOOTING DECOYS

the wage and hour board against our department. During the trial, our departmental higher-ups testified they were not aware our officers were working over forty hours per week, while the officers testified to the opposite. The officers won the case; however, they then had the pleasure of having every report scrutinized for the tiniest infraction and many other activities that seemed to hinge on harassment.

None of that is the reason I will remember the meeting where the law was laid down. The reason was our Chambers County CEO. I had the opportunity to work with the officer on a few occasions and found him to be a comical individual. What made this guy so funny to me was you often couldn't tell whether or not his intent was to be funny. At the no-overtime meeting he was in rare form. The captain (who would later become chief) was laying it on thick about how no one was to work over forty hours per week. He didn't care what kind of call you received, he didn't care if you were writing a ticket, he didn't care what you were doing—you had better be home when your allotted hours ran out. The point was made over and over again. Finally, I feel for effect, he said, "Let me be extremely clear: from this day forward you will work forty hours a week!" It was then the officer, who wasn't one to exert himself, leaned over and in a whisper asked, "You mean we're going to have to start working forty hours a week?" It was all I could do not to laugh out loud.

A few years later, I was attending a firearms qualification in Montgomery with the same officer. I realized he was closely adhering to the work week hour limit. We finished shooting at about eleven in the morning and everyone was at their vehicle putting up their accessories when I asked if he wanted to get some lunch. He replied he needed to head home because he had his eight hours in for the day. I commented he could be home in ninety minutes and asked what time he had started that morning.

He replied, "I woke up at 5:00 a.m. and had the job on my mind so I was on the clock!" He was quite the character!

Back to where I started with cases falling in your lap. I was awakened by my ringing phone. A glance at the clock showed 4:30 a.m. While late night calls were common, early morning ones were fairly rare. Answering the phone, I was greeted by the Goodwater Police Department dispatcher. Goodwater was the largest city in Coosa County. With a population of around two thousand people, Goodwater held almost 20 percent of the population of the entire county. They had the only traffic light in the county and even had a train track running through their town. It was by far the closest thing to urban in our humble county. They were also the only town with a police officer on duty all night! I'm telling you they were big time!

The dispatcher told me her officer had located a vehicle with three deer in the back. She had been right to assume three individuals hauling around three deer an hour before daylight would pique my interest. I jotted down the location and told her I would be en route shortly.

During this time of year, I kept my uniform ready to go and I was headed toward the officer's location in less than five minutes. While en route I was monitoring radio traffic between the dispatcher and officer. From what I could discern, there was one subject at the Goodwater Police Department and two at the vehicle. This seemed odd; however, I would be there shortly and get it figured out.

My trip to Goodwater took me through Coosa County Road 40 or, as we often called it, "the deer gauntlet." During my entire career, County Road 40 was littered with run-over deer every winter. As a matter of fact, at one point the sheriff's office chief deputy ordered the deputies not to travel the road after having half of the fleet in the shop due to accidents with deer. Although I was in a hurry, I took it easy through the deer-infested thoroughfare. (As I am reviewing this story, I had a deer run into my truck on County Road 40!)

Pulling in behind the officer's car, I noticed there were two subjects standing at the rear of a small pickup with the Goodwater officer. The officer came back and began to enlighten me as to what had occurred. He stated an individual had walked to the police department and explained he had run out of gas and asked if they could carry some gas back to the vehicle where his two friends were waiting. Not being extremely busy, although he was in the metropolis of the county, the officer was glad to help and carried the gas to the vehicle. Using his well-honed observation skills, he sort of couldn't help but notice the three dead deer piled in the bed of the small pickup. He had decided this was something we probably needed to look into and had asked the dispatcher to give me a call.

I identified myself to the young men and began to examine the deer. All had been shot and were fairly freshly killed. I went to the cab of the truck and retrieved two rifles and a rechargeable LiteBox flashlight. With these items secured in my truck, we headed to the Goodwater Police Department.

The third suspect, the owner of the truck, was standing out front waiting. Boy was he glad to see me! We escorted the trio into the police department and separated them. I ushered the truck owner into the interrogation room, someone's office, read him the Miranda warning, and began questioning him. I did my best to let him know he was caught with no way out and he might as well give me the details. My first question was, "What time did you leave home?" He explained he had left his home in neighboring Clay County around 10 p.m. en route to his sister's home in Tallapoosa County. I asked what time he arrived there and he said he thought it was around midnight. He said they had stayed there for a couple of hours and headed back home when they had run out of gas and he had walked to the police department for assistance. I acknowledged it was an interesting story, but somehow he had left out the part where the three dead deer had ended up in the bed of the truck. I told him we needed to go through his story a little slower and with a little more detail. I suggested we start with when he left home.

He sat silent for about a minute and finally said, "We spotlighted the fields around my house." I asked if he had seen any deer and he replied he had. I asked, "Did you shoot at any of them?" and he replied, "I missed it." I asked if this was in Clay County and he said it was. He stated they went to his sister's house. Leaving there around 1:00 a.m., they spotted some deer in a field and he shot at them and killed one. They loaded it and proceeded down the road, where they saw another deer. He stated he shot it but when they went to retrieve it, he realized the bullet had passed through the first deer, a big doe, and had also killed a small doe. He made sure I understood he did not intend to kill the small deer. I asked if these deer were killed in Tallapoosa County and he said they were. With his statement complete, I moved on to the passenger-side passenger and took his statement. It was basically the same, including the part about the little deer being killed unintentionally.

I moved to the third occupant of the truck. Seeing how this subject had been sitting in the middle of the front seat, did not possess a firearm, and had not shined the spotlight, it was important I get a statement indicating he was a willing and active participant in the violations. I asked him the same questions as the others and got basically the same story. I asked what his role in the activity was and he plainly stated he had come to help drag the deer to the truck. I asked why he had decided to come along only to do the real work. He hesitated and said, "Well, I love deer

23

meat and I just had a craving and had to try to get some." I thought, Yeah, those cravings will get you in trouble every time.

With all the info I needed to obtain warrants, I told the trio they were free to go. I followed them out and got the vehicle identification number from their truck. I explained I would need that in the event we decided to confiscate the truck. This visibly shook the driver. He asked about his gun and light and I advised him I would be keeping the gun and light as evidence. He quickly stated, "You can't keep that light, it belongs to my dad." I again told him I would be holding it, at least until court. He again said I couldn't keep the light because it actually belonged to Tyson Foods, a local chicken processing plant. I told him it may have used to belong to Tyson but if I didn't miss my guess it would soon belong to the State of Alabama.

Although they admitted hunting in Clay County initially, I set the cases for court in Tallapoosa County, where the deer were actually killed. Having never before appeared in court in the neighboring county and not being familiar with the district attorney, I prepared the case to the fullest. I must admit this was something I did not always have to do in my home court since our judge was well versed on conservation cases. Prior to the court date, I received an interesting phone call from one of the defendants in the case. He explained to me he had been talking with the other defendants and they wanted to know if I thought it would be okay if they tried to get a job before their court date. Although I wasn't exactly sure why they were calling me with this question, I told them I thought it would be a good idea.

The court date arrived and I lugged the two rifles and spotlight into the courtroom. There I met an assistant district attorney (ADA) from Macon County who said he would be handling the cases. I gave him the case notes and he stated he would take it from there.

Prior to the start of court, the ADA called the defendants to the front of the courtroom. Once there he asked to see their hunting licenses, which two of them had. He took the license and, while looking at them, he asked the defendants if they had some nice rifles. They responded they did, to which he replied, "You did have some rifles and licenses but now the State of Alabama owns all of that and you won't be seeing them again." He went on to tell them their hunting privileges would be revoked for three years. I admit this was a much different posture than I was used to. My ADA rarely even spoke with me prior to court and never told the defendants they would surely be convicted.

Obviously, the ADA had set the tone for the cases and the trio pled guilty. The fellows avoided jail time; however, they received about $1,600 in fines and court costs in addition to losing their rifles and licenses. You often wonder whether the conviction and the fines and court costs really get the offenders' attention. Time will tell whether or not they learned their lesson. However, I would bet if they do decide to go night hunting again, they will have a full tank of gas!

Judges

DURING MY CAREER, I was very fortunate to work with some judges who understood the seriousness of the violation of wildlife laws. Any officer learns very quickly that if your judge is weak you will have a hard way to go. While our job was to apprehend violators and the judges' job was to determine their guilt or innocence, it is beyond disheartening to work for weeks to catch a serious violator only to have a judge give them a slap on the wrist or, worse yet, let them go altogether.

The Alabama legislature has sent a strong message to game law violators. I dare say our fines for serious violations are likely as substantial as anywhere in the country. I am often surprised at some of the fines I hear on some of the game warden television programs. Someone who illegally hunts at night in Alabama faces a minimum fine of $2,000, significant court costs, and a three-year suspension of their hunting privileges. That's substantial; however, only if a judge finds them guilty and adheres to the guidelines.

As I stated, I was blessed to work with conservation-minded judges; however, this wasn't always the case. Some of these situations were aggravating, others disgusting, and some outright unbelievable. The very worst judge I had ever had the misfortune to bring a case before was the former district court judge in the north end of Talladega County. This guy was definitely a piece of work.

On a cold winter night, I was working with Conservation Enforcement Officer (CEO) Jerry Fincher attempting to catch some outlaws night hunting for deer in the south part of Talladega County. We had just settled in for what we thought might be a long vigil when the radio crackled to life with the voice of Jerry's partner CEO Greg Gilliland. Greg was still a novice as a game warden and had just started working by himself. Hearing the tension in his voice, we knew we needed to head toward his location. Greg explained he had just apprehended five night hunters and needed some assistance. We advised we were on the way, but it would be a while.

Talladega County is a large county encompassing 760 square miles and is home to over eighty thousand residents. The county was ceded by the Creek Indians in 1832. *Talladega* means "border town" in the Creek language. It was the border between the lands of the Creek, Cherokee, and Chickasaw tribes. Today the county has five cities, and around twenty towns and communities. The county is bordered on the west by the Coosa River and contains a large segment of the Talladega National Forest and a portion of the Hollins Wildlife Management Area. White-tailed deer and wild turkey are plentiful, as is small game, and fishing opportunities abound throughout the county. They also have some kind of stock car race there from time to time! I think they call it the Talladega 500. You may have heard of it.

Like in every county, it was difficult to decide which area to work, seeing how night hunting of deer was prevalent everywhere. This night Jerry and I were along the county line in the southwest corner of the county near the Fayetteville community, and Greg was near the city of Lincoln in the far northeast part of the county. The road distance between us was nearly fifty miles, and to compound things, a dense fog was rolling in.

We were traveling as fast as we safely could, and yet we felt like we were crawling. We kept in radio contact as we strained to even see the road at times. Finally, almost an hour after receiving his call for assistance, we arrived at his location.

It was an interesting scene. There was one guy lying in the road handcuffed and four others sitting in the road beside him. We asked Greg to tell us what happened and he explained that as he observed, the driver of the vehicle had manipulated his SUV in a manner to allow his headlights to illuminate a field on the side of the road. The driver had then backed up and continued down the road in the direction he was previously going.

This was a common technique used by folks hunting deer at night. Using the headlights of their vehicle to spot deer provided a few tactical advantages over the use of a spotlight. Since every vehicle utilized headlights at night, it did not draw the attention of a spotlight. In addition, a spotlight could be seen for miles on a clear night. Furthermore, a driver using their headlights could turn into a field, illuminating it, and back out and go back in the direction from which they had come and if stopped they could claim they were merely turning around and not intentionally shining the field. While this defense normally did not work, it could be viewed as a legitimate excuse for lighting up a field. However, when they turned in and shined a field and then continued in the direction they were headed, they lost this "defense" since it isn't a normal part of driving to turn off the road and shine an area.

Having observed this furtive activity, the officer had stopped the vehicle. Inside the small SUV, he found five young men. He also found a loaded .22-caliber rifle in the back seat. Although five was a lot of folks to be together night hunting, the setup was a typical one in that the group only had one gun. In addition, .22-caliber rifles were used widely by folks hunting at night, partly because of their low report versus that of a high-powered rifle. I advised Greg it sounded like a good case; however, like with all cases, it would be stronger with a confession and I suggested we read the folks their rights and take their statements.

I took the handcuffed driver to our vehicle to talk with him. As I began to read the young man the Miranda warning, he asked if I could please take the handcuffs off, seeing how he was having trouble feeling his hands. I checked the cuffs and found they were snug but not overly tight. However, I was thinking seeing how everything was under control and I did not sense any threat from this individual and he had been wearing the bracelets for over an hour, it would be a goodwill gesture to remove the cuffs and I did. I read him the Miranda warning and asked him to tell me what had occurred. He stated they were just out riding around when the officer stopped them. I asked why he had turned his vehicle crossways in the road and he stated a deer had run across the road and he was trying to get a look at it. When I asked who had the firearm, he said it was in the back of the SUV. I asked if he was night hunting and he assured me he was not. I told him to sit tight and we would be back with him.

I moved to the next individual and basically went through the same scenario. I received a very similar story. I realized that in his excitement of making his first night hunting case by himself, the new officer had forgotten the rule about separating the folks involved to prevent them from getting their stories together. However, reading this individual's body language I could tell something was amiss, so I pressed forward. I informed the man I had been told he was in possession of the firearm when the vehicle had been stopped. He stammered around and said the front-seat passenger had slid the rifle back to him when the officer had pulled them over. I asked why he thought they had the rifle and he did not answer. I asked if it was his rifle and he answered with an emphatic "No." A good technique any time you had multiple subjects was to ask whether or not the gun belonged to them. If it did, you had another strike against them and another set of questions to ask. If it did not belong to them, that told you something as well. I played up the fact this guy was in possession of the gun and again asked what their intent was. He advised he was along for the ride. Giving him my best "I know you're lying" look, I again inquired as to what he thought the front seat passenger's intentions were and he took a deep breath and said, "To shoot a deer."

Armed with this new information, I returned to the driver. This time my tone was more accusatory and I asked him a simple question that had worked for me many times. "Is there any reason why what you said and what your buddy told me are two totally different stories?" This often worked to jar loose the truth. I followed with the quick question, "Was the firearm in the front seat prior to you getting stopped?" Seeing things were going downhill, the fellow hung his head. That was normally a good sign. The guy looked up at me with the "What have I done?" look and I knew the truth was about to come out. I told him to just go ahead and tell it. He stated they had been out riding around, hoping to see a deer. He said he wasn't sure they would have shot it but they might have. I asked, "Why did you bring the gun?" He gave me a pitiful look and said, "To shoot a deer." That was good enough for me. I gave him a pen and piece of paper and asked him to write out his statement. We did the same with the other four individuals and the results were pretty much the same. Greg issued citations for hunting at night, hunting from a public road, and hunting by the aid of a vehicle. That was a lot of tickets.

The court date soon rolled around and I was about to receive a rude awakening. These would be my first cases to be heard in the north district of Talladega County and although I had heard the horror stories from Jerry, I felt, armed with the confessions, there would not be a problem. The cases were called and the five defendants and three officers approached the bench. I got a bad feeling as soon as the judge asked the defendants, "What are you boys doing in here?" I was thinking that was pretty obvious, seeing the charges on the docket. The judge looked at CEO Gilliland and, in a somewhat accusatory tone, asked why he had brought these boys to court. Greg testified he had observed as their SUV moved slowly along the road and turned and illuminated a field with its headlights. The driver backed out and continued the same way it had been going. He stopped the vehicle and found they were in possession of a loaded rifle. He finished his testimony by saying after having been read their rights the defendants had given a written confession stating they were night hunting. I felt the young officer had done a good job and waited to hear the response of the defendants. However, I didn't get to hear it. In a normal court proceeding, the judge would listen to our reason for bringing the charges and then ask the defendant for their side of the story. That didn't happen. Instead, the judge thought for a minute and announced he didn't think that was what these boys were doing. My blood pressure immediately jumped at least fifty points! I'm sure you could have taken my pulse by looking at my neck from across the room. As the senior officer of the group, I stepped up to the bench and informed the judge we had a signed confession in which they admitted they were night hunting for deer. The judge gave me a disparaging look that made it obvious he wasn't interested in anything I had to say and announced he would take the cases under advisement. That was normally judicial code for "These cases are going away!"

I wanted to jump up and grab the judge by his scrawny neck. I had been told he was no friend of conservation. However, I never thought we would lose such a slam dunk case. Unfortunately, this went on for years. I felt so sorry for the officers who had to work in that jurisdiction on a regular basis. One day was just about more than I could take.

Unfortunately, there are many judges who have little regard for the peril of our wildlife resources, much less the fact that CEOs put their lives on the line to protect those resources and the public. When these lawbreakers are let go with a slap on the wrist or less, it promotes the idea that wildlife is of little value. In addition, it's obvious these judges do not care about the danger these violators pose to the public. As I said at the start, I am so thankful I had good, conservation-minded judges. Knowing this sure helped when it was seven degrees at 2:00 a.m. in the middle of nowhere. Conservation officers can and do work day and night to protect the resource, but without a judge that will take the violations seriously, their efforts are often in vain. If you have a judge who is a friend of conservation, thank them. If your judge does not safeguard your wildlife resources, elect a new one!

My First Decoy Experience

To SAY I WAS INTRODUCED to the deer decoy early in my career would be a gross understatement. On my first day of work, my assistant chief instructed me to contact the two game wardens in the county and ask them to teach me how to do law enforcement. Eager to please, I quickly contacted the officers and informed them I wanted to work with them. They were thrilled—NOT. Why on earth would a couple of seasoned officers not want to have a wet-behind-the-ears rookie with no experience accompany them on a dangerous night patrol? Thankfully for me, they allowed me to tag along.

Conservation Enforcement Officers Earl Brown and Hershel Patterson related to me they had received some complaints of people shooting deer at night on Highway 259 and we were going to utilize the deer decoy to try to catch the culprits. As I would quickly learn, Highway 259 was a night hunting hotspot. Earl told me he would come and pick me up at 7:00 p.m.

Keep in mind that my only experience with wildlife law enforcement was riding with a game warden for a couple of hours one night in south Mississippi while I was in graduate school at Mississippi State University. I only learned a couple of things that night. First, I discovered game wardens were good at driving at night without using any headlights. That revelation also helped me realize you should keep your fingernails clipped really short to make them easier to extract from the dash! Oh my gosh! I had no idea that anyone purposely drove at high speeds at night without any lights. It was exhilarating in a scared-to-death kind of way.

I was ready and waiting when Earl came to pick me up. It was a cold late-January night. I was wearing long underwear, my one issued uniform shirt, which was short-sleeved, my issued uniform nylon pants, and my personal coat. I had yet to be issued my large Smith & Wesson .357 magnum pistol; however, I did have a ticket book and had already written my first ticket a couple of days earlier. I guarantee you things were much different in those days. There was no formal training program other than the police academy, which I would attend in a few months. Thinking back, I again realize how fortunate I was that the local officers were willing to assist me. This lack of equipment and training did not dampen my enthusiasm. Have you ever heard of someone who was gleefully ignorant? I just wondered.

I climbed in the truck and we were off on what would be an adventure that changed my life. We traveled south on 259 until we reached Coosa County Road 24 and quickly backed in between two high dirt banks. CEO Patterson and his ride-along were already in the spot which I would learn was called a hidey-hole. I would discover that a good game warden has a hidey-hole on most roads in the county. It's a place that will conceal a vehicle yet provide a view of traffic on the road. These places are essential for working the night hunting of deer, which I quickly learned was prevalent throughout the county.

With our truck properly hidden, I got my first look at "the decoy." I must admit it wasn't much to look at. First of all, it seemed tiny. I had envisioned a nice, large buck with a good set of antlers; however, what I saw was a scrawny little deer with a pitifully small set of antlers. Not to mention that it appeared to have a lot of holes in it. I figured that meant that it worked despite what it looked like.

We set the ragged looking stuffed deer up off the side of the road and hurried back to the truck. The wait began. Having no experience, yet wanting to do a good job, I asked Earl what we would if do someone shot the fake deer. He said we would pull out and stop them, take their gun, and write them tickets for hunting at night, hunting from the public road, and hunting by the aid of a vehicle. While that sounded simple enough, I wasn't sure it would go that way.

It wasn't long until a vehicle eased to a stop and I witnessed my first night hunting incident. Immediately following the shotgun blast, Earl started our truck and roared out into the road behind the shooter's vehicle. A few seconds later, I was right in the middle of my first vehicle chase. Although we never reached high speeds, the driver would not stop until we got in front of him and forced him off the road. Keep in mind, I was about an hour into my first night-hunting work and I had already witnessed someone shooting the deer decoy and was now involved in a car chase. I realized things happened fast in Coosa County!

Earl and I were in front of the vehicle and Hershel and his ride-along, Jim, were behind them. While I was sort of in slow motion, the officers jumped out and quickly moved to the vehicle, took a shotgun from the driver, and pulled the two men out and put them at the back of their car with their hands on the trunk. While the game wardens looked through the vehicle and wrote tickets, Jim and I "guarded" the two violators.

I was learning a lot in a hurry. I quickly realized these guys had obviously not planned on exiting their vehicle. The passenger was wearing a wifebeater T-shirt and blue jeans. As I recall, it was below twenty degrees. Every time he would lift his hands and rub them together, Jim would order him to put them back on the car. I also quickly discovered that folks would hunt with whatever weapon they could find. These guys had shot the decoy with a 16-gauge shotgun loaded with #6 shot. I figured they must have been looking to shoot a rabbit but when confronted with the deer, they just couldn't pass it up. Earl and Hershel finished the paperwork and we headed back to our hiding spot.

It wasn't long until a truck slowed to a stop and within seconds a shot rang out. Earl started the truck and pulled out behind the violator's vehicle as he released another shot toward the stuffed wonder. With all the experience I had gleaned from our first stop an hour earlier, I jumped from the truck and approached the shooter. About the time I reached the rear of his pickup, he fired on the deer for the third time. I did not hesitate to snatch the 30-30 rifle from the man's hands. Fortunately, he was a little intoxicated and a lot shocked that some kid had just yanked his firearm from him. I turned around to see Earl staring at me in disbelief. The look on his face was a combination of astonishment and bewilderment. He quickly snapped out of it and ordered the man out of the truck. Earl approached the man, got his driver's license, and wrote him the appropriate tickets. We were soon back in our hiding spot. It was then I actually starting receiving my law enforcement education. Earl took the opportunity to explain, in a pretty blunt fashion, I might want to let him approach the vehicle first seeing how he had a pistol and knew what he was doing. Having not yet been to the police academy I did not realize just how dangerous the situation was. Looking back, I realize this was the first of many times I would be protected by the grace of God.

Talk about drinking from a fire hose! What a night. I learned many lessons I would see reinforced throughout my career. I discovered the decoy was an effective tool and people shooting at the decoy often exhibit tunnel vision. People night hunting are often also drinking or intoxicated and therefore are highly unpredictable. Thankfully, I realized that veteran officers have a lot of knowledge and if you want to stay alive you had better listen to what they have to say.

The next day, I happened to be in the courthouse when I learned another lesson. As I made my way to the sheriff's office, I could hear a woman who was obviously upset. Once I could make out what was being said, I understood she was upset about her son being caught night hunting the previous night. However, her most fervent request was that she wanted the 16-gauge shotgun he had been hunting with. Although the sheriff had nothing to do with the arrest, he was doing his best to field her questions. The sheriff informed the woman that when someone was caught night hunting, they often didn't get the gun back. To this the woman replied, "My son has to work in the daytime! The only time he has to hunt is at night!" This surely wouldn't be the last outlandish excuse I would hear.

In many respects, the two officers in the county were as different as daylight and dark. However, each of them taught me some valuable lessons about wildlife law enforcement. These lessons went a long way toward making me a well-rounded officer and keeping me alive. Since that time, I have worked with many younger officers and tried to relay to them the lessons I had learned and been taught. Working with these officers made me appreciate all the more the willingness of the two Coosa County game wardens to teach a young kid the ropes.

I would be remiss if I also didn't thank Lt. Alton Boulware. Lt. Boulware was a game warden in Coosa County in the 1960s, a long time before I had ever heard of Coosa County. However, I learned a good bit from the lieutenant. I remember on many occasions CEO Hershel Patterson would say to me, "Alton always said...." Each time, it was something worth remembering. I appreciate all three of them.

Go Slow

OBVIOUSLY, I CAN'T SPEAK FOR every state employee but I would assume most would probably rather not be summoned to the office by the head of the department. In Game & Fish, a call from the director normally wasn't a good thing. In my experience, it was often in response to some outlaw who had been arrested but for whatever reason had the ear of a politician who felt they would have some sway over the higher-ups in our department. I must admit, for the most part we were fairly well insulated from these types of situations. I contribute that to the fact I did my best to make a good case and many (but not all) of the leaders in our department did not cave to pressure. It took me a while to learn they felt obligated to check out complaints and it wasn't always questioning whether or not we had done the right thing but simply what had happened. This is covered in other stories.

In talking with retired game warden Byron Smith, I learned he received several "what happened" calls but also received several calls requesting he go somewhere and catch someone. The director of the department and others realized Byron did a comprehensive job and would put in whatever effort it took to catch a violator.

Byron shared with me one incident where the director called him and told him he had learned of a shooting house in the woods overlooking a small green field. Obviously, we have all seen thousands of those; however, I can count on one hand the ones that had a mercury-vapor light that illuminated the field. For some reason, the director felt this setup deserved a closer look and asked Byron to provide that. I'm sure the fact this property was very near the director's lease had nothing to do with his interest!

Armed with the vague information from the director, Byron began to formulate a plan. His first step was to contact the department pilot and request a flight over the area. The plane was a tremendous law enforcement tool. A quick aerial reconnaissance could reveal a ton of information. When the pilot advised him he was pretty busy, Byron told him the request was coming straight from the director. The next day, Byron and the pilot flew over the area and located the shooting house, complete with green field, light, and feeder. In addition, Byron located an area where he could hide his truck. That was something most people would not think about; however, we dealt with it all the time. Believe me when I tell you a game warden's truck in the area gets the folks' attention. The pair returned to the airport and Byron immediately traveled to the area and stealthily moved into his hiding spot.

As always, the key to making cases for hunting over bait is the ability to get in and out of the area without being detected. In a county that was rapidly growing, with new houses being built in rural areas, this was often a difficult undertaking.

Conducting a thorough investigation of the area, Byron found there was Nomex wire running approximately 250 yards through the woods from a hunting lodge that provided power for the light. In addition, he found a large amount of corn under a feeder in the center of the field. The shooting house was large, with sliding Plexiglas in the front and a Plexiglas non-opening window high in the back. Byron determined what he felt would be the best way to access the property and moved out of the area.

Numerous trips into the area found no one in the shooting house. You must realize that someone wanting to hunt at night has an advantage in that they have a roughly twelve-hour time span to come and hunt the stand. They may hunt it immediately after dark, at midnight, or at four in the morning. The officer, on the other hand, can't monitor the stand for twelve hours a night. Therefore, attempting to apprehend a violator can be both difficult and aggravating. After checking the area a dozen times, Byron decided to try a gadget he had recently seen advertised. You must remember this was at least twenty-plus years ago and way before everybody and their brother had a trail camera that could send the owner an email message if it detected a deer fart within fifty yards.

The Trail Timer was patented in 1985. It was a single-event "high-tech" timer that consisted of a piece of thread hooked to a clock. You stretched the thread across a trail and when something came down the trail, it pulled the string, which stopped the clock. You retrieved the device and read the time on the clock. Simple, yet effective.

Byron ordered one of the devices and set it up to determine when the violator was entering the stand. When he retrieved the unit, the clock read 7:48 p.m. Armed with the new info, the officer adjusted the time he began entering the property to around 6:30 p.m. He would sneak into the area carrying his Remington 870 shotgun and would assume a good vantage point and wait.

Several nights of surveillance had resulted in absolutely nothing. As a general rule, we can only give an area so much time seeing how we are receiving complaints in other areas as well. Of course, this location had been deemed high priority by the director. Ever diligent, another night arrived and Byron once again found himself waiting for the violator to appear. As he sat in the darkness, he soon picked up movement in the shooting house.

Although even with binoculars he could not see well into the house, he finally figured out he was seeing the shadow of someone in the shooting house moving their head from side to side. Realizing he now had someone in the house, he began formulating his plan on how to approach. In the forefront of his mind was the vivid memory of how a deputy game warden had been shot and killed by a night hunter as he approached a shooting house. Byron decided to close the distance between him and the shooting house and then wait on the violator to make a move.

As he sat in the dark watching, the door on the back of the house slowly opened. A man stepped out and put the sling of his scoped rifle on his shoulder. As he turned to latch the door, Byron broke the silence, saying, "Hold it—state game warden."

As was very often the case, the man immediately turned toward the officer's voice. That's when he received a piercing bright light in his face. Blinded, the man asked, "Who's there?"

Byron again announced it was the game warden. He instructed the man to turn around and back down the steps to the ground.

The man protested, "I'll fall."

Byron replied, "Go slow."

The man complied. Once he reached the ground, he was instructed to walk to the middle of the field beneath the light and lie face down on the ground. The man again complied and Byron moved in and took the man's gun from him. Lying facedown with his arms out to his sides, the man asked, "Why are you being so rough on me?"

This fellow was not at all unlike hundreds of folks I have encountered. Although it was obvious he was in violation of the law, actually several laws, he could not understand why he was being treated like a criminal. Notwithstanding the fact the man was breaking laws that if convicted would cost him nearly a thousand dollars in fines and court costs, he was armed with a high-powered rifle and it was in the dark of night. I think that type behavior is reason enough to handle the situation carefully!

The man was arrested for hunting at night and hunting by the aid of bait. After completing the necessary paperwork, the man looked at Byron and asked a familiar question: "Who told you about this?"

Byron's answer was a good one: "You wouldn't believe me if I told you."

War Eagle

ALTHOUGH MY PRIMARY JOB was that of a wildlife biologist for the Alabama Department of Conservation and Natural Resources wildlife section, I had learned early on anyone driving a green truck with a Game & Fish logo on the door was considered a game warden by the public. I learned to accept this and since my position did carry law enforcement authority and responsibilities, I did not mind answering questions and hearing complaints. Some were trivial, some serious, and some hilarious. I'm sure that while reading these stories you have picked up on that I often highlight the humorous aspects. I found a long time ago that keeping it light, if possible, helped my state of mind. Fortunately, there was a lot of funny stuff that went on.

Working in a partnership with the USDA Natural Resources Conservation Service as the private lands biologist for central Alabama, I often traveled to the state headquarters in Auburn, which was sixty miles from my home. I had been in an all-day meeting there and was finally on my way home with a horrible headache. Driving along Highway 280 at about sixty-five miles per hour, I noticed a vehicle behind me flashing their headlights. The vehicle pulled alongside with the occupant frantically motioning for me to pull over. I quickly applied the brakes and pulled to the shoulder of the road, forcing the driver to pull over in front of me. From a tactical standpoint, I did not want the subject coming up from behind me.

While someone trying to flag me down was not uncommon, after having made or assisted on thousands of arrests, you never knew whether it was someone wanting to ask what to plant in their food plot or someone disgruntled after paying their fine. Pulling to the shoulder of the highway, I removed my pistol from its holster, which was in the passenger seat, and held it in my hand under my left arm. I watched closely as the driver exited his vehicle and ran back to me with his phone in his hand. He leaned in my window and quickly explained he had seen a large bird standing in the ditch on a nearby county road and didn't know for sure what it was but had taken a picture of it. As he was pulling the picture up on his phone, he repeated he wasn't sure what it was but thought it could be a "war eagle."

Despite the fact my head was pounding, I couldn't help but get tickled by his thinking the bird might be a war eagle. If you aren't from Alabama, you may not understand that. Wherever you are from, I'm sure you are familiar with a football rivalry. Well, take whatever rivalry you are thinking about and magnify it by about one hundred and you begin to understand the situation between Alabama and Auburn fans. These folks live and breathe college football and they either bleed crimson and white or orange and blue. If you spend any time around an avid fan of either team, they will quickly want to know "Who do you go for?" Translated, they want to know which team you support. It's either the Alabama Crimson Tide or the Auburn Tigers. Seeing how we were about fifteen miles out of Auburn—home of the battle cry "War Eagle"—I understood why he might think it was a war eagle since as far as I know that's the only place they exist!

He showed me the picture of the bird and I told him it appeared to be a hawk. He said it was just sitting there and he didn't want anyone to do anything to it. He gave me directions to where it was. I thanked him and told him I would check it out.

After he drove away, I contacted the county conservation enforcement officer and he stated he happened to be in the area and would look into it. He called back later and told me it was in fact an immature red-tailed hawk that was scavenging on a dead fox. He said the bird was very reluctant to leave the dried-up carcass. I thanked him for checking it out.

Luckily, I never had an Alabama fan stop me thinking they had spotted their school mascot—an elephant!

A quick note. As I said, everybody in Alabama, including kids, wanted to know who you went for. Let me tell you, it threw them for a loop when I told them I went for Mississippi State. They literally would have no answer to that!

You can't make this stuff up—Hail State!

Where Did I Hit It?

A COMMON QUESTION posed by folks who had been apprehended shooting at the deer decoy was, "Where did I hit it?" I'm not sure whether that was an attempt to at least be able to brag about the shot that cost them $1000 or more or if it was just a burning curiosity to know whether or not they would have killed it had it been a real deer. The truth is the shots launched at the decoy ranged from horrible misses to incredible hits.

You must keep in mind the decoy was set up in various locations various distances from the road. This often depended upon whether it was day or night and what the location offered. Based on these factors, we ended up setting the deer as close as 25 yards and as far as 150 yards from the road. While you might be thinking anyone would be able to recognize the deer wasn't real at a distance of 25 yards, either you would be wrong or a whole lot of people recognized it as a decoy but blasted it anyway!

Several memorable shots come to mind. One that got my attention was the fellow who locked down his brakes upon spotting the deer at sixty yards. He literally slid to a stop on the wet pavement, but not before he fired two shots from his lever-action Browning rifle. After we made the apprehension, Wildlife Biologist Gene Carver and I inspected the decoy. While we were skeptical that he could have hit the deer while sliding, we were wrong. We were somewhat amazed when we found two bullet holes in the white spot on the deer's neck. We were even more surprised by the fact that both holes could be covered with a quarter. Even more amazing was the shooter claimed it was the first time he had ever done anything like that! Yeah right.

With the deer set up in the very same location, we watched as a truck rolled to a stop. The front-seat passenger turned around in the seat and lined up his sights and fired on the deer. As we came out of our hiding spot, he fired again. As we were approaching him, he fired for a third time. We apprehended him and the driver of the vehicle. After finishing the paperwork, they were allowed to go on their way. We stepped over and checked the deer. We were once again surprised. The road hunter had missed the deer all three times!

I don't know for sure whether or not the distance of the shot made any difference to the shooter; however, I don't think it did based on their willingness to shoot. I remember one day in Clay County when we had the deer set up 125 yards from the road. A vehicle pulled to a stop with the passenger side of the vehicle facing the deer. Momentarily a shot rang out. Then another and another and another and another. Arriving at the vehicle, we learned the shooter, who was seated in the driver's seat, was firing a 9mm pistol out of the passenger-side window. Surprisingly, he failed to hit the small deer that was only 125 yards away!

Once again, same setup. We had an old guy—he seemed old then, probably about my age now—in a Ford pickup stop in the road and fire on the deer, twice. Upon his apprehension, he of course asked where he had hit the deer. Seeing how the deer was once again 125 yards from the road and the man was firing a 30-30 rifle with iron sights, I seriously doubted whether or not there would be a new hole in the manikin. Once again, I was wrong. The shooter hit the deer with both shots!

One of my favorite stories about someone shooting the decoy comes from Lt. Jerry Fincher. Jerry and CEO Greg Gilliland were both still fairly new game wardens when they decided to utilize the stuffed wonder to hopefully curtail some of the night hunting that was rampant in Talladega County. After checking out a location where they had received numerous night hunting complaints, they located an area they thought would work. With the deer set up about fifty yards from the paved county road, CEO Gilliland took up a position across the road where he could observe traffic and "work" the decoy. As I have mentioned many times, "working the decoy" often meant an officer was going to have to be "on the ground" with the decoy control and a radio, with another officer or two down the road. This was the situation in this case.

After an hour or so, Greg observed a vehicle coming toward his location. Unfortunately, the driver was running at a pretty good rate of speed. Greg thought the car was going much too fast for them to see the deer, much less shoot at it. Therefore, you can imagine his surprise when the passenger began firing at the deer while the car was still moving at about forty miles per hour! The passenger, who was hanging out the window with a .22 rifle, shot five times while Greg was radioing Jerry, telling him to stop the vehicle. Jerry came out of his hiding spot and got behind the vehicle and activated his blue lights. The driver pulled to the side of the road and Jerry moved up and made the apprehension of the driver and the highly intoxicated passenger.

With the paperwork complete, Jerry moved back and met Greg at the deer. Examination of the decoy revealed the inebriated shooter had hit the deer three out of five times, once in the end of the nose, while passing by at forty miles per hour. To say it probably wasn't his first time to do this would probably be a gross understatement!

What Are the Odds?

AS A LAW ENFORCEMENT OFFICER in a rural county, I very well understand that backup is a luxury we normally do not have. Therefore, I would routinely monitor the police scanner just in case an officer needed assistance. Keep in mind, being nosy was part of my job so I also just wanted to keep up with what was going on. If I wasn't out working, I was usually still monitoring the police radio.

One summer night while listening to the scanner, I heard a Coosa County deputy call the dispatcher and report he was making a traffic stop at Hatchett Creek Bridge on Highway 280. Highway 280 was a major highway that cut through the north end of the county. It was the closest thing we had to an interstate and since it was a direct link between Birmingham and Auburn, it got a lot of traffic. As with any major roadway, a lot of the traffic was going way too fast.

The deputy soon came back on the radio and provided the driver's license number to dispatch. The dispatcher came back and told him the license was expired as of May 21. Moments later, he radioed he was back in service after issuing a citation for expired license and speeding eighty-three miles per hour in a sixty-five-miles-per-hour zone.

Approximately three minutes later, the deputy again radioed in he was making a traffic stop at Hatchett Creek Bridge on Highway 280, the exact same location of the last stop. This is not unusual in that officers who are running stationary radar will often set up in a location that will somewhat allow them to dictate where they will be able to stop the violators. Unfortunately, this is often an exercise in frustration seeing how many drivers will roll past a good safe location and either stop just over the crest of a hill or worse yet will pull into the median instead of off the right side of the road, which is what the law specifies you shall do.

The deputy soon came back on the radio and gave the dispatcher a license number to check. The dispatcher came back and told him the license was expired as of May 21. Moments later, he radioed he was back in service after issuing a citation for expired license and speeding eighty-three miles per hour in a sixty-five-miles-per-hour zone.

My first thought was surely he didn't stop the same vehicle minutes apart. My second thought was whether or not this was a *Groundhog Day* movie sort of thing. I guess I had better explain that. *Groundhog Day* was a movie that came out in 1993. It starred Bill Murray as a weatherman who was caught in a loop that forced him to relive the same day, Groundhog Day, repeatedly.

I gave the officer a call and asked if he had realized he had stopped two vehicles in the same spot for the same speeding violation and both drivers had licenses that had expired on the same day. He said he had noticed that. I told him the planets must definitely be aligned. I advised him he might want to buy a lottery ticket.

I would not know how to begin to calculate the odds of something like that happening. However, another set of odds that I often thought about was the odds of us catching a game and fish violator on any given day or night. While it may seem simple to go out and catch a night hunter, you need to consider a few things. When we were at full staff in our county, that meant two game wardens and myself. That was at least one more officer than most counties had. We were supposed to work only forty hours per week; however, during the hunting season, sixty hours wasn't uncommon. That was until a lawsuit that firmly put the forty-hour limit in place. During any given week, there would be two to four days one of us was off duty. So, when we were all working, and if we worked alone, which was not a good idea but was often the case, we could cover three spots in the county for a portion of the night. To put that into perspective, our county was ultra-rural, with only ten thousand residents. There were three incorporated towns in the county and one of those actually had a traffic light. My point is we had very little area that did not get hunted. While people seem to think night hunters would be found in the most remote areas of the county, the truth was they hunted where the deer were and if that was in someone's yard, so be it.

Our county is comprised of 652 square miles, bordered on the west by the Coosa River and on the east by Lake Martin, the largest man-made lake in the country. In between was over four hundred thousand acres of predominately forest dissected by pastures, ponds, wildlife openings, and two federal highways and two main state highways. Any way you looked at it, it was a good setup for violations to occur. When you break the area down by three officers, that is about 135,000-plus acres per officer.

Now think about this. During the hunting season, which definitely was not the only time night hunting violations occurred, a violator had on average twelve hours, 720 minutes, to fire a shot somewhere in 135,000 acres. What are the odds that an officer might be close enough to at least hear the shot much less have the violation occur in their presence? Talk about some astronomical odds! When you think about it that way, it's a little hard to believe we ever caught anybody. That was one reason we weren't very fond of issuing warnings, especially not for a flagrant offense such as hunting at night or over bait.

Those are some crazy odds; however, there is a statistic out that is very simple. It says one out of every one person dies. That includes you and me. Knowing these odds, have you made the necessary preparations for where you will spend eternity? That day is coming. We will all live eternally; the question is where. Romans 10:9 says that if you confess with your mouth the Lord Jesus and believe in your heart God raised Him from the dead, you shall be saved.

You know the odds. It's your decision.

Shelby—Mississippi Game Warden

WITH THE EXCEPTION of being checked one night back when spotlighting was legal in Alabama, I guess my first real exposure to a game warden occurred when I was in graduate school in 1986. A fellow graduate student, Calvin, invited me to accompany him to work on his graduate research project in south Mississippi. I tried to work on as many projects as possible while earning my master's degree in wildlife ecology at Mississippi State University (MSU). Those experiences served me well after I became an area wildlife biologist for the Alabama Department of Conservation and Natural Resources (ADCNR). Calvin's project was a white-tailed deer/vegetation utilization study on a management area near Columbia, Mississippi. Since this project was several hours from Starkville, we would usually stay a night or two. I knew even if I didn't learn anything, we would eat well. Let me assure you, graduate students tried not to miss an opportunity to eat well. While at MSU, I lived on Showboat spaghetti (three cans for a dollar) and deer meat. I didn't miss any meals; however, living on a monthly stipend of $525, it was difficult to pay rent, tuition, and gas and eat high on the hog. However, we knew that when Calvin was headed to Marion County for a couple of days, he stocked up on steak and potatoes!

After arriving at the management area, I learned Calvin had arranged a special bonus for us. We would have the opportunity to accompany the local game wardens on a night patrol. Having never done anything like that before, I was game. Although I had hunted since childhood, I had very little insight into what a game warden actually did. However, I knew if I got the job I wanted as an area wildlife biologist for the ADCNR, I would have to go to the police academy and would have law enforcement responsibility. I felt certain this patrol would prove valuable for me.

We arrived at the Marion County Wildlife Management Area headquarters just before dark. There I met the area manager, Hank Stringer, and a game warden named Shelby. I did not know whether that was his first or last name but it was the only one he offered. Shelby was ancient. He had to be in his fifties, if not sixty! Funny how that doesn't seem so old now for some reason. Shelby explained there had been some night hunting going on and we were going to try to apprehend the offenders. He told us he thought it was a couple of good ole boys who they had encountered in the past. I got into the green pickup with Shelby and we went to set up surveillance. Shelby shared some of what it was like to work as a game warden and it was definitely enlightening.

As I recall, the most memorable story he told was about arresting a man for fishing illegal boxes. I'm not sure that before that evening I even knew people fished with boxes. Evidently, at that time it was common for some folks to build boxes using wooden slats with an entrance on one end. They placed some bait in the box and lowered it into the water. Fish would swim into the box and could not figure out how to get out. There were exact specifications that the boxes had to meet. The slats had to be far enough apart to allow small fish to escape. Shelby explained this guy was fishing "tight" boxes, which I would learn meant the gaps between the wooden slats on the box were not as wide as the law required. This meant smaller fish could not escape from the trap.

Shelby explained he would locate the boxes using a line with a treble hook. He would then pull the heavy boxes up and check to be sure they were the proper size. In addition, I learned a license was required for each box and proof of the license had to be attached to the box itself.

Shelby had located a box and was pulling it up when he reached below the surface of the water and grabbed the box, only to learn it had been booby-trapped with a treble hook that was now sticking through his hand! Due to the weight of the box, he could not let go with his other hand without the hook ripping out. I could understand he was in a bad predicament and couldn't wait to hear how he got out of it. He said he somehow got his knife out of his pocket with his teeth and was able to cut the hook from the box. I was thinking I would have liked to have seen that! The wound required an emergency room visit; however, once the hook was removed, he returned to the lake and waited three days until the fisherman came and checked the box. Although fishing tight boxes would normally warrant a citation, for some reason this guy earned himself a trip to the county jail. I was learning a lot.

Our night patrol was going well, although we didn't see anyone. I assumed you would call it a patrol, although we were actually just sitting in one spot in the dark. I must admit that while I had heard of people shooting deer at night, I was not at all familiar with the practice.

Lo and behold, it wasn't long until we heard a shot. Shelby immediately started the truck and took off, saying he thought we could head them off at the crossroads. As we were barreling down the road at breakneck speed, I was thinking this was really dangerous. It wasn't that I had not ridden at high speeds at night before; the difference was I had always done it with the headlights on! We were flying down a gravel road in the pitch dark. Somehow Shelby must have sensed my discomfort. The fact was that I had frantically dug the seatbelt out from under the seat and put it on and was clinging to the dash with a death grip. Shelby said, "Don't you worry, I know every rock in this road." I was glad to hear that; however, I was wondering whether or not he knew everyone who might be driving on that road. We made it to the crossroads but either were too late or the outlaws had taken another route. The rest of the night was uneventful. Little did I know that a year later I would be flying down the roads in central Alabama with no lights on!

A Haint!

I HAVE OFTEN HEARD IT SAID that conservation enforcement officers (CEOs) are much more likely to be assaulted than any other law enforcement officer. If you think about it, our situation normally works against us in a big way. During the hunting season, almost everyone we encounter is armed. It might surprise you to know that is also true during the fishing season. Many assaults have occurred on the creek bank and in boats! In addition, we often work in remote areas, alone and without any close backup. When you spell it out like that, it really doesn't sound very safe. It's not.

During my career, I had the opportunity to work with several new officers. With many years of experience and a lot of arrests under my belt, I felt as though I had a lot to offer these rookies. Unfortunately, some of our new officers came in thinking they knew pretty much everything. This was especially true for some who had some previous law enforcement experience. While the previous experience was valuable in many ways, they would soon learn wildlife law enforcement was often very different from anything they had done before. Seldom did a police officer or deputy get knocked out of a boat into the lake or sit in the dark in the middle of nowhere without a word of communication for hours. These folks either adapted to it or didn't stay very long.

One important idea I always tried to pass along to new officers was the universal law enforcement rule that we needed to be the ones to go home at the end of the shift. With that in mind, I always tried to communicate to them that although our job would regularly entail sneaking up on or positioning ourselves close to armed suspects, startling those subjects was not a good idea. As hazardous as our job was, and still is today, we sure didn't need to give anyone an excuse to shoot us.

In my opinion, one of the major flaws of our department for many years was a lack of training. Officers were often hired, given a gun and ticket book, and told to go get 'em. I know this because that is exactly what happened with me. I had made many arrests prior to going to the police academy and being told by one of the instructors that I was just asking to be killed working with Game & Fish! Fortunately, I was in a county with two seasoned veteran officers who were willing to work with me. In addition, our county was loaded with wildlife and hunters and I received a lot of on-the-job training in a big hurry. In addition to my county officers, it was my pleasure to have the opportunity to work with another mentor, CEO Byron Smith. Byron was a pit bull game warden. When our office really needed someone caught, Byron was often sent to do the job. I often got the chance to work with Byron on opening day of dove season and we would regularly be suffering from writer's cramp by the end of the day. Byron was also the owner of Conservation Decoy Company and made decoys that were used all over the country to apprehend bad guys.

Byron shared an extreme startled-hunter story with me. Although he had only been working for a few months, like most officers he was working night hunting by himself in the middle of nowhere in Macon County. Working night hunting for deer can be extremely exciting or it can be as lonely as the third verse of a song in a Baptist hymnal. Just in case you didn't grow up in a

Baptist church, let me explain that when singing hymns, it was common practice for the music leader to omit the third verse. It was common to hear them say, "Let's sing the first, second, and the last." Later in my life, it was amusing to some of my fellow choir members when the director would say "On the third" and I would have to reach for a hymn book. I usually knew all of the other verses. I digress.

Another interesting thing about working night hunting was you never knew what might come up. I've had night hunting stakeouts turn in to DUI arrest, domestic violence assaults, arrests for felony theft, and even a murder arrest. You just never knew.

While Byron had not observed any deer hunting activity, he had spotted someone he suspected was coon hunting below his observation point. He decided to check out what appeared to be the lone individual. He moved toward the location on foot and soon observed the hunter's light as he came around the perimeter of a large field. Byron made his way to the field edge, located a good tactical position, and waited on the hunter to arrive.

When the hunter neared him, Byron turned on his Maglite flashlight and said, "Good evening, state game warden." This cordial greeting and identification was answered immediately by loud screaming. As the hunter screamed, he also raised his single barrel shotgun and began trying to cock the hammer on the gun. Byron immediately drew his pistol and dove behind a tree on the field edge. His loud verbal commands for the man to put down the gun were answered by unintelligible screams. After about a minute that Byron said seemed like five, the man quit screaming. Byron again identified himself and told the man to put the gun on the ground. Regaining his composure, the man lowered the gun to the ground. Byron stood up and began to cautiously approach the man, who he could now see was an elderly fellow (eighty-nine years old).

As Byron closed the gap between them, the man placed his right hand behind his back and appeared to be reaching into his overalls, the only garment he had on. Something you learn pretty quickly is not to assume a hunter only has one firearm. I remember learning this after I had arrested a man for hunting deer over bait. I had taken the man's long gun and walked all the way out of the woods to his truck. It was then I asked if he had any other weapons and he stated he had a pistol in a shoulder holster. Once again, a rookie officer was watched over by a loving God.

Byron still had his revolver in his hand when he told the man to keep his hands out where he could see them. The man replied, "I can't."

"What do you mean you can't?" Byron shot back and the man replied, "I have soiled myself."

Byron cautiously approached and his nose soon confirmed what the man said was the truth. Satisfied the man had no other weapons, he allowed him to clean himself as best he could.

With things calmed down, Byron verified the man had permission to hunt the property and that he was in fact old enough that he no longer was required to purchase a hunting license. He then asked the old fellow why he had gotten so shook up. The answer was once again one of those things you just can't make up. The man explained his hunting partner of many years had been buried earlier that very day. He told Byron he thought he was a "haint" (ghost) who was coming back to get him! He went on to tell Byron he wasn't ready to go yet and had he been able to cock the hammer on his gun, he would definitely have shot him! I found it ironic that the man was worried about a ghost coming to take him into the next life and his own actions almost propelled him there!

Friends and loved ones who have passed into eternity will not come back for us. However, if they were Christians, we can take the proper steps to see them again. I am no Bible scholar;

60

however, I do understand it to say that there is a heaven that is reserved for those who know the Lord. It says it is a place of joy and no sorrow. A happy place. It will make me happy to see my loved ones there. I don't know all the details; however, I know I will not live forever. That's a fact that is becoming more real to me every day. Today is the day of salvation. Tomorrow could be everlastingly too late.

Proud Decoy Shooter

THE BARBOUR WILDLIFE MANAGEMENT AREA (WMA) was different from all of the other WMAs in the state. While most of the areas were comprised of land leased from timber companies or other entities, the Barbour area was state owned. This was a major difference.

Many of the entities who owned the land in the other WMAs did not require a monetary payment. Several of the agreements were for in-kind services such as grading roads, replacing and maintaining culverts, and other land services. While this was normally a good situation for both parties, a major drawback did exist. Most of the agreements contained a clause stating the landowner could pull out of the contract with a ninety-day notice. Unfortunately, this meant the state was very reluctant to spend money for improvements on the land, which could quickly be lost. This was often evident when you saw the facilities on the areas.

The checking station at the Coosa WMA was a good example of an area that was not secure. WMA checking stations were normally located near the entrance to the area and were used as a headquarters during deer hunts. Permits were issued from the check station and deer killed on the hunts were brought there to be checked in and have biological data taken. In many cases, the checking station was also the office for the area. When I arrived on the Coosa area, there were two checking stations. The old one was a wooden building that measured about eight feet long by eight feet wide and eight feet high. I would learn it was basically held together by paint. I kid you not! It was rotten along the bottom and eventually fell apart. While the "new" check station was an upgrade, it wasn't a lot better. It was a portable metal building measuring eight feet by ten feet. Inside that building was a wooden desk, two metal filing cabinets, a space heater, and on days of a gun deer hunt there might be four or five people inside as well. To say it was cramped is an understatement. I have forgotten how many times my supervisor told me to develop a list of materials it would take to build an adequate structure. Each time I would come up with the materials list and a cost estimate only to be told we weren't going to spend the money on it. It was frustrating.

Being state owned, the Barbour area had a nice check station that also served as the WMA office. Their check station even had a telephone in it! The check station also had something else I feel certain no other check station had: a large full-body mount of a white-tailed buck. The deer sported a nice rack and garnered many questions from visitors to the area. I think the most frequent question was whether or not the deer was killed on the WMA. However, that's not the most memorable comment I heard. I had a guy come to the office window and when he saw the deer he immediately pointed at the buck and told his buddy, "That's the one I shot the other night!" I wasn't really sure how to respond to that. While I stood there trying to decide just what to say, the guy said, "Wait a minute, I think the one I shot was facing the other direction." He then looked at me and asked, "Is that the dummy deer they put out on the side of the road?" I told him it was not. He said, "Well, it looks just like that one and I shot it the other night!" I had to ask if he had gotten caught and he cheerily

63

said, "Oh yeah, they got me." What really got my attention was how the fellow seemed to wear getting caught shooting the decoy as a badge of honor.

As I would learn, the decoy was quite the mystical animal. Although, initially, all of the decoys were stationary without moving parts, you couldn't tell that by the descriptions many shooters provided. One night CEO Earl Brown and I encountered a young man whose bad sense of direction had caused him to stray onto a property where he did not have a permit to hunt. In addition, a record check showed he was also well known to other law enforcement agencies, who had warrants for him. Therefore, we were giving him a ride to the only public lodging in the county, the jail. At that time, we only had standard cab pickups. Therefore, the fellow was seated between us. Not a great way to transport a violator but we did what we had to do. The fellow was doing his best to strike up a conversation with us. He asked if we knew the game warden in Elmore County and I told him we did. He said a friend of his had shot the decoy deer down there. He said he knew it was a decoy because sparks were flying off of it when he was shooting it! That was a new one. A lot of the people we caught had a lot of "friends" that evidently violated a lot of laws and then told their friends all about it! Their friends evidently provided a tremendous amount of detail since hearing them tell the story you would swear they had been there!

There He Goes, Shannon

SOMETHING I REALLY ENJOYED during my career was working with new officers. Some were better than others. The ones who wanted to learn were a lot of fun. The others, not so much.

Working with these new guys helped me to understand how my wonderful wife could work in a school classroom for thirty years. There definitely is something special when you see the light come on and realize you've taught them something.

The years following the turn of the century (man that sure makes me sound old) were a busy time for me. The two veteran county game wardens had both retired, which resulted in a revolving door of new officers. Considering I had been in the county for about fifteen years, I received the majority of the complaints that came in since I was the only department member familiar to the local folks. This situation resulted in me working closely with the officers and I normally very much enjoyed it. This was prior to our department establishing a formal field training officer program.

Opening day of the 2002 deer season found me once again with a brand-new, green-as-a-gourd officer in tow. We will call him Shannon. Shannon finished the police academy just in time to be able to work the opening day of the Alabama gun deer season. And an eventful day it was.

Prior to opening day, I had noticed the evidence of some traffic on a secluded road in the town of Rockford, the county seat of Coosa County. Before you get to thinking that it is unusual for someone to hunt in town, let me provide some clarification. Rockford is a neat town; however, to call it a town may be a little bit of a stretch. The population is around four hundred folks scattered through about a ten-square-mile area. Like many small towns, the "town" of Rockford went way beyond the actual town limits that constituted just over three square miles. To call it rural doesn't do it justice.

When I initially came to Rockford, I lived "in town," meaning I could literally throw a rock from my house and hit the county courthouse! Many times, I would have deer eating in my yard so close to the window I could hear them crunching the pecans from inside the house. I kid you not. To help you understand that we were really rural, we did not have a 911 system of addresses. Everyone in "town" had a post office box. Shortly after I arrived, the state decided everyone must have their physical address on their driver's license. When my wife went to the courthouse to surrender her Tennessee driver's license and get one for Alabama, the lady asked her for her street address and she told her she didn't have one. The lady asked her where she lived and she told her our house was just two blocks from the courthouse. When the woman asked her in which direction, she told her "behind the old jail." The old jail is a three-story rock building that then and still today serves as a county museum. They prepared her temporary license and told her she would receive her hard copy in the mail. When she looked at the license, she was surprised to see her address listed as "behind old jail." I kid you not! I digress.

Seeing fresh tracks in an area just prior to deer season would often throw up a yellow flag for the local game warden. Yes, normally that would be a red flag, but since what it indicated to me was the likely presence of yellow corn being used as deer bait, in my case it threw up a yellow flag. Concluding my wildlife management area duties a little early one afternoon, I made my way to the suspect area for a look.

I walked in on the property via the main road, which traversed the whole tract from west to east. This was before every road on every property had a camera placed on it. Believe me when I tell you the evolution of the cameras was and is a bane for game wardens. I had not gone far when I found a ladder stand overlooking a green field. The stand was a little bit unusual in that it was only about six feet off the ground. Most were about fifteen feet and some higher. Looking on and around the field did not reveal any problems. I continued down the road and eventually came upon a small green field with a shooting house on the west end. Calling a hunting structure a shooting house is akin to calling Rockford a town. That's what it is but it isn't a very big one. Most shooting houses are relatively small structures, normally measuring eight feet high by four to eight feet long and four to eight feet wide. I have sat in shooting houses that were half that size and a few that were twice that size. My youngest son and I were afforded the opportunity to utilize a hydraulic shooting house. The house was about six feet by six feet by six feet. You stepped inside of the house on the ground and then pushed the lever and raised the house to the desired height up to about fifteen feet. It was nice and Caleb was able to take his first buck that day. I appreciate that opportunity afforded to me by certified wildlife biologist Brian Walker, who managed the property. I digress. I'm bad about that.

When checking a property, it was important to check inside a shooting house if the house was located on the ground, as this one was. A quick glance in the open window of the shooting house revealed several loose kernels of corn on the floor. Walking around the food plot, I found it to be fairly well covered with bait. I gathered a sample of the corn and quickly left the area.

Opening day rolled around and after a pretty eventful morning, Shannon and I headed toward the baited property. We parked at the gate and started down the main road. As we came over a rise in the road, I spotted a hunter sitting in the tree stand overlooking the first green field. As soon as I spotted him, he spotted us and immediately jumped out of the stand and out of our sight. Assuming he was running from us, I said to Shannon, "There he goes, Shannon." I did not have to say anything else. Being fresh out of the academy and in excellent shape, Shannon took off down the road wide open. However, he didn't go that far. He had covered about fifty yards when the guy who had jumped out of the stand topped the hill running at us. It turned out the man had seen our orange hats and had mistaken us for someone illegally hunting the property. It was an interesting meeting. When the fellow said he had spotted our orange hats, I mentioned that I had not seen his. A sheepish grin came upon his face and he realized he should have had one himself.

I left Shannon with the man and I hurried on down to the shooting house on the property. There I found the man's adult son. As there was corn all under his feet, it was difficult for him to deny knowledge that the area was baited. I filled out his bond for hunting by the aid of bait and allowed him to sign it. I explained the area could not be hunted until all the bait had been removed for at least ten days. I then made my way back to Shannon.

Shannon and the first man had made their way back to our truck. I asked Shannon if he had handled the paperwork for no hunter orange. The blank expression on his face gave me the answer. As he stood looking at me with a deer-in-the-headlights look, I asked if he had his ticket book and he replied he did. I told him to go ahead and get the fellows driver's license. Although he was doing everything I asked him to, it was obvious something was amiss. As he stood with the license and ticket book in his hand, it dawned on me what the problem was. He had never written anyone a ticket and wasn't exactly sure what to do. I began walking him through the process and could not help but get tickled when I realized his hand was shaking so badly I could barely make out anything he had written. I wrote the license number down in case I needed to retrieve any more info. I explained the bond to the fellow and had him sign it.

First tickets are big. I remember the date, location, defendant's name, and charge of my first arrest. I had been working three days. While I've probably forgotten more of them than I remember, that one still sticks out in my mind. Your first arrest sort of makes everything real. It helps you understand the awesome responsibility you have been saddled with. Fortunately, the majority of our arrests were not custodial. The first time you took someone into custody really made you understand and appreciate freedom. I remember that it often stunned me how nonchalantly people accepted being arrested. It took me a while to understand getting arrested is very common for a lot of folks. In that regard, I recently checked a couple of young guys on a public use area. They were both about forty years old. When I ran them through the database, it revealed they had eighty-five prior violations between them! I guess after that many you do sort of take it in stride. Now their total is eighty-seven!

I thank God that I survived my first arrest and the thousands that came after it. I know I survived it only by His grace. As I am reviewing this story, I received a text telling me that an Alabama state trooper in my area was killed in a motorcycle wreck. He was only twenty-eight years old. Don't take life for granted. Remember we will all spend eternity somewhere. Where that is, is up to us.

Long Time Coming

FOR THE MAJORITY OF MY CAREER, deer were overpopulated in much of the state. This often prompted people to comment they did not understand why we worried so much about people hunting deer at night. Whenever this came up, it was a good opportunity to explain that night hunting was as much of a public safety issue as it was a resource concern.

In countless presentations, I used a picture of a home that had been shot into by someone shooting at a deer at night. Buckshot had peppered the brick, blown out the picture window, and struck the mantle above the fireplace. I witnessed multiple houses hit by bullets during my career.

The Shelton house in Coosa County was the photo I often used. Mr. Shelton had died years earlier but Mrs. Shelton still lived there. One night I received a call stating someone in a small, dark-colored car had once again shot at a deer in front of her house. If you have read many of my stories, you have learned that in my experience, contrary to popular belief, many night hunters drove small cars. I got dressed and headed toward the location.

During this time, the dispatching through our county sheriff's office left a lot to be desired. I radioed the jail and told them I was 10-81, which was the code for in the vicinity of the complaint. As I came up to County Road 36, I observed a small, dark vehicle coming from the direction of the Shelton house. As the vehicle passed by me, I noticed it was occupied by three white males. I pulled out behind the vehicle. I radioed the jail and told them I was stopping a vehicle matching the description I had been given and gave them the tag number. The driver pulled the vehicle to the side of the road at an intersection with a gravel road that led into the adjoining county. It was interesting how often we received calls that were right on the county line. Evidently folks thought the hunting would be better in an adjacent county. I guess it was the grass-is-always-greener kind of situation. I exited my vehicle and began to slowly approach the car. This was always a dangerous time and especially so when you were in the middle of nowhere and outnumbered three to one by armed suspects.

As I reached the rear of the car, the driver hit the gas. The rear wheels began to spin, filling the air with gravel. I quickly retreated and jumped back into my truck. Although it was obvious the driver was going to flee, I was not prepared for what happened next. Instead of going in the direction he was headed, the driver spun the car around and came back right past me. A lot of things are going through your mind at a time like that. I was trying to get a look at the driver, a young blond-headed kid. I also had to make the decision whether or not to ram into the car, stopping the pursuit but also damaging both vehicles. I put my truck into reverse but knowing how long it would take to get it repaired and the grief I would get for it, I decided to wait until the vehicle cleared mine and then spun around and gave chase. I knew the road well; however, that advantage was short lived when the driver turned off his headlights. It was pitch dark and I'll never know how he stayed in the road. Once I reached the intersection of County Road 31 and County Road 60, I realized I had lost the vehicle.

I called the jail and told them the vehicle had eluded me and asked who the registration came back to. The dispatcher responded with, "Can you give me that tag number again?" As a good friend from college was fond of saying, "I hit top limb!" I was fit to be tied. I was in the middle of nowhere, risking my life, and they had not even written down the tag number I had called in to them. I pulled off the side of the road and tried to regain my composure. As I tried to calm down, a local state trooper came on the radio and asked the dispatcher if I needed any assistance. Their immediate reply was "Negative." I wanted to scream. I guess calling me and asking if I needed any assistance never crossed their pea brain. Although I was incensed, I was able to visualize the tag on the vehicle and come up with the number. The dispatcher ran the tag and gave me the information. The car was registered to a female in the adjoining county. I immediately headed to the address. I staked out the address for several hours; however, the car never returned there.

The next day I gathered up my partner, and we went to the home where the car was registered. We learned that the owner was a young girl. We spoke with her and her parents. She stated her boyfriend, Dwayne Carney, had been using her car on the night in question. She said he was accompanied by two friends. Other than that, she didn't know very much. We looked up Mr. Carney and I identified him as the driver of the car. I met with the clerk and obtained warrants for attempting to elude, driving while suspended, and driving on the wrong side of the road. I gave the warrants to my partner and he and the Elmore County game warden pursued the subject for two or three weeks but to no avail. Time moved on and I pretty much forgot about the case.

Four years later, I had just returned from church on Wednesday night when the phone rang. It was the dispatcher from the sheriff's office. He told me a deputy had picked up a fellow on a game and fish warrant. I asked who it was and he replied, "Dwayne Carney." I asked to speak to the deputy who had brought him in. Deputy Josh Jones got on the line and I asked him what the fellow had to say. He said the man had declared he was innocent and he would fight the charges in court. I asked if he would hold him until I could get there and he said he would be there.

As I got dressed, I was thinking about whether or not I would be able to identify the man. I had only seen him as he quickly drove by me in the dark four years earlier. I knew if I couldn't positively identify him, I would have to dismiss the cases. However, there was always the chance the man would plead guilty, although that sounded highly unlikely. We would just have to see how it would go.

I soon arrived at the jail. As I walked toward the holding room, I spotted the young man standing behind the glass. I secured my gun in the security locker and was buzzed through the heavy metal door. I came around the corner and faced the young man at a distance of about twelve feet. I stopped and gave him my best "Don't I know you?" look.

I held the gaze for probably ten seconds. Just long enough for the man to turn to the jailer and say, "He knows I'm the one that ran from him!"

I immediately said, "Yeah, it's you buddy." He just bowed his head.

As I walked up to the man, he said, "Man, I was drunk and I was crazy and I'm sorry." I told him I would appreciate it if he would give me a statement to that effect, and he did. He said the jailers had told him I was a fair man and it would be best for him to be honest with me. He told me he wanted to try to get his life straightened out and I told him I would give him what help I could.

The court date rolled around and I asked the judge to drop one charge and allow the man to plead guilty to the other two. The judge agreed and Mr. Carney was fined a total of $1,224. I must admit I was shocked by what happened next. The man told the judge he didn't have the money and would need thirty days to get it. I could not believe he came to court without the money knowing the judge would put him back in jail. However, I received yet another even bigger shock when our hardline, hardnosed judge granted his request. As I stood there with my mouth hanging open in disbelief, the judge told him if he did not come up with the money, he would start serving his thirty days in jail. The man assured me and the judge he would have it paid by the due date. I wanted to blurt out to the judge that it had taken four years to get this man to answer the charges and only then because a deputy happened to check to see if he had any warrants on him while he had him stopped. But I knew it would do no good so I held my tongue, which wasn't easy with my mouth gaped open like it was.

The thirty days came and went and sure enough, Mr. Carney did not make good on his promise to pay his fines. As I began following up on the cases, I learned he had also not made good concerning his promise to turn his life around. A little research revealed he now had added to his list of warrants. In addition to the failure to pay warrants I held, he now had two felony warrants in adjoining Elmore County. I again began the process of locating this fugitive from justice.

I would soon learn this guy was as slippery as a moss-covered rock in a fast-moving stream. (If you've never stepped on such a rock, they're slippery!) Although he had to make court appearances in an adjoining county and our failure-to-pay warrants were in the system, he remained on the loose. Once again, the trail grew cold and I became preoccupied with trying to cover the eighteen counties I was now covering as a private lands biologist. However, one day while at the jail I decided to run the name just to see if anything popped up. Lo and behold, the record showed Mr. Carney had been charged with two felonies in Lee County within the last week. This was seven years after the attempting-to-elude incident had taken place. I immediately got on the phone and eventually spoke with an assistant district attorney who was handling the case. She advised me he had been released on bond awaiting a grand jury indictment. I explained my interest in the man and that she would be lucky if she saw him again. I asked her to contact me if he was indicted and I would be present at the arraignment.

Once again, I was busy. With the retirement of my cohort wildlife biologist, I was now attempting to cover forty counties. It was obviously more than one person could handle but I was trying. During this time, my law enforcement activities were severely curtailed. There just wasn't enough time in the week. However, I eventually did check the Law Enforcement Tactical System and learned that Mr. Carney was in fact incarcerated in an Alabama prison. Obviously, I had not been contacted about his indictment. Of course, she may have tried to contact me. I was going in multiple directions. I went to our county jail and asked them to place a hold on Mr. Carney. This would mean the Department of Corrections would contact us when it was time for him to be released and we could transport him to our jail.

Months passed and I again checked the system and learned that Mr. Carney had been released. Once again, I was ready to hit top limb! Actually, I was more ready to throw in the towel. I don't give up easily; however, this had rocked on for years and the fellow had been in custody at least three times. It was frustrating. I put it on the back burner and didn't give it much thought.

Fast forward another three years. I'm at home watching the evening news from Montgomery. As is very common, the station aired a Crime Stoppers segment showing a picture of a man who was wanted for questioning by Elmore County authorities. I looked at the picture and thought the fellow looked familiar. Of course, by this time I had made or assisted on probably over three thousand cases and therefore everybody looked a little familiar. I didn't think too much about it.

The next night the news again showed the wanted individual's picture and stated the man, Dwayne Carney, had been placed in the Elmore County jail thanks to tips from the public. I sat with my mouth hanging open. I immediately called our jail and asked them to contact Elmore County and place a hold on Mr. Carney.

A couple of months later, Mr. Carney was finally returned to the Coosa County jail to await a hearing on his failure to pay warrants. Ten days later, Mr. Carney appeared before the district court judge. The judge asked him if he was prepared to pay his fines and court costs from his now more than ten-year-old cases. He replied he didn't have any money. The judge did not skip a beat and told him he could spend another twenty days with us. The man protested, saying he had already been in our jail for ten days. The judge explained that taking the ten days from his thirty-day sentence left twenty days and that he would serve every day of it.

I have used this case to train young officers concerning the need to make good notes on your cases. Who would think it would be four years before you would get the defendant into the courtroom? Who would think that it would take twelve years for a couple of traffic cases to come to fruition? It also teaches something else that is very important. A review of Mr. Carney's rap sheet shows he has had over fifty felony and misdemeanor cases. As conservation officers, we always have to remember our criminals are often criminals in general.

I was thankful to Montgomery Crime Stoppers for helping get these cases to a conclusion. Without them airing the segment on the nightly news, I might still be looking for the guy!

Sitting in the Truck Window

LIFE AS A WILDLIFE BIOLOGIST and conservation enforcement officer (CEO) changed dramatically for me after the two longtime CEOs in my county retired. It wasn't long until I found myself in a new unofficial role of CEO training officer. I learned to love this role and did so with a few exceptions. As I have stated many times, I am very thankful that I had several officers who were willing to "train" me. Although I finished at the top of my class at the police academy, they taught me very little about conservation law enforcement. There was a lot to learn and I did my best to teach the new officers that were willing to listen.

The first officer I spent a lot of time with was Shannon Calfee. Shannon had worked construction prior to being hired with us and had limited experience in the woods. Our association was a good one and I really enjoyed it. We had many interesting cases I have chronicled. One cold winter day found us at one of the most productive areas in the county for game law violations, a place known as the skating rink. Before my time, there had been a skating rink in the middle of nowhere on County Road 56 west of the Weogufka community. The area held plenty of deer and for several years the area offered a good hiding place from which you could observe the road. Unfortunately, the pine trees eventually grew too high and obscured the view. The landowner, a county forest ranger and good friend, Buddy Adcox, gave me permission to operate the deer decoy on the property and it normally produced results. On this afternoon, Shannon had positioned the fake deer south of the road in a small opening in the thick pines. We were hidden in a fire break across the road. We had very little traffic; however, around four o'clock we heard a slow-moving vehicle approaching our location. I told Shannon to ease out toward the road so he could observe the vehicle while I stayed in the truck ready to pounce out on the violators. For those old enough to remember, the situation reminded me of Marlin Perkins and Jim Fowler on the *Wild Kingdom* television show! If you aren't familiar, Marlin always watched from the observation point while Jim fought with an anaconda or wrestled an alligator.

Shannon hurried up toward the road and watched as the truck drove by. As the vehicle passed the decoy, I heard the telltale sound of deceleration and knew they had spotted the target. While some road hunters would slide to a stop and shoot, most would ease by and then return. The vehicle eased down the road and I listened as they turned around and headed back toward us. With my hand on the ignition key, I anxiously awaited the shot I felt certain would come. The vehicle slowed considerably and then pulled away. Shannon turned and looked at me and raised his hands in an "I don't know what happened" gesture. I motioned for him to come to me. I have had many vehicles make numerous passes before shooting; however, that normally occurred more at night than in the daylight. Shannon hustled back to my location and said, "I don't know why they didn't shoot."

I asked, "Did they see it?" and he replied, "Yeah, the passenger was sitting in the window with his rifle over the cab of the truck."

Sitting in the Truck Window

"Get in!" I yelled as I cranked the truck and slammed it in gear.

Fortunately, Shannon was young and in good shape; therefore, he was able to jump into the truck as I was quickly pulling out of our hiding spot. I rapidly explained that sitting in the window was not a normal way to ride and coupled with having your rifle in hand over the cab of the truck proved intent to me. Granted, I would much rather they had shot; however, this was enough for them to receive a talking to at the very least.

A few seconds later, I was behind the vehicle with my blue lights flashing. As the driver pulled over, I told Shannon I would approach on the passenger side first and he needed to keep an eye on the driver. I did this because his report of the passenger sitting in the window led me to believe the firearm and likely some other evidence would be on that side. Since Shannon was still new at this, I told him to hang back and keep an eye on the driver. Two young men and a young boy occupied the truck. I took the rifle from the passenger and noted it was unloaded. As I looked at the numerous shells lying in the floorboard, I noticed the passenger was visibly shaken. The fact they only had one rifle between them was an obvious road hunting indicator.

With everything secure, I escorted the passenger to the rear of the vehicle while Shannon solicited some identification from the driver. I took the card from my wallet and read the man the Miranda warning. This intensified his nervousness as I had hoped it would.

You never knew how reading the Miranda warning to a suspect would affect them. Overtime, I learned to read body language and could guess how the warning would be taken. If we wanted to use the suspect's statement in court, then we had to advise them of their rights. However, if you started off by reading them the warning, many times they would not say anything. Very often we did not need a statement since the violation had occurred in our presence. However, it was normally always good to get a statement.

It was obvious this fellow was pretty shaken up. I began our conversation by asking, "Do you always carry your ammunition in the floorboard?"

He hurriedly replied, "No sir, no sir, Mr. Glover."

When I asked, "Why was it there?" the man admitted he had unloaded the gun because he knew we would be coming after them. "But it was loaded when you were looking at that deer back there?"

"Yes, sir, it was."

With the information flowing easily I began trying to calm the man down by telling him I appreciated his honesty. I then said, "Why don't you tell me the whole story?" He did not hesitate.

He said they had been watching the football game on TV and at halftime he and the driver decided to "ride the loop" and see if they could see a deer to shoot. I said, "You do know that it's illegal to hunt from the road and from a vehicle and you don't have to shoot to be considered hunting?" He replied he understood. I took his driver's license and began writing him a ticket for hunting from the road and from the vehicle. I asked if he had a permit to hunt on this property and he once again became shaken. He said he did not but he knew Mr. Adcox (the landowner) and he might be able to get one. I told him since he had been honest with me I would just let that violation go with a verbal warning. He thanked me profusely and then asked how soon he could be at the courthouse to pay his tickets. I told him it was up to the judge as to whether or not they could pay off before court; however, my recommendation would be for a minimum fine and to let them pay it early. He again thanked me. Shannon finished with the driver, who was not nearly as thankful as the passenger, and the trio went on their way.

We went back to our hiding spot and I provided Shannon some training concerning probable cause and how that once you had that, you often could end up with something else. It was one of many lessons he would learn while working in the wilds of Coosa County.

Taking Them to the Vet

"YOU CAN'T MAKE THIS STUFF UP." I've often used that line when referring to incidents that have occurred during my career and to accounts related to me by other officers. A highlight of my career was to return to my alma mater, Mississippi State University (MSU), and speak to wildlife classes and the wildlife law enforcement club. My dear friend Dr. Jeanne Jones was a fellow graduate research assistant who earned a PhD and became a highly esteemed professor of wildlife at MSU. She requested I provide her students with a "lecture" concerning the realities of being a wildlife biologist for a state agency blended with many of her favorite stories from the law enforcement side of my position.

As often as possible, I would have my family accompany me when I spoke with the classes. After one of the lectures, my wife, Melanie, Jeanne, and I were walking across campus when Melanie asked a question that had never crossed my mind. She said, "I wonder if they [the students] realize all of those stories are true?" I had never considered they might think some of what I told them was actually fictitious! However, after I thought about it, a lot of what I've experienced is hard to believe!

A retired conservation enforcement officer (CEO) related a story to me that definitely would fall into the hard-to-believe category. The CEO had a long career and during that time made literally thousands of arrests. A couple of those arrests came on a late summer day and involved a fellow who was quick on his feet and had a good imagination.

Late in the afternoon, the officer was contacted by a complainant who stated someone had just shot a couple of deer and was headed to their house with them. They provided a vehicle description and the name of the fellow involved. Being close by and familiar with the individual and the location of his house, the officer was able to intercept the truck.

Let me tell you, when you worked in a county comprised of over 650 square miles, the odds were definitely against you being in the right spot at the right time. Sometimes you were so far from the call you wondered if it was even worth heading toward it.

The officer pulled in behind the truck and activated his blue light and the driver slowly pulled to the side of the road. The CEO approached the vehicle and observed two deer lying in the bed of the pickup. As soon as he reached the cab, the driver began to plead his case. He started with a phrase that was very familiar to those in our profession: "This is not what it looks like." Our officer responded, "I hope not because this doesn't look good!" The driver proceeded to render what he felt was a very plausible explanation.

It seems his grandmother had a couple of apple trees in her backyard and she couldn't get a single apple since the deer kept eating everything within reach. Therefore, granny had solicited junior's assistance in running the deer off. The officer told him there was no problem in running deer away from an apple tree; however, it appeared these deer had been shot in the head! The fellow did not miss a beat and explained how his intention had been to shoot over the deer's heads but evidently his sights were off and he had hit the deer in the head.

The officer was fairly quick as well and asked, "Did you not figure that out after you shot the first one?"

As the guy struggled for a reply, the officer examined the obviously dead deer and asked what he had planned to do with them. His response was classic: "Oh, I was taking them to the vet to see if there was anything he could do for them!" And people actually think we make some of this stuff up!

Obviously, these deer were beyond any help a veterinarian could provide. That is the same for us. Once life ends here, our eternal life will begin. The decision of where we will spend eternity is a decision we must make before it is everlastingly too late. Today would be a great time. Ironically, as I am doing the final edit on this story, I received word that the officer in this story had passed away. That sort of puts an exclamation point on it, doesn't it? Rest in peace, Don.

Prison Chase

IN AN EFFORT to bring the chase to an end, the game warden rammed the vehicle. When the driver careened into the ditch and came back up into the road without ever letting off the gas, the officer knew this wasn't your typical night hunter.

A critical skill the conservation enforcement officer (CEO) must possess is a good power of observation. A multitude of wildlife law violations occur in remote areas off the beaten path. These areas are often far from anyone who might see and report nefarious activities. Therefore, the CEO must be observant when in these areas to pick up on any evidence that suggests someone has been lurking and messing around. Noticing where someone has turned crossways in the road or pulled off on a side trail or spotting a spent hull in or along the road often leads to an eventual arrest.

Elmore County CEO Byron Smith was a keen observer. On a cool fall night, this skill resulted in a high-speed, hair-raising chase. Byron had noticed an area near the state prison in the county where it appeared someone had repeatedly backed into an opening which would allow their headlights to illuminate the field across the county road. He had seen this technique before. Folks would find where deer were using a field with a corresponding location where they could sit in their vehicle and periodically turn on their headlights, illuminating the field and hopefully a target. Of course, this didn't always indicate someone was hunting deer at night. I feel certain every officer has checked out a situation like this and found shooting a deer was the last thing on the couple's mind! However, you never knew what might be going on and this type of activity was worth checking out. Byron decided he needed to keep a check on the area. He scouted around and located a hiding spot or "hole" where he could conceal his vehicle and observe the area.

While "lounging" on the hood of his Ford Bronco hidden in his hole, he watched as a car pulled past the area and backed in with its headlights illuminating the field across the road. When the driver turned off his headlights, the officer thought things were just as he had suspected. After a few minutes, the driver turned on the headlights and almost immediately turned them off. The car sat motionless for a couple of minutes and Byron decided to go ahead and check things out. He moved into position directly in front of the vehicle and activated his blue lights.

Pulling up head-on to a vehicle was always a dangerous proposition; however, it was not uncommon for us to have to approach in this manner. The vehicle's driver decided not to stick around and immediately hit the gas and spun past Byron's truck. The officer immediately pursued the vehicle.

While many of our chases were of fairly short duration, others were multimile marathons. We were often at a disadvantage during a chase in that we were normally in a four-wheel-drive truck, which wasn't the most nimble pursuit vehicle. However, CEOs were normally very good drivers. That reminds me of the time that we all went to the state trooper pursuit driving school. When we were about halfway through the driving part of the course, my instructor looked at me and said, "Y'all are the best drivers." He went on to say that when training municipal police officers, he could ride with about three of them and would then be sick from spinning in circles. We discussed it and decided the difference was possibly due to the fact that we all regularly drove on muddy and gravel roads. Driving on those roads would teach you how to get straightened out when the rear end of your vehicle tried to get away from you. You quickly learned to turn the steering wheel in the direction your rear end was sliding in order to straighten things out. If you turn the wheel in the opposite direction, you would quickly spin around in a circle. Since I have gotten way off of my story, let me go ahead and say that it always interests me when people speak about a NASCAR race and say they don't see what's so difficult about somebody driving around in a circle. I always try to ask them when was the last time they drove at speeds over 100 miles per hour? I do not recommend it but I can tell you that at 140 miles per hour things get pretty squirrelly! So, I appreciate those guys that drive at 200 miles per hour six inches off each other's bumpers! I digress.

Back to Byron's chase. Once the driver of the car had reached his top speed and realized the Bronco was hanging right with him, he decided to change tactics. As Byron pulled up close on the vehicle and his headlights illuminated the interior of the car, he noticed the driver was turning his whole body to look at the officer and his right hand was down behind the seat, where Byron couldn't see it. Thinking the fleeing driver might be preparing to shoot at him, Byron backed off and the driver again accelerated and sped off. Byron again closed the gap between them and the driver once again slowed and turned to engage the officer. Byron again backed off and the driver sped away. When Byron decided to close the gap again, he also decided he would try a different technique. When the fleeing vehicle slowed, Byron didn't and rammed the vehicle, knocking it off the road. The driver never slowed down as he went down an embankment and came right back up into the road. Byron said at this point he realized he wasn't chasing your run-of-the-mill night hunter.

During the course of the chase, Byron had contacted the local sheriff's office (SO) and state troopers and had them coming toward him. As he stayed behind the driver, the man took a turn Byron knew led to a dead end. This put him on high alert. As the road played out, the man slid the car to a stop. Byron had already stopped and exited his truck and took cover behind the vehicle. The subject's driver's-side door flew open and the driver slid out onto the ground, went under the door, and came up on the other side with a pistol in his hand and looking for a target! When the man couldn't spot the officer, he turned and ran into the woods. Byron moved back to the truck and called the SO and asked them to contact the prison and get the dog team en route to his location.

The dog team arrived soon. Byron explained the chase had begun near the prison and had covered a few miles. He advised the man was armed with a handgun and had run into the woods in front of where his car was currently setting. He told them he had not contaminated the track. The man was found within three hundred yards of the vehicle. Interestingly, he was found in possession of the pistol and a bag full of drugs.

Byron was later contacted by the Alabama Bureau of Investigation, who informed him the subject he had chased had been under investigation for supplying drugs to correctional officers who were smuggling them into the prison. This incident again enforced the idea you never knew who you might end up dealing with in the middle of nowhere in the dark of night!

There Are No Deer Left!

DURING A LONG CAREER, I had many opportunities for folks to point out that they knew a little more about what should be done with the deer herd than I did. Sure, I had a BS degree in environmental biology and an MS degree in wildlife ecology and at one time I worked with eighty clubs on the deer management program. While I felt that gave me a fairly good insight into deer management, others would disagree. I received a complaint from a landowner in the southern part of the county who was upset over our season-long either-sex deer season and two-antlerless-deer-per-day limit. The avid hunter claimed we had allowed the deer herd to be decimated to the point that he had trouble locating even a track on his property where there used to be plenty of deer. He requested we immediately stop the either-sex deer hunting. He also stated he had heard our department was allowing bowhunters to take deer from Oak Mountain State Park near Birmingham to try to reduce the population. He suggested we trap the deer in the park and relocate them to his area.

I assured him we still had plenty of deer in the county. I acknowledged the numbers were not nearly as many as there once were. I attempted to explain the either-sex season was in place to try and reduce the deer herd, which we considered to be overpopulated. I also attempted to explain trapping and relocating deer was a very expensive and time-consuming activity and we would not be doing that. I assured him I understood his concern, appreciated his input, and would pass it on to the powers that be in Montgomery.

A week later I was in a meeting in Montgomery and did pass along the man's concerns. Meetings at the state headquarters were not my favorite thing. Unfortunately, since I was only forty-five miles north of the office, I frequently had to attend meetings there. The meeting did not adjourn until late and I was hurrying home along Highway 231. Although 231 is a major artery through Alabama, the majority of it in our area is all two lanes with limited areas suitable for passing. As I entered the south end of Coosa County, I had been following a slow car for several miles. As I passed County Road 10, I finally got an opportunity to go around the slow mover. I pulled into the southbound lane and had begun to overtake the car when I caught movement on the left side of the highway. A fairly large deer was running toward the road. Although I immediately decelerated, I realized there was no way to avoid the deer and my goal quickly became to keep from hitting the car beside me.

The deer hit my left headlight and destroyed the light, grill, and bumper. The impact spun the deer around, causing it to go down the left side of my vehicle, ruining the front fender and both doors. Fortunately, I was able to hold the vehicle in my lane and not collide with the vehicle that was directly beside me when the collision occurred. I was able to get slowed down and pulled over in the next driveway. I hope you haven't got ahead of me: it was the driveway of the man who had called to complain there were no deer left in the area. I kid you not. That nonexistent deer did in excess of $4,700 worth of damage. You can't make this stuff up.

One That Got Away

ALMOST EVERY STORY I have written details an incident where we were successful in apprehending someone. As I'm sure you are aware, we were not always successful. As a matter of fact, if you divided the number of nights we worked by the number of nights we apprehended someone, the result would be a very small percentage. This story is about one of those unsuccessful times.

I was in my favorite night hunting honey hole near the site of the old skating rink in Weogufka in west central Coosa County. Working alone, which was not a wise decision, I had placed the deer decoy on the south side of the road. Due to the trees coming up to the road, I had to put it much closer to the road than what I would have liked. Despite this, I hoped the good luck I had experienced there in the past would hold. The skating rink locale had proved to be a productive spot for me. I pulled into my normal hiding spot on the north side of the road and began my wait.

We had recently had a good rain and, although my hiding spot was pretty wet, I did not have any problem getting into it. Standing outside my truck, I heard a vehicle coming from the west. Little did I know I was about to have a couple of things happen that I had never experienced. I listened as the driver let off the accelerator as he passed the decoy. This was always a good sign. However, what happened next erased my good feeling.

I quickly got into my truck. Although I could not actually see the road in front of me, there was no mistaking that the truck was going to turn into the woods road I was sitting in. I held my breath and hoped he would not pull far enough up the road to illuminate my truck. Those hopes were quickly dashed when his headlights hit me in the face. I slammed my fist down on the steering wheel as the truck reversed back into the road and went back the way he had come. I was so aggravated that he had pulled up far enough to see me. As hard as it was to be in the right place at the right time, I could not believe I had messed this up. As I was fuming over what had just occurred, I did not know things were about to go from bad to worse.

The truck pulled back toward the decoy and suddenly a rifle blast split the night. I couldn't believe it. How on earth did the driver not see me and my truck as we were plainly lit up in his headlights? At the same time, I could not believe my good fortune. I cranked the truck and slammed it into gear and mashed the accelerator to the floor. However, instead of flying down the hill and into the road after the shooter, I simply sat there and listened to my tires spinning. I put the truck in reverse and it still didn't move. Unfortunately, although my truck was a four-wheel drive, as a cost-saving measure it had been special ordered with manual locking hubs. Therefore, I had to get out and lock both hubs in and then put the truck in four-wheel drive and pull out into the road.

While the violator had not been observant enough to see me sitting in my truck in his headlights, it didn't take him very long to figure out the deer, which just stood there after he had shot it, was a fake. He was quickly hightailing it up the road. I saw his taillights once. There was an intersection about a mile up the road and when I reached it, he was out of sight and I had no way of knowing which way he had gone. I returned to my setup, threw the decoy in the back of my truck, and went home totally dejected.

Although I worked hundreds of nights that I didn't catch anyone, this one really hurt. However, it was a valuable learning experience. I learned that just because a violator lights you up, he may not see you at all. I also learned not to park in a wet place where a would-be violator is apt to turn into! Fortunately, my next night at the skating rink ended a whole lot better. Well, better for me anyway.

One thing this episode did was let me know what it felt like to ride the game warden roller coaster. That was what I called it when a violator experienced the high of seeing a deer and having it stand there long enough for them to shoot it, and then the low of realizing it wasn't real and seeing the blue lights in their rearview mirror. That is a bad feeling. There will always be highs and lows in life. There will be gain and loss. There will be life and death. There will be heaven or hell. The choices we make will determine the outcomes. The choice is ours. Choose you this day who you will serve.

Close Call at the Dog Track

WE ALL FACE THREATS on a regular basis. Some we are aware of and others not so much. When you have a law enforcement job, you are probably a little more on the lookout than other folks. At least you should be. You may not know it, but a lot of folks don't appreciate being arrested. It's true. Many of them hold it against the officer, even though they deserved it. Another group who isn't well liked by these outlaws are the judges that send them off and/or get in their pocketbooks. I learned our judges receive their share of threats. It's the ones that creep up from behind that are often the most troubling.

If you have read many of my stories, you have likely come to understand my first district court judge was a colorful fellow. The Coosa County District Court was the first stop for those violators we apprehended. Thankfully, our judge held wildlife law breakers in low esteem and had no qualms about hammering the outlaws we brought before him. Believe me when I tell you those who broke the conservation laws did not want to come before our judge and I very much appreciated that.

During the hunting season, I was in the courthouse on a fairly regular basis and it was not at all uncommon for the judge to stop me in the hall and relate some interesting tale. One day he shared that he had encountered a close call over the past weekend. I

94

wasn't sure what type of close call it might have been. As you can imagine a judge who handled hundreds of cases a month probably has some enemies. As mentioned earlier, rather than accept responsibility for their actions, people very often blame the officer for their arrest and later blame the judge for the consequences of their actions.

I listened intently as the judge told the story. It turns out he had gone to a nearby county to visit the dog track and maybe see how his luck would run. During a lull in the action, the judge made what he thought would be a quick visit to the restroom. As he stood at the urinal, he was startled by the voice of a man standing directly behind him. Obviously, anyone who has ever utilized a urinal realizes the design of the apparatus leaves you in a pretty vulnerable situation. Your back is to everything and your hands are—well you understand. The judge explained he was the only person at the line of urinals and with several open slots it was obvious the fellow was not waiting for a position to become available. That made what came next all the more troubling.

An ominous voice asked, "Aren't you the judge from Coosa County?" Instantly, the judge thought he was trapped like a rat. He said as soon as he heard the question, he could anticipate the knife slicing through his back and could visualize dying a slow death on the dirty floor of the dog track men's room. As his life was flashing before his eyes, he quickly realized there was nowhere to go to escape the inevitable. Not knowing anything else to do, he said he simply replied "Yes" and braced for the worst. He said the seconds passed like cold molasses as he awaited his fate. The fellow hesitated for a few seconds that seemed like a week and said, "Well, they caught my brother night hunting up there and you really laid it to him and I appreciate it." The judge said it was as if his legs were made of spaghetti as he fell forward and caught himself on the wall. Regaining his ability to speak, he did his best to utter, "You're welcome." The guy turned and left and after a few moments the judge regained his composure enough to walk out under his own power!

This incident happened many years ago when things weren't like they are today. As I am editing this story, I am watching the news. It is disheartening, to say the least. One of the topics discussed was how it is offensive to many for someone to state a phrase such as "blue lives matter." I have to wonder, does that mean blue lives (the lives of law enforcement officers) do not matter? We are obviously living in troubling times. I can tell you, the Creator of life believes all lives matter. Many areas are calling for the abolishment of the police. I think those need to realize that there will always be someone in the role of authority. I fear the people in areas where the police are abolished will regret that action. Please pray for law enforcement officers.

In this incident, the judge truly believed his life might be in jeopardy. He had every reason to believe that. As a matter of fact, we all should feel that way. I'm not saying we should live in fear, but we should live with the understanding that tomorrow isn't guaranteed. Today is the day of salvation.

Cow Shooters

AUGUST IN CENTRAL ALABAMA is no picnic. The temperature often hovers around one hundred degrees and the humidity seems much higher. At least it feels that way! On a hot August day, I placed a call to Conservation Enforcement Officer (CEO) Jerry Fincher in Talladega County, which bordered Coosa County to the north. As a greeting I asked, "What's going on?" I must admit, his reply of "night hunting" took me totally by surprise.

Although I know night hunting of deer has occurred in every month of the year, it was relatively rare outside of deer season and the month prior to and after. The fact that daytime temperatures were in the high nineties and nighttime lows in the upper seventies made it seem like an odd time for someone to hunt at night. Any deer killed would either have to be dressed or moved to a cooler immediately to keep it from spoiling. Of course, an unfortunate truth is that many deer that are shot at night aren't even picked up. I asked for details and Jerry explained he had received a complaint in the Fayetteville area, near his home, and had located the carcass of a doe that had been shot. He gave me a couple of other details and I told him I would work the complaint with him during the coming weekend.

While Jerry had a few seasons under his belt, I still considered him to be a rookie. I had served as his unofficial field training officer and he was a dang good student. He possessed the strong work ethic needed to be a good game warden and I enjoyed getting to work with him when possible.

Saturday night at 11:00 we were sitting overlooking a large field and sweating profusely. It was eighty-five degrees and I was having trouble visualizing anyone hunting in such weather. We kept our vigil until two in the morning and called it a night without seeing or hearing anything.

A couple of weeks later, Jerry again received a call concerning night hunting in the area; however, this time it seemed the target had changed from deer to cows! Although shooting deer at night is egregious, shooting cows kicks things up a notch. In this case, the culprits made a bad choice of whose cows to shoot. I can tell you for a fact the county sheriff doesn't appreciate someone shooting cows in his county, and when the cows belong to him, it's even worse! We were about to receive a lot of assistance with our investigation. As a matter of fact, Jerry was contacted the next day by the sheriff's investigator stating they had a line on some suspects and would be questioning them that afternoon. I asked what time and told Jerry we needed to be there.

We arrived shortly before 6:00 p.m. and learned two of the suspects were already there and had already admitted to shooting the cows. We set up our video camera and called the subjects in separately. We advised them of their rights and Jerry began the questioning. Both defendants talked freely concerning shooting both deer and cows. Their excuse was they were just stupid. I couldn't argue with that.

During each defendant's statement, they mentioned going to an area where the road turned to gravel and shooting at deer in a field there. This caught my attention since where the road turned to gravel was the county line and they had just admitted to night hunting in Coosa County. My county. In addition, each defendant listed two other subjects who had taken part in the night hunting forays. Jerry asked a few necessary questions to fill in gaps in the story. The subjects wrote out their statements and the interviews were concluded.

We asked the defendants if they would contact the other parties involved and ask them to come to the sheriff's office. They called the subjects and learned one subject was at work, but the other was in town and would come in. He and his girlfriend arrived shortly thereafter. Our information was these subjects were not involved in shooting the cows but had taken part on one of the first nights of deer hunting. We decided to question the girlfriend first. We advised her of her rights and began questioning. She readily admitted she had been with the defendants when they went spotlighting deer in the Fayetteville area. When asked if they had taken a gun with them, she stated they definitely did not have a gun. She went on to say the game wardens had caught her daddy shooting the dummy deer in Coosa County and she knew better than to have a gun with them.

Of course, this piqued my interest and I asked who her daddy was and she replied "Larry Wilton" and asked, "Do you know him?" I told her I did. She replied, "That's not good." I told her I knew a lot of people. We wrapped up her questioning and excused her.

I looked at Jerry and told him I was old as dirt. He said, "Because you are now catching the kids of previous violators?" and I said, "It's worse than that, I've caught her dad and her granddad! Twice!"

Prior to the boyfriend entering the room, I told Jerry we currently only had hearsay evidence against him and really needed a good statement. The young man entered the room and we advised him of his rights and he agreed to speak with us on camera. It was obvious he and his girlfriend had come up with the "we were just looking" defense together. During a lull in the questioning, I told Jerry I would like to ask a few questions. I started by telling the young man that killing cows was a serious thing. He quickly responded he hadn't shot any cows. I pushed forward as if I hadn't heard his reply and said killing cows could very likely lead to a felony charge. He again stated he had not shot any cows. I told him I understood that but he was out with the group that had shot the cows. "Not when they shot the cows I wasn't." I asked if he realized not only was shooting cows a possible felony but the cattle owner could request double the amount of the value of the cows in restitution. Once again, he said he wasn't with them when they shot the cows. I acted as if I hadn't heard his denial and reiterated that Alabama law 9-11-258 stated that anyone who killed livestock while engaged in night hunting would be required to pay the owner double the value of the livestock. It was obvious he had heard enough about paying for the cows and was getting irritated that I insisted on bringing it up. He again, in a much more forceful tone, stated he was not with them when they shot the cows. I immediately came back with "Yeah, but you were with them when they shot the deer" and he said, "Yeah, but not the cows."

Almost immediately he realized what he had just said. He hung his head for a few seconds and then looked up at me with a sheepish grin. I said, "Why don't you tell us about it?" He proceeded to tell us they had used his vehicle and he had shot a seven-point buck and the other defendants had killed a doe and a four-point and had missed some deer in another field. Further questioning revealed the other field was in Coosa County. He gave a written statement and the interview was concluded.

Although we entered court armed with one side of a seven-point rack, a picture of a decomposed doe, four written statements, and video confessions, we were still worried about the outcome. Normally this would have been a pretty easy conviction; however, prior to the court date, we checked on the cases and learned the Talladega County cases had been continued at the request of an attorney in the case, Robert Rumsey. Seeing how almost everyone, myself included, considered Robert to be the best defense attorney in the county, this turn of events gave us a little discomfort.

I had known Robert my entire career. He had been the district attorney in Talladega County when I went to work. Rumor had it he had sent plenty of people to death row and rarely lost a case. During his tenure, it was my good fortune to have him prosecute a couple of my cases and he definitely knew how to do it. However, after twenty-five years of prosecuting, he had retired and gone over to the dark side. That was how we sometimes referred to defense lawyers.

Robert and I had a very good officer/attorney relationship. Unlike many attorneys, he didn't try to show me up and I didn't try to blindside him. We were able to lay our cards on the table and if I had the upper hand, he would concede and ask for leniency, if he had me beat, he would tell me how and if nothing else, I would get a good education in the law. I went to Robert on more than one occasion to ask for advice. Many officers, attorneys, and even judges feared Robert. Upon hearing that Robert had taken the case, I had immediately began to wonder if I had I crossed all my t's and dotted my i's.

As fate would have it, the Coosa County cases came up first. I had to keep reminding Jerry we had started with nothing and anything we got would be good. It turned out two of the three defendants had attorneys and we agreed to a plea. The third defendant received the same deal, although he had not had to pay an attorney, which likely saved him a significant amount. We waited for the cases to be heard in Talladega.

The next month, the cow shooters entered plea agreements to pay restitution for the cows in lieu of being charged with felonies and pled guilty to the hunting charges. Then came the charges against the last night hunter—Robert's client. Once again Rumsey's power was evident when the assistant district attorney came to us wanting to drop the charges. When I asked why, he stated Robert had told him he was going to beat it and he didn't want to be embarrassed in the courtroom. I told him I didn't feel we should give the cases up without a fight. When it was evident he was ready to concede, I told him I would like to talk with Robert about it. Although he didn't like it, he called Robert over and I asked him point blank how was he going to beat us and he said we had no corpus delicti. *Corpus delicti* is a Latin term meaning "the body of the crime." It refers to the idea that before someone can be tried for the crime, the requisite elements of a crime must be proven. In our case we needed to be able to prove a deer had been killed illegally. I reminded him we had statements of codefendants. He told me he could beat that as well. Seeing the writing on the wall, I asked if he would settle for pleading to the hunting at night and us dropping the other charges. After thinking for a moment, he said he would propose that to his client. He soon came back and said that in the interest of time, they would plead to the one charge.

This was an enjoyable case for me and a great learning opportunity for Jerry. As usual, he did a great job pursuing the case. Obviously, having the possible felonies to hold over their heads and having the sheriff's office bearing down on the defendants didn't hurt anything. However, I've witnessed a lot of officers with a lot more evidence than we had who would not pursue such a case. When all was said and done, we had taken a complaint and some determination and ended up collecting $27,000 in fines, court costs, and restitution!

Who All Has to
Know about This?

"WHO ALL HAS TO KNOW ABOUT THIS?"

That was the question the ticketed hunter asked me. He wasn't the first to want to know this, nor would he be the last. I have made several arrests in my career when the violator was extremely interested in knowing whether or not their arrest would be public knowledge. It normally did become public knowledge, but it wasn't because *I* told somebody.

The phone rang and the caller explained he knew where someone was hunting turkey out of season. Our spring season had indeed been closed for five days; therefore, this caller had my full attention. While I did my best to apprehend anyone violating the law, those who tried to take turkeys illegally were on the top of my list. The man said the people were currently on the property and I told him I would be en route.

I am passionate about turkey hunting and I found it hard to stomach someone trying to take turkeys by illegal methods. Unfortunately, many folks pursued turkeys whenever they would gobble, whether in February prior to the season or in May and June after it had gone out. My former partner Hershel Patterson once caught a "well-known" turkey hunter hunting on the second day of June. The season had closed on the twenty-fifth of April!

Many nonhunters have several misconceptions about turkeys. I have had many adults ask me whether or not turkeys can fly. I'm sure the only live turkey a lot of folks have ever seen was either in a barnyard or at a turkey farm. They are not at all familiar with the wild turkey, which can indeed fly at fifty-five miles per hour and can see you blink your eye at twenty yards. I feel certain, based on their erroneous ideas about turkeys, a lot of folks believe hunting a turkey would be less than sporting. Those who believe that are wrong. Due to the fact wild turkeys are pursued by a multitude of predators literally before they hatch from the egg, an adult turkey is the wariest of game birds. An adult gobbler is a true trophy when taken legally.

I was familiar with the farm the informant named and I quickly phoned my partner and advised him of the situation and told him I would meet him there. The property was in the north end of Coosa County, approximately fifteen miles from my home. The property was owned by a local doctor and encompassed several hundred acres. I had been on the property previously and knew it was a mixture of pastures, pine plantations, and hardwoods. On that much acreage, it would be difficult to find a fully camouflaged hunter. I crossed my fingers and hoped we could find the suspects' vehicle.

We arrived on the farm and quickly located a Jeep Cherokee, which contained hunting paraphernalia. After a brief search of the area, we decided to set up on the vehicle and wait for the person or persons to return.

This type of stakeout was very unpredictable. If we had the right vehicle, and it looked as if we did, we felt confident the folks would eventually show up. However, it could take minutes or hours. If they were to spot us or our vehicles, they might not come back at all. We settled in to wait. Fortunately, our wait was a short one. Two camo-clad individuals emerged from the woods with their shotguns in hand. Experience had taught us to wait until the pair reached the vehicle before making our presence known. If you stepped out too quickly, it could prompt a foot chase and someone in full camo was often difficult to find in the woods.

As the men reached the vehicle, we stepped out of our hiding spot, identified ourselves, and asked for their guns, licenses, and permits. The fellow we identified as the vehicle owner immediately took a belligerent tone and asked if there was a problem. We explained since turkey season had ended five days earlier, yes, there was a problem. While the first guy continued to bluster and fume, the other was contrite and apologetic. I asked the ornery man about the turkey tail that was visible in his vehicle. He immediately belligerently informed me that was the tail from a Rio Grande gobbler and we didn't have that species around here. He then added, "We hunt easterns here." I did not bother to inform him that I was a certified wildlife biologist and I was well aware of what species the tail had come from and what species we had here. Neither did I inform him that I really appreciated him confirming he was in fact hunting in closed season. I did advise him he and his partner were under arrest for hunting turkey in closed season.

It turned out the polite subject was a county commissioner in an adjacent county. By this time, I had arrested numerous "somebodies" and I was not impressed. While this fellow was very nice, he did ask, "Who all has to know about this?" We told him that although it was a matter of public record, we would not publicize his arrest. We allowed the men to sign their bonds and be on their way.

As usually happened in this type situation, my phone rang the next day and the caller asked if I had arrested the county commissioner. Although my partner and I had not mentioned the arrest to anyone, we both received calls concerning the arrests. Surprisingly, this was the norm when folks didn't want the word to get out.

I once responded to a report of a baited area and a trip to the spot revealed it was indeed baited with corn. I returned on Saturday morning and found a bow hunter about twenty feet high in a pine tree overlooking the baited site. I spotted the fellow in the tree from about seventy-five yards away. He was sitting looking in the direction of the bait and away from me. I slowly and quietly eased my very large carcass toward him. When I was about twenty yards away, I intentionally broke a stick to get his attention. He never looked my way. This was not at all unusual. I whistled and the fellow did not acknowledge it in any way. I moved to within ten yards of the base of his tree and he still had no idea I was anywhere on the place. I again whistled. This always amused me. I had walked all the way to this fellow's tree and for the last twenty yards I had made no effort to be quiet. I had whistled at him twice and now he ever so slowly turned his head only to spot my large frame standing almost directly below him. I instructed him to let his bow down and to descend the tree safely. While he was performing these tasks, I walked over to the baited area and was surprised to see all of the corn was gone. Although our regulation stated all bait must be gone for ten days before the area could be hunted legally and I was within that window, I didn't like making a case when there was actually no bait present. I said I didn't like it, I didn't say I hadn't done it!

As the camo-clad man lowered his bow and was gathering his gear in preparation to climb down the tree, I was debating whether or not to write him a ticket or to tell him just to stay up there. I walked back toward the base of his tree, which was alongside a sandy logging road traversing a pine thicket. As I looked down in the dusty road, I noticed several nice white oak acorns littering the ground. I must admit it took me a minute to realize there was something wrong with this picture. I looked around to confirm there were no white oak trees in the area.

Once the hunter was safely on the ground, I asked to see his hunting license. He dug it out and handed it to me. As I confirmed the license was valid, I asked if he had been aware there was corn nearby. He wasn't a good liar but did his best to deny knowledge of the corn having been there earlier. I gave him my "I know you're lying" look and he did his best to hold it together. I could tell the deception wasn't coming easy for him. However, I decided not to belabor the point but instead to move on to the new evidence. I asked if he could possibly tell me where the acorns littering the ground around our feet had come from. He paused for a few seconds and pointed to a green canvas bag on his stand. I unzipped the bag and found it contained several acorns. He acted as if he was baffled and asked if it was illegal to hunt over acorns and I told him it was if he had placed them there as an attractant. I no longer had any doubt about whether or not he was getting a ticket and I requested his driver's license and began writing him a citation. When I asked for his occupation, he got a panic-stricken look on his face and immediately asked, "Who all has to know about this?" I told him it would be a matter of public record but I wouldn't tell anyone. He said he would really rather that his engineering firm didn't find out. He then made an interesting request I had not heard in the past. He asked if I would mind putting on the ticket that he was hunting over acorns and not corn. I quickly considered he might try to use this as a defense in court, yet I reasoned he was in violation either way and so I granted his request.

In my experience, there are normally three reasons why someone will ask "Who all has to know about this?" The person is a known public figure or they think they are; the person knows an arrest and conviction may affect their job; or the person has friends, family, or church members whom they don't want to know about it.

We all have done things we would rather others not know about. However, it usually happens just like it did with these hunting cases. That is, it gets out without the officer saying a word. That is the irony of it. The people who worry the most the word will get out end up telling it themselves.

The engineer may have thought he could sell his colleagues and others on the stupid game warden that actually wrote him a ticket for hunting over acorns. When I think of this, the beginning of several Bible verses comes to mind. Those first words are "be not deceived." Paraphrased, don't kid yourself. God so often inspired biblical writers to begin verses with that admonition. Why? Because we are so good at deceiving ourselves! This is illustrated by the reasons people don't want their violation found out.

First, we often fool ourselves into thinking we are somebody. The Bible makes it clear in Proverbs, where it says anyone who does wrong will be repaid for their wrongs, and there is no favoritism. God is no respecter of persons. We must remember the Bible says our righteousness is like filthy rags. We are not "somebody."

Next, we fool ourselves into thinking if no one finds out there won't be a consequence. I have had many people tell me it's only illegal if you get caught. That is so untrue. Sin has consequences. Even though we may be forgiven, there are consequences to sin. Everyone will have to give account on the Day of Judgment for every empty word they have spoken. Galatians 6:7 says, "Do not be deceived: God is not mocked. A man reaps what he sows."

Mark 4:22 reads, "For everything that is hidden will eventually be brought into the open, and every secret will be brought to light." That is followed by an insightful admonition: anyone with ears to hear should listen and understand.

The 139th Psalm says it all.

> [2]You know when I sit down or stand up. You know my thoughts even when I'm far away. [3]You see me when I travel and when I rest at home. You know everything I do. [4]You know what I am going to say even before I say it, LORD. [5]You go before me and follow me. You place your hand of blessing on my head. [6]Such knowledge is too wonderful for me, too great for me to understand! [7]I can never escape from your Spirit! I can never get away from your presence! [8]If I go up to heaven, you are there; if I go down to the grave, you are there. [9]If I ride the wings of the morning, if I dwell by the farthest oceans, [10]even there your hand will guide me, and your strength will support me. [11]I could ask the darkness to hide me and the light around me to become night— [12]but even in darkness I cannot hide from you. To you the night shines as bright as day. Darkness and light are the same to you.

He knows it all. Jesus has already come as a Savior, he will return as judge.

He knows all we have said and done, but through the ultimate sacrifice He made on our behalf, He offers forgiveness. That's the good news and if you ask me who all has to know about that—the answer is everybody!

Hunter Education

IS HUNTING SAFE? I have heard it said that golfers are more likely to be injured while golfing than a hunter is while hunting. I used that in several hunter education classes; however, I would always follow that by saying most people survive a golfing injury but that often isn't true with hunting injuries.

On many occasions, I've had someone tell me there was no way they would hunt on a wildlife management area (WMA). Although I knew the answer, I would often ask why they would say that. The answer was almost universal. They would reply they were not going to get out there with all those nuts. They would go on to claim how unsafe it was. I often took that opportunity to let them know that statistically, hunting the WMA was safer than hunting on private property. This revelation was often met with a bunch of disbelief. During my thirty-five-year career, I had to work several hunting accidents. To the best of my memory, I worked two hunting accidents on WMAs.

One of the reasons we had few hunting accidents was the requirement that everyone born after 1977 was required to successfully complete a hunter education course. The courses were often referred to as "hunter safety" classes. While safety was a dominant theme, the courses encompassed ten hours of instruction and covered everything from wildlife management to

110

trapping to wildlife identification to first aid. The courses were normally taught by a group of instructors that included both volunteers and departmental personnel. It was my good fortune to work with some excellent instructors.

Each county handled things a little bit differently when it came to teaching the courses. In Coosa County, the classes were handled in a couple of different ways. Fortunately, the vocational agricultural teacher at the high school taught the course in his class, which caught the majority of the young folks who had to have it. However, there were always other young folks and adults who needed a course. These courses were normally coordinated by me for the most part, with the help of conservation officers and volunteers. Since we were a small county, we normally only offered one course per year.

Let me take you on a little rant for a minute. For many years, our hunter education section would give instructors who had taught a thousand students a nice commemorative belt buckle. While it wasn't anything fancy, it was a nice thank-you. Midway through my career, it was decided it would be unethical for departmental instructors to receive the belt buckle since teaching the classes was part of our job and receiving the gift would be profiting from our position. Well, I found that to be really aggravating seeing how when the ruling was made, I had taught 980 students!

Even though there was no hope of a belt buckle, I still enjoyed teaching the classes. Later in my career, I became a member of the Tallapoosa County Hunter Education Instructors team. They were a top-notch group of instructors who gave unselfishly of their time and talent. Jerry and Genelle Brown were the driving force behind the group. They graciously allowed the use of their property and provided the majority of materials for the courses. Jerry decided to develop a shooting range on his property for use during the hunter education instruction and allowed my oldest son to assist with the development of the range, which assisted him in earning his Eagle Scout recognition. Jerry and Genelle became two of my dearest friends. Many of the instructors in the group won the Alabama Wildlife Federation Governor's Conservation Achievement Award as Hunter Education Instructor of the Year. In addition, Jerry and his nephew Lee both won National Instructor of the Year Awards. They were a tremendous group of instructors and Tallapoosa County and the state of Alabama owe them a debt of gratitude.

Several years ago, the decision was made to provide the hunter education course online. While I understood the reasons for allowing this, I did not support it. The reason being that it had much of the effect I thought it would in that the participation in the in-person courses dwindled to the point there were no longer enough folks to keep the courses going. I hate this because I feel there was much to be said for the in-person courses. It is more than a little scary when you realize that with the online version someone can be certified as a "safe hunter" without ever having touched a firearm. I understand things change but it isn't always for the best.

Of course, even those who attended the in-person hands-on course didn't always comprehend everything. While the courses were normally made up of teenagers, there were several older folks who took the class as well. I always encouraged the parents to take the class with their child and many did. Several times I had parents come to me and thank me for encouraging them to attend since they had learned a lot. Some parents, not so much.

As I have said many times, one of the best parts of my job was you never really knew what might be coming next. This was true whether you were working a night hunting detail, plowing up a food plot on the wildlife management area, or teaching a hunter education class in a rural central Alabama county.

teenager armed with a shotgun into the mix, it's totally unnerving. Once again, I have to thank the Lord for keeping me safe and for all the other blessings He has bestowed on me. There is no way to know how close I was to death on so many occasions. I'm sure if you think about it, you've probably had a few close calls yourself. Now is a good time to thank Him.

Courtroom Etiquette

DURING THIRTY-FIVE YEARS of visiting courtrooms in multiple counites, I have learned while all are similar, no two are exactly the same. This is true for several reasons but I believe the primary reason is that the judges who preside over the courtrooms are all different individuals with their own ideas of how a court should be handled.

The judges I have known have run the gamut from very laid back to extremely straitlaced. I have been in courtrooms so loud that you could not hear what the judge was saying while you were standing at the bench and those where you could hear a pin drop and anyone who uttered a word out of turn was either reprimanded, removed from the courtroom, or both!

For many years of my career, my home county had a circuit judge I knew was adamant about three things in the courtroom. Actually, two of them were in the courtroom and the other was about people trying to get into the courtroom. The judge was definitely a stickler for people being on time. To that end, at the start of court, 9:00 a.m., he would instruct the bailiff to lock the doors at the front and rear of the courtroom. The door at the rear of the courtroom was a glass door. As the court would get underway, people would begin to line up at the door. Of course, they would initially try to open the door. Then they might knock on the glass. This would prompt the bailiff to instruct them not to do that by placing his finger to his lip and/or shaking his head no. The judge would address everyone in the courtroom, advising them why we were there. He would also explain the etiquette he expected and would make it clear that he would enforce what he said. With the preliminaries out of the way, he would instruct the bailiff to open the door.

When the door was opened and the people would begin to file in, the judge would advise them to come to the bench and form a line. The people would nervously move to the front of the room and the judge would normally address them one at a time. His question was "Why were you late for court?" As you can imagine, there was a wide range of answers. However, the judge was pretty good at getting his point across and that usually cut down on people trying to come up with a plausible reason.

I once heard the judge ask the question and the fellow he was addressing stated he had a flat tire on the way to court and had to change it. The judge asked if he had changed the tire and come straight to court and the man said he had. The judge asked the man if an officer was sent to check the trunk of his car would they find a flat tire in it. There was silence in the courtroom, including the fellow to whom the question had been posed. Of course, this was a great example of the saying "a picture paints a thousand words." His face was saying, "Oh no, I've lied to the judge and I'm probably going to jail." It did not help the man when the judge continued saying that in the event there was not a flat tire in his trunk, he would be held in contempt of court and could be placed in the county jail. The judge looked at the next person in line and asked what their excuse was and they immediately said they did not have one. The judge then told the people, including the fellow who claimed he had had a flat, to find a seat and to never be late for court again.

The folks who were in the courtroom on time were still not necessarily out of the woods. The judge was adamant that there would be no babies or small children in the courtroom. He always made this known at the beginning of court; however, from time to time someone would end up bringing a child in the courtroom. I remember once during the middle of a hearing there was the slightest cry from a baby. The judge immediately stopped everything and excitedly asked, "Where is that child?" Of course, everyone turned and looked at the woman who had the child. The judge told the woman that she needed to remove the child from the courtroom. She replied that it was her son that the hearing was about. The judge, in a much sterner tone, again told her to remove the child from the courtroom. As she was leaving, the judge addressed the courtroom saying he had nothing against children but the courtroom was not a place for them. I wasn't sure what caused the judge to be so adamant about removing babies from the courtroom; however, he definitely was. Obviously, an unruly or upset child in the closed confines of a courtroom would be a hindrance and nuisance.

The other pet peeve of the judge was that no one in the courtroom could have anything on their head. While the court bailiff normally did a good job of instructing everyone who entered to remove their hats, things sometimes got past them. I remember an incident when the judge was going through his routine when he suddenly came to an abrupt stop. He pointed into the crowd and instructed the woman with the head covering to approach the bench. The woman had what I would refer to as a scarf covering her head. The woman walked up to the judge's bench and he asked her why she had the scarf on her head. She replied she had a skin condition. I thought that was probably a sufficient answer. Evidently, I was wrong. The judge replied, "Take it off." The woman stared at the judge with a bewildered look on her face. The judge offered a clarifying comment when he said, "Now." The woman removed the scarf and he advised her to return to her seat.

Another judge whose courtroom I often visited had an interesting style. Something different about this court was they normally had about four different dockets for court. One would handle game and fish cases, another had felonies, another for misdemeanors, and the last one was traffic offenses. The judge would often change what order the cases were taken up. Another thing that was very different was this judge wasn't too concerned with being punctual. Many days we waited thirty-plus minutes for the judge to show up. Of course, it was his courtroom.

The strangest quirk of this judge was how he handled people with traffic citations. He would announce to the court that anyone who was there for a traffic ticket needed to line up along the wall of the courtroom. He would clarify that they were to stand alongside the wall but not to lean on the wall. He was serious about it. In the event, someone was caught leaning against the wall, they would not only be instructed to move to the end of the line, but this wall-leaning infraction also seemed to have a bearing on their case. While the judge was way too lenient for my taste, the "wall leaners" often seemed to take it on the chin. At least it seemed that way to me. Go figure.

Conservation Enforcement Officer Ryan O'Meara was attending a city court proceeding and related to me an incident that had occurred. He described the court as being extremely formal. He said the local police department was represented by several officers who were all wearing their class A uniforms, complete with ties. Fortunately, we were not required to wear ties in court during the summer. As the court was getting underway, the police lieutenant noticed that a couple of women in the audience had sunglasses on top of their heads. Evidently this was not acceptable. The lieutenant made eye contact with one of the women and motioned for her to remove the glasses and she did. However, he was unable to get the attention of the other woman. Therefore, he summoned one of his young officers, gestured toward the woman, and instructed the officer to go over and tell the woman to remove the glasses from her head. Unfortunately, the young officer did not understand exactly which woman the lieutenant was speaking of. He promptly walked over to a woman seated in the front row and told her to remove her eyeglasses. With a confused look on her face the woman removed her glasses. With his task completed the officer returned to the lieutenant, who was now incensed. He, in no uncertain terms, explained to the officer he wanted the sunglasses removed from the top of the other woman's head not the eyeglasses removed from the woman's face! I'm telling you, courtrooms can be confusing!

Picture This

ABOUT FIFTEEN TO TWENTY YEARS into my career, something happened that would forever alter the way we worked hunting. It was not a change in the law or a division directive or policy, although it did initiate the development of new policies. It wasn't necessarily a new technology; it was an old technology being utilized in a new way. It was one of those things that made you ask, "Why didn't I think of that?"

They were first called trail cameras and later game cameras. Unfortunately, over time they became known in our circles as game warden cameras. They were definitely a pain in the rear for those whose success often depended on the ability to move in and out of areas undetected. Do not misunderstand me, in some regards the cameras were a good thing in that they would often reveal to hunters there were some good bucks on their property, thereby giving them an incentive to put forth more effort. The primary reason we disliked cameras was they made it easier for hunters to "catch" us when we were trying to catch them. This was especially true when we were looking for baited areas. As if it wasn't difficult enough trying to find a needle in a haystack, now the haystack had eyes! As cameras evolved and got smaller and smaller, detecting them became more and more difficult. On our first trip into a property, we had to initially spend our time watching for cameras before we could concentrate on locating shooting stands and feeders.

In the beginning, the cameras were normally always set up watching an area where bait had been placed. However, as time went by and cameras became more affordable, they started showing up in other areas. A few years into the camera craze, it became apparent the cameras were not only placed to photograph wildlife, but also game wardens.

"Mr. Joel." I knew when I heard that greeting on the phone it had to be one of my 4-H kids. For twenty years I served as a coach for the Coosa County 4-H Wildlife Habitat Evaluation Program teams. A highlight of my career was watching these young people develop into productive, successful adults who had a good grasp of wildlife management. Many of them became my friends and some my coworkers. Even though at the end of my career some of these "4-H kids" were over forty years old, they were and always will be my 4-H kids.

When the caller stated, "Mr. Joel, I think my neighbor has bait out for deer," I immediately recognized the voice and began picturing the property. The young man explained he had noticed some activity on the property just to the north of his and had reason to believe the area was baited. After a couple of clarifying questions, I knew where to go. I thanked the engineer (I told you these kids were successful) and told him I would check it out.

The next day I made my way to the property. I walked the area and located the baited site, complete with a ladder stand and a camera attached to a nearby tree. I photographed the set up and hurried out of the area with plans to return on Saturday morning. During this time, it was totally illegal to hunt by the aid of bait. Years later, people would be able to purchase a "bait privilege license," which allowed the hunting of deer and wild hogs by the aid of bait.

Picture This

Shortly after daybreak on Saturday, I stealthily approached the baited area. I was moving slowly along a logging road that was slightly above the location of the feeder. Once close enough, I used my binoculars to ascertain there was no one in the stand. Knowing folks don't always hunt from the obvious stand, I checked other trees in the area and, not seeing anyone, turned to leave the area. And there it was. I spotted another camera set up on the trail leading to the stand. Although I had not seen the "warden" camera on my first trip, I have the feeling it saw me, seeing how the corn dried up and in several subsequent trips I never found anyone in the area.

Obviously, being caught on camera normally would bring compliance since the folks would either remove the bait or wait until it was all consumed for ten days before hunting the area. And while we were glad the violation was no longer taking place, that really wasn't the way we had hoped to correct the illegal activity.

Interestingly, we did eventually figure a few ways to work the cameras to our advantage. Conservation Enforcement Officer (CEO) Drake Hayes was working a baited area in Coosa County and finally found someone in the shooting house overlooking the bait. He approached the man and asked to see his hunting license. He asked the man if he knew why he was there and the man replied he did not. The officer pointed out the very obvious feeder in the field and asked if that was his feeder. The man did his best to appear shocked that there was a big honking corn feeder in the middle of the field directly in front of his shooting house. Drake asked the fellow to accompany him to the feeder. As they walked across the field, Drake pointed out the fresh corn that had been poured in the field. He reached down and picked up some corn, stating it was interesting the corn was dry while the grass in the field was wet. The man again claimed to have no knowledge of the bait being in the area. As they surveyed the feed on the ground and in the feeder, Drake spotted a camera on a nearby tree. Thinking quickly, Drake advised the man of his right to remain silent. He then pointed at the camera and asked the man, "If I take the card from that camera and view it on the computer in my truck, will I see you pouring this corn out?" The man paid the tickets off prior to court!

I am not implying that the cameras were all bad. While the cameras did a good job of catching us on properties, it also caught a lot of poachers as well. Many times, I received calls from hunters who had viewed the card from their camera and found photos of intruders on their property. This wasn't limited to hunting. The cameras were also handy around fish ponds, hunting camps, and residences. Many times, I have questioned a suspect who vehemently denied being where I was accusing them of being. I must admit, when I was able to lay their picture on the table in front of them, the old saying about a picture being worth a thousand words often proved true.

Stop or I'll Run You Down

I DON'T KNOW WHO was the most surprised. Was it the folks who were being stopped by the game warden standing in the road or the game warden standing in the road trying to stop the night hunters? Either way it was one of the most unorthodox stops I had ever made and I couldn't believe it was really happening.

Probably no other county in Alabama has more name recognition than Talladega. Whether or not you are a NASCAR fan, almost everyone has heard of the Talladega 500 stock car race. Coosa County was bordered to the north by Talladega County and I had the opportunity to work there during most deer seasons. I had spent a lot of time and effort training Conservation Enforcement Officer (CEO) Jerry Fincher and enjoyed being able to assist in his county. Jerry had hit the ground running in Talladega County and had caught a lot of folks hunting deer at night; however, it was obvious he had not caught them all.

I have lamented many times concerning how hard it was to find a good place to set up and work night hunting. This appeared to be a universal problem. Jerry contacted me saying he had located a great-looking night hunting spot just north of the city of Sylacauga. The lush green field lying adjacent to the paved county road with no houses in sight would no doubt be more than anybody trying to shoot a deer at night could pass up. It was a good spot except for not having a good place to sit and watch the green field. There was a road at one end of the field; however, it had a couple of problems. First, it had a gate on it and if you wanted to sit up the road you would have to leave the gate open in order to get out. While many would pay it no attention, an observant night hunter would probably notice the open gate. Second, if you backed up the road far enough not to be seen, you could not see the field. This meant you would have to come and stand at the edge of the field and watch to see if someone was hunting the field and if they were, you would have to run to your truck and give chase. This would unfortunately take a long time and might let the violator escape or lead to a chase, which we always wanted to avoid.

Jerry and I kept looking and finally located an area right across the road from the field where, with just a little heavy trimming, we were able to back his truck between the trees and hide it. It was a great observation point, but it took some care to get in and out without doing any vehicle damage.

The weekend rolled around and I was scheduled to assist Jerry. We discussed the areas that needed to be worked and it was decided I would work the tight spot on Riser's Mill Road and he would work a couple of miles away at another likely spot. We split up and headed for our hidey holes. I knew my place was a tight squeeze; however, I had not taken into consideration that my vehicle, a Chevy Tahoe, was much wider than Jerry's Dodge Dakota pickup. I literally had to pull my side mirrors in and they still rubbed the trees on both sides of the entrance. I backed into the hole knowing it would take me forever to get out. However, I didn't have much of an alternative.

I sat and watched the field for over two hours with not the first vehicle coming by. As I sat, I pondered the situation and knew the good visibility the spot offered was trumped by the fact

I would not be able to get out in a hurry. I eventually surmised there had to be a better place and I decided to ease along the wood line and find it. I realized this would slow my response time even more if someone came along; however, I felt I had to find a better place. I eased up the road and again realized why we had selected the place we had. After you left our hole, the road bank continued to get higher, making it nearly impossible to back up on. I kept moving along the road but could not find a better location. Exasperated, I turned back toward my truck only to see the glow of headlights coming in my direction. Here I was, two hundred yards from my truck with a vehicle coming down the road, and I could not believe what an amateurish mistake I had made. I immediately started running down the road toward my truck but as the vehicle's headlights illuminated the road, I had to get up in the woods. With the vehicle at the end of the field, I made my way through the woods as best I could in the darkness. I couldn't believe what was happening.

As I watched the vehicle, the driver pulled a few yards off the road into the end of the green field. He maneuvered the vehicle in such a way the headlights illuminated different areas of the field. This shining was repeated and continuous. I realized I had a night hunter but as he pulled back into the edge of the road and proceeded toward my location, I realized he had me. I radioed Jerry and told him to come to my location.

I had to lie on the ground as the vehicle passed by. As soon as he passed me, I jumped up and started hurrying toward my truck. Did I mention it was difficult to hurry through the dark woods without turning on a light while at the same time trying to watch over your shoulder to see which way the violator was going? I knew if the driver turned to the right at the end of the field, he would likely meet Jerry on the road. I was thinking that might be the best thing that could happen. Of course, that wasn't to be.

The Jeep Cherokee—I had got a good look at it as it passed by me at a distance of about fifteen feet—went to the other end of the field, turned around, and headed back in my direction. Realizing I wasn't going to make it to my vehicle and knowing Jerry would be coming from the opposite direction than the Jeep was now traveling, I had to make a decision.

In keeping with my track record of bad decisions for the night, I stepped out in the road and began waving my flashlight at the approaching vehicle. I did not know how the driver might respond. Once I knew they saw me, I raised the light above my head and illuminated the badge on my chest. Knowing if they sped past me there would be nothing I could do, I hoped letting them see I was an officer would get them to stop. I held my breath and waited.

Thankfully, they stopped. I approached the driver's side of the vehicle and identified myself as a state conservation officer and instructed the driver to turn the vehicle off and place his hands on the steering wheel. The Jeep was occupied by a young man and young woman. I asked if there were any firearms in the vehicle and the driver stated there was a rifle in the back. The passenger, who turned out to be the owner of the vehicle, said, "I don't want to go to jail." I wasn't sure, but I felt her statement might indicate she thought they were up to no good and she just might want to tell me about it. I told the young woman to get out and step to the front of the vehicle. I stepped to the rear of the vehicle and opened the hatch and retrieved the scoped rifle, which was fully loaded. I unloaded the rifle and placed it back in the Jeep. I would have rather placed it in my vehicle but that would have meant a fifty-yard hike!

As I started toward the front of the vehicle, I heard a vehicle quickly approaching and was glad to see Jerry coming around the curve. I know he had to be confused seeing this vehicle stopped in the road with my vehicle nowhere in sight.

He approached wearing a puzzled look that I surely understood. I apprised him of what I had witnessed and asked him to watch the driver while I spoke with the passenger. I advised the young woman of her Miranda rights and asked her to tell me what they were doing. She stated they were just riding around. I asked why they had pulled off the road and she said the driver had told her you could usually see some deer in this field. She stated they had been riding for about an hour. I asked her why they had the rifle and she said she did not know. When I asked if she knew they had brought the rifle along, she replied she did. I felt this was important information since it was often difficult to convict a passenger who had not fired a shot or held a light. I asked her to go back to the vehicle and I asked the driver to come to me.

I advised the young man of his Miranda rights and he stated he understood. He asked what he was being held for and I told him we were conducting a night hunting investigation. He stated he was not night hunting. I explained he had in fact fulfilled all of the elements of a prima facie night hunting case. In order to make a good case for hunting deer at night, you had to prove four elements were present. It had to be at night, in an area where deer were known to frequent, there had to be a light source, and a weapon had to be possessed. Once those elements were met, the officer needed to be able to prove to a reasonable person there was intent to take a deer. The last element was the toughest and was where a good statement came into play.

The young man again replied he wasn't hunting, they were just riding around. I asked how long they had been riding and he said three hours. I asked why he had the gun and he said he was going target shooting the next day.

Having made a lot of night hunting cases, I knew explaining the presence of the gun was often difficult for defendants. It was true they had every right to possess a rifle; it was deer season and it was not at all unusual for a hunter to leave his rifle in the truck. However, it was often the case that if you would just let them talk, they would trip themselves up. I asked the guy where he was planning on going target shooting and he replied at a friend's house. I mentioned he must not plan to shoot a lot seeing how he only had four bullets. After allowing that to hang in the air for a minute, I said I found it odd he would put his loaded rifle into his friend's vehicle only to have to take it out and put it back in his later. At this point, he was beginning to get confused and couldn't keep his answers straight. I knew it was time for my patented line and I asked, "Why is your story so different than the one your friend told me?" You could see in his eyes he was having trouble coming up with an answer.

I asked why he had pulled off of the road with his headlights shining into the field and he replied he was having a problem with the brakes on the vehicle. I immediately went to his passenger, the vehicle owner, and asked if there were any brake problems with the vehicle and she said there was no vehicle problem. I returned to him and advised him the vehicle owner said there were no problems with the brakes. As a general rule, when you could quickly shoot holes in a violator's story, the tale would unravel fairly quickly. In addition, knowing his accomplice wasn't going to corroborate his story pretty well took the wind out of his sails.

I gave the nineteen-year-old my best "I know you did it" look and told him his story did not make any sense. Knowing he was had, he hung his head and admitted he had come to the field to look for deer. I again asked why he had brought the gun and he said he did not know. I asked when he had loaded the gun and he said before they left home. Based on his having admitted coming to look for deer, having shined the fields with his headlights, and possessing a loaded rifle, I informed him he had fulfilled all the elements of hunting at night and he was under arrest for it. He stated he did not want to go to jail and I told him I did not intend to take him to jail. I asked if he had a permit to hunt the property and he stated he did not. I began writing him tickets for hunting at night, hunting from a public road, hunting without a permit, and hunting by the aid of a vehicle.

After learning he was not going to jail, the young man seemed to relax and become more talkative. We asked him to give a written statement and he did. I asked him if he had seen a deer in the field, would he have shot it and he replied, "Yes sir." I finished his tickets and explained the bonds to him. He signed the bonds and stated he understood the procedure.

I discussed with Jerry whether or not to charge the young woman. Based on her cooperation and the fact she was a passenger, we decided not to charge her at the time. She was advised her vehicle was subject to being confiscated and there was a one-year statute of limitations on charging her with the hunting offenses. The pair were allowed to leave.

The cases were set for district court in Sylacauga a month later. The court date rolled around and the young man entered the court room accompanied by his father. The defendant pled not guilty. You would be surprised how many times I had acquired a signed confession only to have the defendant come to court and plead not guilty. In the bench trial, I explained what I had observed, that I had read him his rights, and that he had given a statement saying he was night hunting. When the judge looked at the defendant for his defense, his father, who was not present at the time of the offense, spoke up using a defense I had not heard in the past. He said his son wasn't deer hunting; he was trying to entice the young lady into an erotic interlude. That isn't at all how he phrased it, but you get the idea. The father went on to claim we had held his son on the side of the road for three hours until he agreed to sign a statement. When the judge looked at me, I simply rolled my eyes and shook my head. I must say the father was fortunate he was before the judge that he was, seeing how most judges I had known would not have let the man speak at all. Since the man had not been on the scene, all he had to say was hearsay and was not admissible. Not surprisingly, this "just looking for love" defense did not work. The judge gave the father's assertions little credence and found the young man guilty. I'm sure at that point the young man wished he would have just driven around (or maybe over) the big game warden and gone on his way. Hindsight is twenty-twenty!

This Far Out

HUNTING WITHOUT A PERMIT was a common complaint in Alabama. When I was growing up, you could pretty much hunt wherever you wanted to. Although my daddy made me request permission from any landowner whose property I wanted to hunt on, it was pretty much just a courteous thing to do. That was before there were deer in the area. The presence of deer and turkey on a property definitely changed things.

Fast forward almost fifty years and add in a good population of deer and wild turkey and land that used to be open for anyone to hunt now generates a lot of money in hunting lease fees. Many people would probably be astounded at the amount of money people spend for a place to hunt. In our county today, hunting lease prices range from $5 to $20 per acre and compared to some other counties, that's pretty cheap. I once knew a guy that leased eight thousand acres in the fertile black belt of the state for $10 per acre. Believe me, when someone pays $80,000 for a deer and turkey lease, they don't want someone hunting on it without permission!

Alabama state law 9-11-241 states that anyone hunting on lands other than their own must have written permission from the landowner in their possession. Anyone found guilty of breaking that law faces a minimum fine of $1,000 and, at the discretion of the judge, may have their hunting privileges revoked for one year. That's pretty serious. Another important detail is all land in Alabama is posted by law. It is the hunters' responsibility to know where they are at all times.

One would think, with that kind of penalty in place, you would not have much of a hunting-without-a-permit problem. Anyone who believes that would be wrong. I often wondered why so many people wound up in places they weren't supposed to be. I had a guy relay to me a story that helped me understand.

A fellow in Elmore County who owned a large amount of property told me he had been checking on some of his holdings on a dead-end road. As he was leaving, he met a small car occupied by two young men wearing camouflage heading into his property. Since he owned all of the land on both sides of the road, he knew they did not have permission to be on the property. He turned around and followed the vehicle. When he arrived at the dead end, the men were out of the car and were taking long guns out of their cases. He pulled alongside the vehicle and asked the driver what they were doing. The man replied they were about to go hunting. He said when he asked if they had permission from the landowner, the two fellows looked at each other with a bewildered look and then the driver replied, "We didn't figure anybody owned the property this far out!"

So that's what it is. You can't make this stuff up.

What about you? Have you ever thought that something didn't necessarily apply to you? I've met a lot of people who lived their life as if man's laws and God's law did not apply to them. Many of these have found out they were wrong on both counts.

Folks get by with a lot in this life. You have no doubt read where I have lamented about how few of the game law violators we actually apprehended. I've had many folks boast to me about what all they had gotten by with. I knew we were only catching a few. However, there is something else I know. The Bible says every knee will bow and every tongue will confess. That doesn't leave anybody out. There is a day of reckoning coming. For all we know, it could be today. To me, one of the most significant verses in the Bible is Galatians 6:7, which says, "Be not deceived, God is not mocked, you will reap what you sow." That day is coming. It applies to everybody.

Firsthand Information

RECEIVING GOOD INFORMATION concerning illegal activities is a welcome gift for all law enforcement officers. Notice I said "good" information. I'm sure everyone has received the cryptic, jumbled information that only serves to cause you to waste a lot of time. It seemed some informants wanted to tell you what they knew but could only bring themselves to give a partial story or sketchy directions. However, every once in a while, we would receive some info that was right on the money and those were some sweet times.

There were several motivations for someone to become an informant. One of the most common was the desire to shut up the bragging outlaw. Others wanted to limit their competition. Some were motivated by a true concern for what the violator was doing to the resource and understood he was stealing from the law-abiding sportsman. I had the occasion to meet a person with this motivation one Saturday afternoon at the check station on the Coosa Wildlife Management Area (WMA).

While someone more eloquent and less familiar with the WMA check station might describe it as quaint, I would call it old, cramped, and totally insufficient. During the course of my career on the WMA, I continuously requested a new check station and was allowed to draw up plans for one on several occasions. It

138

never happened. Ironically, within two weeks of my retirement I was told there were plans to build a new one. My cynical reply was I would believe it when I saw it.

The check station was an aluminum building that measured eight feet by ten feet and often times during a deer hunt we would have as many as six folks inside of it, not to mention a desk and a couple of file cabinets. These cramped quarters offered no privacy so when a fellow approached the window and asked to speak privately, I ventured out into the cold to hear what he had to say. You never knew what an individual might want to tell you in this situation. I have had folks report everything from someone hunting over bait to someone who did not like the way a food plot was planted, and much more you would not believe!

Getting a sufficient distance from the building, the man asked who he needed to talk to concerning some illegal hunting activity. I told him I would be glad to hear his complaint. Even though we were "alone" in the parking area, he said he was not comfortable talking there and asked if I could meet him somewhere else. Although a little leery of this situation, I told him I could. He asked me to meet him at the four-way stop in Weogufka at three o'clock that afternoon. I advised him I would be there and would likely have fellow wildlife biologist Gene Carver with me. He said okay and left.

At 3:00 p.m., Gene and I pulled up to the four-way stop and spotted the man in his vehicle sitting in front of the Weogufka Fire Department. We all exited our vehicles and the man immediately began saying what was going on just wasn't right and he had to do what he could to put a stop to it. This sounded like a good start but I knew a lot of folks were hesitant to give complete information. Fortunately, this guy was ready to talk. He reported a fellow he knew who worked for a local utility department left work each day at 2:30 p.m. and headed to Coosa

County to road hunt. His route consisted of traveling south on Coosa County Road 29 then west on County Road 56 to Unity Crossroads. From there he would turn right on Lay Dam Road and follow it to County Road 29. He advised the violator was making this route in a red Ford Ranger pickup and shooting any deer he saw. If a deer was spotted in the daylight, he would shoot it with a Remington .270 rifle but after dark he would use a Marlin .22 magnum rifle. At this point he stopped and took a breath. It was all I could do to keep myself from sarcastically asking if he could give a little more detail!

Seriously, I had never received such thorough information about anything. We assured the fellow we would take care of the situation. He told us he didn't want his name involved and I told him that would not be a problem since I didn't know his name. Gene and I returned to the WMA discussing the plethora of info we had just received.

I couldn't wait to set up and try to apprehend this guy. The violator obviously did not know his route led right through the middle of our favorite honey hole. Therefore, we knew exactly where to set up. Tuesday afternoon was our first chance to get to the location. We arrived around 2:00 p.m. and hurriedly set the decoy up approximately sixty yards from the road. We hid our trucks in our usual place just over a small rise across the road and I nestled down in the wood line adjacent to the road and tested the remote control. With everything working well, we began our wait. It wasn't a long one.

Shortly after three o'clock we noticed a small red pickup as it slowly made its way toward our location. The driver was moving slowly, scanning the woods. He spotted the deer and was easing to a stop when a big yellow school bus came rumbling along behind him. The driver accelerated and drove away. I was heartsick. Although I knew the driver might come back, it was always a gamble when they got more than one look at the deer decoy in the daytime.

Within a couple of minutes, I saw the truck approaching once again. The driver slowed down and almost turned all the way around in his seat looking at the small six-point buck that stood on what was now his passenger side. I had turned the deer's head to make it look like he was following the truck as it went by. As I observed, the poacher drove about three hundred yards down the road and turned around and started back to us. One thing I loved about this place was you had really good visual coverage. I radioed Gene that the suspect was coming back and to be ready. This would be his third look at the stationary deer. I hoped he wouldn't take too long of a look. We normally placed the deer one hundred yards or more off the road during the daytime; however, this placement had worked well in the past.

The man hurried back to a spot adjacent to the fake deer, stopped abruptly, and shot with a high-powered rifle. I immediately came out of the woods moving toward the truck. Another round blew through the stuffed deer and the man realized he had been had. He stomped the accelerator and the rear tires lit up spinning on the pavement. At the same time, I tapped on the passenger side window with the barrel of my .40-caliber Beretta pistol. The man raised his hands and mouthed the words *you got me*. I told him to keep his hands up as I noticed the .270 rifle across his lap and the .22 magnum in the passenger's seat. Gene pulled his truck into the road in front of the violators truck and we took him out of the vehicle. He again stated, "You got me, you caught me."

We wrote tickets for hunting from the public road, hunting without a permit, and hunting by aid of a vehicle. He pled guilty in district court and paid hefty fines and court costs. Seeing how he was caught at one of our favorite places to work, we might have caught him without receiving the tip. However, I would have given a lot to have received that type of information every year. People often forget three important things. Those who are breaking the game laws are stealing from the legitimate hunters. They are damaging the resource and anyone shooting from the public road not only puts anyone in the road in jeopardy but also runs the very real risk of hitting someone legally hunting in the woods. And that's not to mention the horses, cows, vehicles, houses, and barns I've seen shot. These folks are outlaws. If you know of something going on, report it!

While You Were Shining That Field

IT'S NOT AS IF the case was ever in jeopardy; however, if the judge needed corroborating evidence, the clueless defendant was doing his best to provide it. The courtroom was often a stage for some bizarre happenings and this was once again the case.

Conservation enforcement officers (CEOs) were often fortunate in that many of their cases were on-view arrests requiring little or no investigation. It was relatively easy to articulate to the judge that someone was hunting or fishing without a license. Of course, this often depended on which judge was hearing the case. Some judges had a much better grasp of conservation cases than others and some ran a much tighter courtroom than others. I remember well the day the Honorable George Simpson asked me what statute gave the conservation commissioner the authority to promulgate a regulation. Luckily, my fellow wildlife biologist, Gene Carver, had warned me that might happen and I was prepared with the answer. No one likes to be embarrassed in court.

No matter whether the judge was lax or strict, there was no substitute for a well-placed word during a trial. Since the majority of our cases were bench trials and the defendants were

143

normally not represented by counsel, we could usually interject a word here or there. I observed this handled masterfully on several occasions. I was in Elmore County District Court when CEO Byron Smith was the arresting officer on a night hunting case involving a state corrections officer.

While I can't speak for all CEOs, I will provide my view on law enforcement officers who break the law. I understand no one is perfect and everyone makes mistakes. I understand there are slipups that occur every day. However, I did my best to treat everyone the same. If a warning would suffice, so be it. However, many of our cases were not minor oversights or something insignificant. When it was a flagrant and/or premeditated violation, the fact the violator was a law enforcement officer was irrelevant. It is my contention that an officer should know better than anyone else the consequences of breaking the law. If an officer was willing to attempt to illegally kill a deer at night, we were willing to arrest them for it. Such was the case in this situation.

The defendant pled not guilty to the charge of hunting deer at night and the judge had asked Byron to explain what had occurred. He stated he was observing a field where he suspected someone was shooting deer at night. As was his custom, Byron poured himself a cup of steaming hot coffee from his thermos and crawled up on the hood of his Ford Bronco to wait for the violator he hoped would come. In less than five minutes he observed a Toyota pickup as it slowly moved toward his location. The vehicle came to a stop and the driver illuminated the field with a spotlight. He eased down the road and repeated the procedure in the next field directly in front of Byron. Sliding off the hood and tossing out his cup of perfectly good coffee, Byron pulled out behind the slow-moving vehicle. He activated his blue lights and the driver pulled to the side of the road.

The man immediately exited his truck and started back toward the officer. Byron quickly gave the unmistakable loud verbal command for the man to stop. I know of no officer who wants anyone who has just been stopped to hurriedly exit the vehicle and start toward them. It is a good recipe for getting a good look at the business end of a Glock!

With the man standing at the rear of his truck, Byron asked if he had a firearm in his vehicle and he stated he did not. The fellow quickly informed the officer that he was a law enforcement officer. Byron told him to place his hands on the side of his truck and patted the subject down. Finding no weapons, he checked the cab of the truck. There on the seat he found a spotlight and a loaded 7mm rifle. This was often the reason someone would quickly jump out and come back to meet an officer hoping they would not check the vehicle. Byron placed the rifle in his truck and began filling out the paperwork for a hunting at night charge while the suspect was explaining he was a corrections officer and he was checking the field to make sure no one else was hunting there. When Byron asked why he possessed the rifle, the man did not provide an answer. He again reminded the officer that he was an officer and that should make a difference. It didn't. At least not in the way he had hoped.

Once Byron finished his testimony, the judge asked the defendant if he had any questions he would like to ask the officer. The man, who had pled not guilty, said he did and turned to Byron and asked, "How far from me were you?" Byron immediately responded with, "While you were shining that field?" "Yeah," the man replied. I almost laughed out loud. Byron replied he was close enough to see what had happened.

The judge told the defendant based on the testimony, including his, she had no choice but to find him guilty. She also commented his actions were very unbecoming of an officer. The man seemed unfazed by the judge's comment and responded by asking the judge if she would ask the officer if he would be sure to put some oil on his rifle. Byron replied, "You don't need to worry about the rifle." Before the man could reply, the judge ordered the rifle be condemned and awarded to the Department of Conservation to be used by them as needed. I could tell that the man's first instinct was to argue; however, in what was probably a wise move, he dropped his head and left the courtroom.

Lake Wind Advisory

AS A CERTIFIED WILDLIFE BIOLOGIST, one of my many responsibilities was making recommendations to landowners to improve the wildlife habitat on their property. One of the most frequently recommended practices was prescribed burning. I'm sure to those not familiar with the practice, being told to intentionally set the woods on fire sounded a little crazy. Anyone watching the horrific wildfires that devastate the country every year would reason fire is the worst thing that could happen to a property. That is understandable, but incorrect. Prescribed fire is a great technique for managing pine woodlands. However, it must be practiced by someone familiar with fire behavior. To implement this technique, the practitioner must consider a wide array of factors, including available moisture, relative humidity, wind speed and direction, mixing height, and several other important factors. It definitely is not as simple as just setting the woods on fire.

As with any endeavor, you always have some who jump in headfirst with little knowledge and less forethought. When you are literally playing with fire, this can be catastrophic. I have witnessed several "prescribed" fires that have gone astray. This can happen even under ideal conditions; however, it is much more likely when folks fail to plan properly.

One of the difficulties of prescribed burning is often a lack of days with good burning weather. While some burning practitioners will tell you every day is a burn day, most will tell you the number of ideal days is normally very limited. While certified burn managers understand different sites require different atmospheric conditions for a burn to render the desired results, many laypeople don't understand that.

On more than one occasion, I've had a landowner pose the question "You aren't going to burn today, are you?" Normally, this query is accompanied by a near-panic expression on their face. On the occasion that I say yes, I normally know the question that is coming next. "What about the wind?" This reveals a widely held misconception: you should never burn when the wind is blowing. Now while I think I understand where this thinking stems from, that doesn't make it true. The truth is you need wind when you are burning.

I think back to a warm early spring day when I topped a hill on the Coosa Wildlife Management Area and came face-to-face with a raging inferno. Flames were running across an open field of broom sedge like a hot knife through butter. I immediately grabbed my radio microphone and called the sheriff's office and told them I needed a fire truck dispatched ASAP. I followed that call with one to the Alabama Forestry Commission (AFC), telling them I needed the bulldozer with the fire plow to be on the way. Although thirteen round bales of hay were lost and a lot of ground was burned, they were able to save the landowner's barn, tractor, and implements. The landowner made a comment I've heard many times, "The wind wasn't blowing when I lit the fire."

This episode brings up a couple of good points. One, a certified burn manager (CBM) knows they must get a weather forecast prior to setting a fire. The fire weather gives many important pieces of information for the CBM. In addition, they know a fire can and does make its own wind. Wind is often a necessary component for fire to perform as it should. This is true when performing an understory burn and especially when young pine trees are involved. Fire needs to move through the area and a prevailing wind assists it in doing so. Without wind, the fire may stay on or around a seedling longer than is desirable. Therefore, you need to have some wind.

During my career, I worked very closely with the members of the Alabama Forestry Commission. One of their primary duties was fighting wildfires. It wasn't a job I envied. Coosa County AFC Ranger Milton Ellington related to me a story of how he was dispatched to a fire one night around 10 p.m. He arrived on scene and realized the landowner had been burning a brush pile but due to the high winds, the fire had gotten out and was wildly burning out of control. He unloaded the unit, a bulldozer with a fire plow attached, and plowed the fire out. Returning to his truck, he was met by the landowner. The man explained he did not know how the fire had gotten out since he had a break around the pile. Milton suggested it might have been due to the high winds, to which the man replied, "The wind doesn't blow at night." Met with such a profound statement, Milton was taken aback; however, he quickly responded and said, "Well, the winds have been pretty high and as a matter of fact a lake wind advisory was issued." The man replied, "Yeah, I saw that on the news but I knew we were far enough from the lake it wouldn't affect us." Milton decided it was time to load the unit and head for home.

Wind is often an integral part of prescribed burning. Landowners should use a certified burn manager who understands how wind affects a fire and what type fire is needed. Prescribed burning is a tremendous, relatively inexpensive tool. Always keep the wind in mind or burn at night when the wind doesn't blow!

You can't make this stuff up!

Close Correlation

MY FIRST DISTRICT COURT JUDGE was unpredictable at best. Although he normally always did a good job for us, you never knew what might happen next. One day as I made my way past his office, he motioned me in. I entered the room and he told me he had received a call from a woman whose husband had been arrested for hunting deer at night.

From around the first of November until mid to late February we spent a lot of time attempting to catch folks hunting deer at night. The deer were plentiful and the sight of them standing alongside of the road often proved to be more temptation than many of the folks riding along the road could withstand. Unfortunately, many had no qualms about shooting at the deer whether they were in a remote area or standing beside the US highway that traversed our entire county.

Apprehending these folks was difficult, seeing how the illegal activity was so widespread and we were able to cover such a small area. When we were fortunate enough to be in the right place at the right time and apprehend some of the culprits, we would normally leave them with a handful of paperwork in the form of tickets for hunting at night, hunting from a public road, and hunting by the aid of a vehicle. Many times, this would prompt a call to the district judge in an effort to take care of things through the mail and skip the hassle of appearing in court.

When these folks reached the court, they would quickly learn that while the judge would allow some defendants with minor infractions to pay through the mail, those charged with hunting at night were required to appear in court. Evidently one recent arrestee had not even wanted to talk with the judge and therefore had his wife call. The woman explained her husband had received tickets for hunting at night, hunting from a public road, and hunting by the aid of a vehicle and she needed to know the amount of the fine so she could mail it in so her husband would not have to appear in court. The judge said the lady had become upset when he told her that would not be possible since he did not allow anyone charged with night hunting to pay off prior to court. Having served on the bench for many years and having heard every excuse in the book, the judge had little tolerance for those who questioned his authority. Therefore, when the woman took a belligerent tone and informed the judge he could not do that, she quickly got on his last nerve.

I always found it interesting the number of folks who evidently thought it was a good idea to argue with the person who was obviously in authority. This regularly happened in the field, where violators would inform officers they could not arrest them. Let me assure you, this rarely ended with the defendant not being arrested. I can understand that someone realizing they were about to be arrested might try to persuade an officer not to charge them. However, belligerently telling the officer he could not do what he was doing normally did not work out for them. Acting that way in the field was one thing; however, telling the judge, who held all the cards, what he could and couldn't do was a good way to end up in a small room with bars on the windows.

The night hunter's wife plowed forward, telling the judge she had received traffic tickets in the past and had always been able to pay them off prior to court. The judge acknowledged that was a common practice and he allowed that for minor infractions but he did not allow it when it was a night hunting charge. When she asked, in a belligerent tone, "And why not?" the judge quickly got her attention when he replied, "Because of the close correlation between night hunting and child molestation."

"What?" was her startled reply.

The judge, a strong conservationist and animal lover, told her that, in his opinion, "anyone who would stoop to shining a light in a deer's eyes and shooting it would likely do anything."

After regaining her composure from her initial shock, she fired back, "Well my husband is not a criminal!"

The judge asked, "Are you not calling me to try and pay for his criminal behavior?" Before she could answer, he continued with "I'll see him in court."

Before anyone starts to think our judge would equate someone illegally hunting with the heinous act of child molestation, let me assure you he was hard on any law violator. I think in this instance he used the first thing that popped in his head that would in fact get the woman's attention.

Many times during my career, I had people belittle the significance of a wildlife law violation by saying it was just a deer or a rabbit or a raccoon that was affected. Those folks would often have it pointed out to them that I had responded to numerous houses that had been shot into by someone shooting at a deer in the dark in someone's front yard. I responded to multiple cases of livestock being killed by someone shooting at night. I had apprehended folks whose actions had definitely put other people in serious danger. CEOs have arrested numerous individuals who were selling parts from endangered species. I hope you get my point. No, I definitely don't equate the life of an animal with that of a human. However, I definitely do believe anyone illegally taking wildlife should be punished. Not only for the damage to the resource but also for the potential damage to the public. I'm thankful my judge felt the same.

CRASH!

THE TRAFFIC CRASH wasn't necessarily severe; the injuries were limited to their pride and ego. Of course, there was significant vehicle damage. That coupled with the illegal hunting fines and court costs put a large dent in their wallet.

During the first several years of my career, the deer decoy was a new and tremendous tool. Since it was so effective at catching violators, it generated many great stories. My fellow wildlife biologist and conservation enforcement officer, Jeff Makemson, related the details of an incident he witnessed that illustrates my point. At this time, Jeff worked on the Oakmulgee Wildlife Management Area, which is located on the Oakmulgee district of the Talladega National Forest. He would later serve as the district supervisor. Like me, Jeff worked a lot of enforcement on his area. Working the decoy on the national forest one afternoon turned out to be very memorable.

Due to recent complaints, Jeff and others had set the decoy about one hundred yards from a US Forest Service road in the national forest. Jeff was positioned in the woods where he could operate the decoy and observe the violators. A chase vehicle was stationed down the road to intercept the violators in the event they decided to make a run for it. Things had been progressing slowly when a pickup truck loaded with lighter wood approached the setup.

CRASH!

Now I must admit when I moved to central Alabama, I had never heard of lighter wood, fat lighter, fat wood, or "lighterd," as many folks called it. Having not grown up in a home where wood was used for heat, I never really had a need to quickly start a fire. However, I soon learned the lighter wood was actually heart pine that would ignite in an instant. It was great for lighting a fire, hence the name. As a matter of fact, I was so fascinated by the product and the fact you could find it lying around in the woods, I began collecting it. One year at Christmas, I decided it would be good to split some into little pieces and give a boxful to my wife's grandparents, who used a wood-burning heater in their home. Unfortunately, her grandparents weren't familiar with the potency of the product and her grandfather put the entire box of wood in the stove at one time. It's an episode we don't talk about much! Needless to say, I didn't give them any more lighter wood and I understand granddaddy made a contribution to the volunteer fire department for several years! I digress.

As the lighter-wood-laden truck approached the decoy, Jeff was thinking about how it was illegal to remove the wood from the national forest and debated whether or not to leave his hiding spot and discuss the violation with the driver.

As he observed, the truck driver spotted the decoy and came to a complete stop in the road. This was not at all uncommon. Often your less experienced road hunters would slam on the brakes and slide to a stop upon sighting the stuffed deer. Your more refined road hunters would simply ease off the gas and roll to a stop so as not to spook the deer look-alike.

While watching the driver, Jeff noticed another truck was coming up behind the lighter-wood-loaded truck. It appeared the driver of the second truck had also spotted the decoy. Unfortunately, he evidently had not spotted the truck sitting in the road in front of him. As Jeff watched, the second truck slammed into the stationary truck. With the sound of the crash reverberating through the woods, the officer in the chase vehicle radioed Jeff and asked, "Did they shoot?"

Although laughing uncontrollably, he replied, "No, they wrecked!"

Jeff could not believe what had just occurred. However, what happened next was even more of a shock. As Jeff watched, the driver's door on the second truck flew open. The man did not go to check on the occupants of the other truck. No, with rifle in hand, he ran to the rear of the truck, took a steady rest, and proceeded to shoot the "deer" that amazingly continued to stand dead still watching the trucks the trucks in the road. Astounded, Jeff keyed the mike and said, "Now he's shot. Come on down here."

As it turned out, the two vehicles were driven by a father (front) and son. The collision did about $2,000 worth of damage to the trucks and the tickets for hunting from a public road and hunting by the aid of a vehicle did about another $1,500! To add a little insult to injury, Jeff had the fellow unload the lighter wood. Man, what a hardnose.

Now according to Jeff, the father never exited his vehicle until the son had shot at the decoy. Therefore, I can't help but believe the pair were in it together. At least I am sure if I were going to do something like that, I wouldn't do it in front of my father and especially not after I had just rammed his truck with mine!

This of course isn't an isolated incident of a father "training" his son. We have caught night hunters who told us they were teaching their son how to hunt. This same thing has occurred with folks hunting by the aid of bait. These cases are very blatant and most people would not condone this type of behavior. However, I also have fathers who allowed their son to take a doe when it wasn't doe season and fathers who have bragged about how their son took two bucks running together on opening day. I've known fathers who allowed their kids to take over the limit on doves and to take them over bait.

I've met a lot of people who were, as far as I could tell, as straight as an arrow. Unfortunately, for each one of them, I've met several that were as crooked as a snake. This father-to-son "training" doesn't only take place in hunting. If you want to check the deacon of the church's resolve, arrest his son and see how he greets you on Sunday morning. Worst yet, catch the deacon's grandson or the pastor's son. I have done those things and lived with the fallout. Don't misunderstand me. A father can do a great job raising a child and have them turn out wayward. However, that's a lot more likely if the father condones and/or promotes bad behavior.

If it wasn't enough being a conservation enforcement officer, I was also a little league umpire for fifteen years. Believe me when I tell you as a game warden and little league umpire, I could write a great book entitled *How to Lose Friends and Negatively Influence People*. There probably aren't that many other folks who are hated just for showing up! Maybe IRS agents.

Today, we all need to take a look in the mirror and decide if we are the examples Christ wants us to be. When we look in the mirror, we need to ask ourselves, "Am I doing what God wants me to do? Do my kids, and other kids, see Jesus in me?" And as the old Royal Ambassadors' pledge said, do I "have a Christlike concern for all people"?

We need to think on things that matter. Luckily, the folks in this story survived the crash without physical injury. However, we know tomorrow isn't guaranteed. Choose you this day who you will serve.

I appreciated Jeff sharing this story with me. He is a good friend with a compassion for people. Interestingly, his son is now an Alabama conservation enforcement officer. I pray God watches over him.

I Could Not Believe It

WE HAD A NEW conservation enforcement officer (CEO) hired around 2007 or so. He was a seasoned police officer. He made the comment to me that he had seen it all and I replied, "Not yet you haven't." There were several times I too felt I had seen it all; however, each time that occurred, something would happen that would help me realize I hadn't.

Early in my career as a wildlife biologist /CEO, I spent every weekend of the deer hunting season working on a wildlife management area (WMA). This meant I was on either my area, the Coosa WMA; the Hollins WMA, which was in Clay County about twenty miles from my home; or the Barbour WMA, located in Barbour County, which was about 110 miles away in southeast Alabama.

I made the trip many times. The Barbour WMA was the crown jewel of the WMA system. This was true largely to the fact the area was owned by the state, unlike most other areas, which were leased from private landowners or were made up of national forest property. The Barbour area often received the lion's share of equipment and had more personnel than any of the other areas. This was due in part to the fact that the leased property could be lost within ninety days of notice from the landowners. Another major factor that made Barbour so popular was that it was located in the black belt of Alabama and therefore produced some great deer.

I would be remiss if I did not mention the area manager at Barbour. Billy Sharp was a one of a kind. He was a hoot. He did a good job of managing the area and supervising "the hands," as he called them. The hands were three men who lived on the area and did everything from planting the fields to working the roads to working the hunts. They were a good team.

As a general rule, when I had to go and work at Barbour I would leave my house around seven in the morning, which would put me on the WMA by 9:00 a.m., which was when the deer started being brought to the check station. Checking the deer, weighing, and aging them was my primary job on the hunt. After the first wave of deer came through, we would normally go and check hunters on the area until about dark, when we returned to the check station to begin checking in the afternoon's harvest. After that, we would go out and work night hunting for a while and then return to the lodging at the headquarters and try to get three or four hours of sleep before getting up to open the check station the next morning at about 4:30 a.m.

My turn to make the trip south had rolled around once again. I did not know this trip would be an extremely memorable one.

Let me take you back a few years. I grew up with a great desire to hunt. However, there were no deer anywhere close to my home in the Greenhill community in northwest Alabama. Therefore, like many folks, I learned to hunt by chasing the squirrels that were abundant around my home and community. While I enjoyed hunting squirrels, I really wanted to deer hunt. Although my dad did not deer hunt, he realized my desire and made arrangements with a fellow he had worked with to take me deer hunting. It turned out there were three guys that often hunted together and they took me under their wing and taught me the basics of deer hunting.

I'm sure taking a teenager hunting probably wasn't high on their bucket list; however, I guess Don, Freddie, and Jerry were up for a challenge and they got one. Things went well with only a few hiccups, as far as I was concerned. The day I was climbing down a tree with my climbing tree stand and the stand fell off my feet to the ground, leaving me hanging in the tree on my hand climber, comes to mind.

While Don and Freddie were primarily weekend hunters, Jerry did not work during the deer season. He did not want work or anything else interfering with his deer season. It cost him a lot monetarily and in relationships. It taught me a lesson. However, the most significant thing I remember Jerry telling me was, "If you spend a lot of time in the woods, you are going to see things that people will not believe, and it's usually best just not to tell them about it." Going into a career that had me spending a lot of time in the woods, I saw that proven true many times.

While en route to the Barbour WMA, I encountered something unlike anything I had ever seen before or since. I had entered Barbour County and was getting pretty close to my turnoff in the town of Midway when I spotted a pickup truck across a large field in the edge of the wood line about two hundred yards from the road. Spotting a truck parked in such a place at 9:30 in the morning, I automatically assumed it belonged to someone who was hunting and I instinctively began scanning the wood line for a hunter. Within seconds, I noticed movement that I quickly realized was someone walking. Someone who wasn't wearing any hunter orange. I spotted the road that led to the pickup and I turned in. As I was now quickly moving down the field road, I keyed in on the "hunter" just in case he realized he wasn't wearing any orange and decided a quick exit was needed.

As I honed my focus, my mouth fell open in disbelief. It was one of those "I'm sure I didn't just see that" moments. As I got closer, I could verify that my eyes were in fact not playing a trick on me. The man was carrying a rifle in one hand and a rope in the other. The other end of the rope was tied around the neck of a six-point buck that was walking behind the man. As happened several times in my career, it would have been interesting to have had a picture of the look on my face!

I quickly exited my truck and started toward the man. My first words were, "What is going on?" The fellow stopped and the deer stopped. The deer's nose was almost on the ground and the animal was panting heavily. The man explained he had been hunting down in the hollow and had shot the deer. When he had got to the deer, it wasn't dead. Not wanting to have to drag it up the hill out of the hollow, he had tied the rope around its neck and got it up and walked it out. I must admit I was now scanning the area to see where the folks were with the cameras since I knew this wasn't happening for real and had to be some type of setup. I was thinking, "I don't believe that story at all"; however, there he stood with a live deer with a rope around its neck. I again looked at the deer and noticed it did have some blood on its side. I could tell the animal was suffering in that it had its eyes closed and was panting hard. I told the man that he needed to put the deer out of its misery.

Little did I know I was about to witness another first. The man placed the muzzle of his 30-30 rifle against the deer's side and pulled the trigger and there was basically no sound. There was a very muffled thump and the deer fell to the ground. The deer did not kick or quiver. I think it was dead when it hit the ground.

With the deer taken care of, I turned my attention to the hunter. I asked to see his license and addressed his need for some hunter orange. He explained he had forgotten to put on his orange cap. He explained he was the only one who hunted the property and knew the local game warden very well. I explained to him that although he may have been the only one with permission to hunt the property, that definitely did not mean he would be the only one hunting on it. As far as being a friend of the game warden, in my short career I had met many people who claimed to be friends of the game warden, many more "friends" than game wardens had. Interestingly, about the only time people claimed to be a friend of the game warden was after they had been caught in a violation!

Seeing how this was taking place in Barbour County and having learned that many game wardens were quite territorial, I decided it might be best to contact the local officer and see how he wanted to handle the situation. While I was well within my statewide authority to arrest the violator and I had no qualms about doing so, I did not want to alienate the local officer. Once again, the "us versus them" that was prevalent between the enforcement section and the wildlife section was in my mind. I contacted the local CEO and he said he was familiar with the man and he would handle it. I let it go at that.

I left the scene and headed to the WMA. There, while telling the story and getting the "What have you been smoking" looks, I remembered the advice of not telling everything you had seen. I have rarely told this story but I assure you it's the truth. It would not be the last hard-to-believe episode I witnessed. I guarantee you that!

I owe my dad a great deal. He was a wonderful father and I miss him each day. One of the things I appreciated the most was that although he wasn't much of a hunter, he knew how much I wanted to hunt and he made it happen. It was a good gift that led to a career and a great life. The Bible says if we give good gifts, just imagine the gifts that God has in store for us—the greatest being the gift of salvation and eternal life. The greatest gift my dad ever gave me was to take me to church and tell me about Jesus. I can't thank him enough, but I look forward to thanking him again when I see him in heaven.

When You Put It That Way
(Special Task Force Needed)

WHILE MANY SKILLS are necessary to be a successful game warden, a good understanding of human nature is a good place to start. I've been asked many times by young people who thought they wanted to be a game warden as to what courses they should take in school to help them. One thing I've often suggested is that they take some sociology and psychology courses. Understanding people and why they do what they do is helpful. Of course, some things folks do I will never understand. Something I have told people many times is when you hear an account of how an officer mistreated some violator, never assume the violator was acting rationally.

Many times, I have said you can't get inside the head of a violator. That is true to a point. What I mean by that is it is often difficult to figure out what a violator is going to do or when they may do it. Those who will violate the law come in all shapes and sizes. They literally run the gamut from the hardcore violator that will shoot a deer anywhere at any time to the guy who shoots a deer out the window on a sudden impulse.

When dealing with these folks, it is imperative you make a quick evaluation of them and develop a plan of action when speaking with them. Violators, like all people, respond to different stimuli.

Washington County in southwest Alabama was well known for wildlife law violators. For many there, it was simply a way of life and they took it seriously. While working on a hunter education project in the area, wildlife biologists/CEOs Jinks Altiere and Ray Metzler decided they would assist the local CEOs in trying to get a handle on the night hunting of deer that was rampant in the area. The local officer advised Jinks that many of the residents took their poaching very seriously and, in the event they attempted to apprehend someone, they better be prepared for a fight. Having worked in Butler County, another night hunting hotspot, for several years and having caught plenty of night hunters, Jinks knew some folks could be a handle and appreciated the heads-up.

While driving down a rural county road the Washington County officer had suggested, the two officers spotted a couple of deer on the side of the road. Not far past them they found a dim road that looked like it might be a good surveillance spot. They backed into the road and found that it was indeed a good vantage point. With a limited knowledge of the area, and with some deer along the road close by, they decided to monitor the area for a while.

It wasn't long until they spotted a vehicle slowly making its way toward their location. They watched as the driver maneuvered the vehicle so the headlights were shining off the side of the road. Within seconds, a rifle blast split the calm night. The officers took off toward the vehicle. They radioed the local officer and told him they were headed toward someone who had just shot and he advised he was en route.

Like most night hunters, the shooter was surprised to see the officers arrive on the scene so quickly. They exited their vehicle, as did the shooter. Jinks advised the man that he was under arrest for hunting at night. While he wasn't happy, he understood, like most, that he had slipped up and was now going to have to pay the price. They asked for his driver's license and he reluctantly handed it over.

While they were writing the tickets, the local officer arrived on the scene. Although most violators know very well who their local officers are, it appeared this guy had not really realized the two officers who had apprehended him were not local. That realization, coupled with Jinks telling the man they would be confiscating his rifle, changed the landscape, so to speak. The man immediately informed them they would not be taking his firearm.

During this time, it was common procedure for us to take the weapons used by night hunters. This was distressing for the violator since they knew they might not get the gun back. Alabama law 9-11-252.1 reads, in part, "Any motor vehicle, or any gun, rifle, ammunition or other hunting equipment which has been or is used for illegal nighttime deer hunting shall be contraband, and, in the discretion of the circuit court may be forfeited to the State of Alabama."

On many occasions, I have had men beg me not to take their firearm. I have had more than one offer to give me another, much more valuable, firearm if I would allow them to retain the one they had used to break the law. This was normally because the gun was a family heirloom that had been passed down over time. This brings to mind a story where CEO Hershel Patterson and I had apprehended some night hunters in Coosa County. As I looked at the unusual rifle I had taken from the front-seat passenger, the man commented, "If that gun could talk, it could really tell some stories." When I informed him we would be confiscating it and he probably wouldn't get it back, it was as if I had kicked him below the belt. He immediately started pleading with me not to take the gun. I told him we would be holding it until court and it would be up to the judge as to whether or not he would get it back. That was one upset fellow. I digress.

Back to the story. Seeing how the man had taken a fighting stance, it was blatantly obvious to even the most casual observer he had no intention of turning over his firearm. To emphasize his intention, he stated he wasn't about to give his gun to a couple of game wardens he didn't even know. If you remember what I said at the start of this story about sociology and psychology, you are about to understand what I'm talking about.

The violator's statement that he didn't even know who these game wardens were gave Jinks an idea. If you are a game warden, you must be able to think on your feet in order to use what lawbreakers say to help achieve your desired outcome. Realizing this man was upset that these obviously "out of town" wardens had apprehended him, Jinks quickly formulated a ploy to hopefully defuse the now testy situation. He told the man he was correct in thinking they were not local officers. He said, in fact, he was from Greenville and his partner was from Montgomery. He informed the man they were members of a special task force that had been put together to try and catch him. Jinks could see the wheels turning in the man's head and knew he may have hit on something. Therefore, he moved forward, saying it had become obvious that he was such a good night hunter that it was going to take more than the local effort to apprehend him.

The fellow's posture had suddenly changed from a fighting stance to one of a proud outlaw, with his chest swelled with pride. Jinks then landed the final blow when he said, "We are just thankful we were able to catch you." With his ego properly massaged, it was obvious the situation had turned a full 180 degrees. It was as if the violator said, "Well, since you put it that way." The now proud violator said they could have his gun.

166

Whether we want to admit it or not, I think everyone enjoys hearing a little praise now and then. I have always remembered something I was told in one of the required classes for supervisors I attended. The instructor said, "Everybody understands two things: raises and praises." While we did not praise violators, it was helpful to try and understand their psyche. That often wasn't easy. However, it was imperative that we learn to read people. There are experts who read people's body language for a living and then there is everyone else who reads people's body language every day. We all do that. Whether you think about it or not, you are doing it. Some folks are much easier to read than others.

Reading body language isn't restricted to other people. We read the body language of animals and animals read our body language. Your dog can likely read you like a book. It's a necessary skill you can sharpen if you work at it.

We all make an evaluation of other people we come in contact with. While we may not think about it in depth, we do make an initial evaluation. So, how do people see you? I've often heard people say they don't care what people think about them. I do not believe that is true. I think we should consider how people see us. You have heard the adage about putting your best foot forward. Another saying that is so true is "You never get a second chance to make a first impression."

As a conservation officer, a lot of the public was against you from the start. Often the best you could do was to be known as someone who was fair and who treated everyone the same. When you were accused of being someone who would give their own mother a ticket, which I heard on more than one occasion, it was refreshing to hear someone add the phrase "but he was fair."

Interestingly, Jinks did end up on the Alabama Department of Conservation and Natural Resources Special Task Force with me after we had both retired and then returned to part-time duty. We

Good Ole Boys SHOOTING DECOYS

worked several cases together, which gave us the opportunity to swap stories. I appreciate him telling me this one and allowing me to share it.

168

Training Bennett
(WMA Meltdown)

I HAD NEVER SEEN anything like it and never have since. Sure, I have witnessed many folks who have gotten upset. Nobody likes being arrested. When you arrest someone while they are enjoying themselves, they take it personally. But most of them don't go ballistic.

The two game wardens in Coosa County had worked the Coosa Wildlife Management Area (WMA) their entire careers. Once they realized I was willing and eager to work with them on the area, they had shared their law enforcement expertise with me. While similar to enforcement activities outside of the WMA, there were some nuances to working on a WMA.

Because the officers had taught me well and because I worked the entire county, not just the WMA, my arrest numbers were normally the highest in the state among officers working in the wildlife section. For this reason, our wildlife chief would on occasion send new employees to the Coosa WMA for us to "train" them. Obviously, it wasn't rocket science, but it helped to work alongside someone who had been doing it for a while.

I received a call from the chief, who informed me he was sending a new biologist to work a deer hunt on the Coosa WMA.

169

He was going to have the new man, Bennett, to come on the date of an either-sex draw hunt since he knew there would be plenty of people there.

In the late eighties and early nineties, I had pushed for and been allowed to have some either-sex deer hunts on the Coosa WMA in an effort to lower our population and thereby improve the condition of the deer. The data we were keeping on the health of our herd had shown our deer were twenty-five pounds or more below optimum weight. That told us there were more deer than there was food to adequately meet their needs. Since our hands were pretty much tied as far as making habitat improvements, increased harvests were our only mechanism to try to improve the condition of the herd. Since the majority of our hunting, and therefore our harvest, was bucks, we were not putting much of a dent in the deer numbers. To do that, we needed to increase our antlerless harvest.

Although they were coming around to the idea, getting our leadership to agree to increasing the number of either-sex hunts we offered on the WMAs was not the easiest thing to do. Often, instead of having an either-sex hunt where every hunter had the opportunity to take either a buck or a doe, we would determine that a percentage of the permits would be either-sex and the remainder would be buck only. This was deemed necessary in part due to the fact that we might have two thousand people show up for the hunt. Although the success rate was always rather low, we didn't need to take the chance on killing five hundred does when we were hoping for two hundred.

The mechanism we used to determine whether or not folks received a "doe tag," as they were commonly called, was pretty advanced. We had a box that the hunters would reach into and pull out a tennis ball. If they got a green one, they were given an either-sex permit; if they pulled out a red ball, they got a buck-only permit. If we wanted the percentage to be 50 percent, we put two green and two red balls in the box. If we wanted 33 percent, we put in one green and two red, and so forth. Yes, we were on the cutting edge! The system basically worked well. However, I must admit it was pretty comical when we first started. It was hilarious to me that we had several guys who were very reluctant to stick their hand into the box where they could not see. Some flatly refused to reach into the box and just asked for a buck-only permit instead. Initially, the hesitance to reach into the box would quickly become a problem when you were trying to hurriedly move a thousand people through the line. Luckily, the problem was short lived. Once they had participated, they were no longer wary, but you always would have a couple who would balk when you told them to reach into the box. Of course, I always thought it would be really funny to either put a rubber snake in the box or cut a hole in the back side so I could grab their hand when they stuck it in. However, I didn't want to have to fight some guy because he had been embarrassed in front of the crowd. I digress.

Bennett was stationed in southwest Alabama, which meant it would take him about two and a half or three hours to make the trip north to Coosa County. I told him we would be at the WMA check station at 4:30 a.m. but he didn't need to be there until about eight o'clock.

As had become customary, there was a line containing roughly two hundred hunters at the check station when I arrived at about 4:15. Anticipating a large crowd, we would have everything ready the night before. We quickly got the station opened and the drawing apparatus set up. We would have to check each hunter's license before allowing them to draw for their permit. Since most of these folks hunted the WMA on a regular basis, things went relatively smoothly. Of course, you always had a newcomer that, although he had just watched a hundred people present their license and draw for a permit, would not have his license out and ready and would inevitably not be able to find it, which threw a wrench in things. From time to time, you would have someone who, when they finally reached the front of the line, would ask if they could buy a license. The answer was yes, they could, at the store eight miles south of our current location. The parking area would normally stay pretty full for a couple of hours. After that we had a lull.

Bennett arrived and we got in my truck and headed across the area to set up a roadblock. I decided we would go to the west side of the 38,000-acre area and set up on the ridge road. Road number 11, aka the Ridge Road, traversed the entire west side of the area. That part of the area normally received a good amount of hunting pressure and I thought we would likely have a lot of traffic. I went down to road number 114 or, as it was known by some, the Bloomer Road. As you might guess, many of the roads on the area had several unofficial names, some of which were more interesting than others. When I arrived on the area, it was all I could do to find my way around the two hundred miles of roads using the map with the numbered roads on it, much less learn all of the unofficial names. However, I did learn that someone had once left a pair of underwear, bloomers, hanging in a tree at the entrance of 114 and the name had stuck.

The intersection of the two roads was just north of a curve in the gravel road that would keep oncoming traffic from seeing us too soon, giving them the opportunity to unload their gun. Having a loaded gun in a vehicle was our most common violation on the WMA. Since it was not illegal to have your gun loaded in the vehicle outside the WMA, many folks forgot to unload them when on the area. I do not mean to imply that we were set up immediately around a blind curve. We had learned that stopping the traffic too close to the curve would result in a traffic hazard.

Furthermore, we learned over time that it didn't make a lot of difference where you placed a roadblock, you usually ended up catching some loaded guns. However, I have seen several attempting to unload their gun while waiting in line to be checked!

As normal, around nine o'clock folks began making it back to their vehicles and moving around on the area. We had explained to Bennett what we were looking for. He was familiar with the WMA regulations and I found he already knew what he was doing. Little did I know we were all about to experience something unlike ever before.

As a four-wheel-drive pickup rolled up to our checkpoint, I recognized the driver. Since I was present on every hunt and gave out every permit on most hunt days, I was familiar with the majority of the hunters on the area. I didn't necessarily know them by name but I recognized them. As I stepped to the driver's-side window of the truck, I asked the driver to see his permit and to check his gun to make sure it was unloaded. He handed me the permit and reached for his gun. He worked the bolt to show me the gun was empty. While I was paying attention to the gun, I was a little more interested in the permit. I distinctly remembered that during the drawing for permits, this individual had failed to pull out a green ball and had been issued a buck-only permit. I remembered this because he had been very disappointed that he had failed to get a green ball. However, the permit I now held in my hand was in fact an either-sex permit. I asked the fellow to pull his truck to the side of the road. He complied and I asked him to step out of the truck. Bennett was watching intently since he had not seen anything obviously wrong.

The fellow was a young kid, probably around twenty years old. Of course, I was only a few years older than that. I asked him where he had obtained the either-sex permit and he said he had got it at the check station. I told him I had issued his permit and I

173

remembered it was not an either-sex permit. I could see he was getting a little upset but I knew I was right. He again claimed that was the permit he had received earlier that morning and I again refuted his claim. While I figured it was somehow illegal to swap permits with someone else, I did not have in mind to try to arrest him for it. However, the fact that I knew he was lying to my face was quite aggravating.

Instead of continuing to push the permit situation, I decided I would search his vehicle. This was before extended-cab pickups were the norm and I leaned his seat forward and there found a box of shotgun shells. The box contained birdshot. Since this was a deer hunt, it was illegal to possess any shotgun shells other than rifled slugs. This was not normally a violation we wrote a ticket for so I left the shells there and continued to look through the rest of the vehicle.

I completed my search without turning up anything else illegal. I approached the young man and again asked him to tell me how he had come up with the either-sex permit. Evidently, he had heard enough about the permit. I could see he was grinding his teeth and his fists were clenched. As I stared at him, he blurted out, "I swapped with my buddy when he was leaving, okay?" Then he basically screamed, "What's the big deal? I didn't even kill anything!" I had heard this defense several times in the past. Many people were of the opinion that if their violations of the law did not result in the death of an animal then they should not be charged with anything. This was often true for folks hunting without a permit who adhered to the "no harm, no foul" philosophy. As I viewed it then and now, the problem with this type of thinking was it leads to no one being responsible for their actions. That was a problem then and it's worse today.

I wanted to take the time to tell the young man that we were doing our best to manage the deer herd and someone manipulating our permitting system was a problem. However, the more I thought about the man repeatedly lying to me the more agitated I became. I'm not proud of what happened next. I returned to his truck and retrieved the box of shot shells. I advised him the shells were illegal to possess and asked for his driver's license. He removed his license from his wallet and handed it to me, all the while protesting that he did not even remember those shells were in his truck. I took the license and started writing him a ticket. He was trying to keep calm but I could tell he wasn't very good at it.

I completed the citation for possession of illegal ammunition and showed him where to sign it. He signed the ticket and I gave him his copy and told him he was free to go. He got in his truck, snatched it in gear, and tore out, throwing dirt and gravel everywhere. We watched as he flew down the road for about 150 yards, then he abruptly slid to a stop. I advised Bennett we had better keep an eye on him since I wasn't sure what he might do. I wasn't ready for what he did.

The best way I can describe it is to say he got out of the truck and pitched a fit. He was screaming and hollering, spinning around and then proceeded to beat on the side of his truck with his fists. This went on for almost a minute. Once again, I wish I had a picture of my face while this was happening.

After he finished beating the side of his truck, he just stood still for about a minute. After that, he got back in his truck and drove away. We stood looking at each other with our mouths hanging open.

As I mentioned earlier, I wasn't much older than this kid. It was interesting that while I was supposed to be "training" Bennett, I was the one that learned something that day. I should say something I had been told previously was reinforced that day. One of my mentors, CEO Hershel Patterson, had told me, "If you don't feel good about writing a ticket, don't write it." Looking back, while the ticket I wrote that day was legitimate, it was not something I would normally write. I should not have allowed my emotion to dictate my actions. I regretted the decision I made.

Fortunately, I learned a lesson I have tried to pass on to all the officers I have had an opportunity to train since that time. The majority of people dislike the game warden to start with. Game wardens are normally enforcing the law alone, in the middle of nowhere, with backup basically nonexistent. The odds are obviously against us. If we really want to stack the odds against us, all we have to do is arrest someone for something they feel is not legitimate. Let me give you another example. A few years before I went to work, a local game warden arrested several employees of a local company for hunting doves over a baited field. Whether or not the field was baited was a matter of debate even among officers. Therefore, the folks who received tickets strongly believed they had been wronged. They believed this so much that I heard about it on almost a yearly basis for the next thirty years! It taught me that if I was in doubt, I needed to think long and hard before writing the ticket. Luckily for me, most of the time there wasn't a lot of doubt!

I feel certain that Bennett probably never forgot that episode. Several years later, we both ended up working together as private lands biologists. I enjoyed working with him. Unfortunately, Bennett developed some serious health problems that eventually took his life. It was difficult losing him. However, I know that I will see him again. Bennett deeply loved his wife and daughters; however, he loved the Lord more. While it is never easy to say goodbye to friends and loved ones, when you know they have chosen Christ as their savior, it makes it a little easier. See you soon my friend.

A Federal Shotgun

IT WAS MY GOOD FORTUNE to learn my decoy utilization techniques from the decoy guru, Conservation Enforcement Officer Byron Smith. While I haven't researched it, I would be surprised if anyone has caught more people shooting a decoy in Alabama than Byron. Byron began the decoy revolution in Alabama and later sold decoys to most of the states in the country. Everyone has heard the adage that experience is the best teacher. I learned a lot from Byron's experience.

When the decoy first arrived on the scene, the violations were often almost automatic. Folks who had road hunted all of their lives could not resist it. Besides revealing just how much road hunting was taking place, the decoy also uncovered who the typical road hunter was. In actuality, it revealed there is no typical road hunter. Those apprehended using the decoy ran the gamut from the female nurse to the career military man and from the kid to the retiree. To be honest, after working in conservation law enforcement for a short time, I learned not to put anything past anybody. The sight of a deer standing alongside the road was just more than a lot of people could pass up.

Byron related to me a story of a fateful night in east Alabama when he and his partner could not write fast enough. With the deer placed along a highway that led to a popular wildlife management area, the violations were coming fast and furious and the deer soon resembled a piece of Swiss cheese. When a sedan passed the deer and let off the accelerator but did not touch the brakes, Byron told his partner to buckle up.

While wildlife law violators are a diverse group, some were obviously more experienced than others. This was often evident when the decoy had been deployed. It was always interesting to observe the reaction of a potential violator when they spotted the decoy. The range spanned from those that simply eased off the accelerator and coolly coasted to a stop to those that stood on the brakes and slid to a stop. You also had those who gave no indication at all but soon came creeping back toward the stuffed wonder. And then there were those who drove off the road toward it! I witnessed all of these and more.

Within a minute, the car was coming back toward the motionless manikin. With the car still moving at a high rate of speed, a shotgun blast split the night. Did I mention some of the shooters didn't stop at all? Byron immediately pursued the vehicle and was quickly closing the distance when he realized the sedan had three antennas across the trunk lid. He knew this was a good indication he was likely in pursuit of a law enforcement officer. The car quickly slowed and came to a stop on the edge of the road. Byron told his partner "Just like anybody else" as they exited the truck. The driver door opened and Byron told the driver to stay in the car. The driver called back, "We are law enforcement," and Byron responded, "Put your hands up where I can see them." The officers complied and Byron and his partner moved in and removed the men's handguns and a shotgun. A federally issued shotgun!

With everything secure, the shooters were allowed to exit their federal vehicle and immediately began pleading their case. Byron quickly assured the men the charges would not be dropped and the gun would be held as evidence. The men anxiously explained if they lost the gun they would likely lose their jobs as well. Byron told the driver the best he could offer was he would be at the courthouse at eight o'clock Monday morning and if the district attorney (DA) wanted to accept a guilty plea and give the gun back, that would be okay with him. The pair looked pretty pitiful as they limped back to their vehicle with a handful of paper. Byron moved back to the setup to wait on the next taker. It didn't take long. The night culminated with twenty-six arrests!

When Byron arrived at the courthouse the following Monday, the now familiar sedan was parked out front with two nervous-looking fellows seated on the hood. The trio walked into the district attorney's office and the officer relayed the facts of the case and informed the DA the violators were federal law enforcement officers and were there in hopes of having their federally issued shotgun returned to them. Byron said he felt the chances of them getting the gun back were slim to none and he was taken by surprise when the DA stated they might be able to get it back. He said the attorney picked up the old Remington 870 pump-action shotgun and gave it a good examination. He pondered the situation for a couple of minutes and announced he felt the gun was probably worth about $800. Although both agents knew they could buy a brand new 870 for around $200, they also knew they would be glad to pay $800 for the one the DA was holding. The fellows paid their fine and court costs, which included $800 for the gun, and thankfully went on their way. That wouldn't be the last law enforcement officer that the decoy would reel in.

Go Call Your Momma

LATE IN MY CAREER, my job duties had changed, which cut deeply into the time I had to work law enforcement within the forty-hour work week I was limited to. During this time, I joined the Coosa County Sheriff's Reserve and began working regularly with deputies. I quickly learned they dealt with as many or maybe more weird characters than we did.

While on patrol one summer night, Coosa County Sheriff's Deputy Josh Jones and I responded to a call of an assault in the Lake Martin area. We arrived on scene and were met by a woman who greeted us with "It's about time you got here." I'm sure the woman did not know and did not care that we were the only unit covering the 652 square miles that comprised the county. Nothing like getting off on a good foot! The woman turned around and hollered at the mobile home and an elderly looking man came out the back door and slowly and painfully made his way toward our location. We asked the fellow what was going on and before he could speak, the woman, who turned out to be his wife, stated their son had beat him up. I was beginning to wonder why she had called him outside if she was going to do all the talking. We asked the fellow where he was hurt and he said primarily his neck. After he stated he did not want any medical attention, we asked him to tell us what had occurred and again his wife began chiming in. We had

180

to tell her to let the man speak. He finally said his son had come in and attacked him as he lay in the bed. He advised he was dying of cancer. We gathered he had gotten onto his son for not working and helping around the house as he should and in return the son had grabbed him around the neck and choked him.

We asked where the son was now and they stated he was down at the other house, which was just down the road. We moved down to the next house and stepped onto the porch and called through the open door, telling the man to come out. The man appeared to be in his midthirties. He was about five feet seven inches tall and might have weighed 150 pounds. He was accompanied by his wife, who was a little shorter and a little heavier. We asked the man to tell us what had gone on with his dad and he explained they had just had a verbal argument but nobody had touched anybody. You always need to listen closely when someone tells you the events that have occurred. While you hoped you would get the whole truthful story, that rarely happened. You were also listening for any details that sounded suspect, such as someone adding that nobody had touched anybody. That part of the fellow's statement caught our attention.

As he was finishing his sentence, his sister and her husband pulled up in the front yard. The mother had told us the sister was on her way. This was quickly becoming the worst kind of family reunion. Josh asked me to stay with the suspect while he spoke with the sister. While the deputy spoke with her, her husband came onto the porch with us. Our suspect started telling him how if he got arrested, he would have to go to prison for twelve years. He explained he was already on probation and they had told him if he got arrested again, he would have to go to prison for twelve years. The brother-in-law was really helpful as he exclaimed, "Man, that's a long time!" The suspect stated he wasn't worried about going to prison but he just didn't want to be away from his wife and kids for that long. The brother-in-law stayed true to the course as he chimed in, "Man, in twelve years your kids will be full growed!" Just as I was thinking I really could do without this guy's comments, the wife decided it was time for her to add her two cents' worth. I didn't know what she was going to say but I sure wasn't ready for what came out of her mouth. She said, "Yeah, if you go to prison for twelve years, I'll probably be pregnant again!" Talk about biting a hole in your lip. It was all I could do not to laugh out loud. I thought surely that didn't come out the way she meant for it to. However, they didn't seem to miss a beat and kept the conversation going.

Shortly Josh came onto the porch, followed by the man's mother. Josh gave me the signal to go ahead and cuff the man so I told him to stand up and put his hands behind his back. His mother began to protest, saying he didn't need to go to jail. Keep in mind this is the same woman who couldn't wait to tell us about what he had done just minutes earlier. As I applied the cuffs, the man's wife abruptly stomped her foot and screamed, "I'm calling my momma!" She stormed off into the house. While it crossed my mind that she might be calling her momma to tell her she might be getting pregnant again, I thought it best not to ask. I escorted the man to the car and we headed to the county jail. You can't make this stuff up!

Several years ago, I was accompanying Coosa County Sheriff's Deputy Mike Rudd one night running radar near the Kellyton Fire Department. In addition to the fire department, there were three intersecting roads nearby, which necessitated a low speed limit. Unfortunately, many drivers did not adhere to the limit, which generated a lot of complaints. Therefore, we frequently worked the area.

We had not been there very long when our radar indicated a vehicle was traveling twice the posted limit. We pursued the vehicle, which pulled into a nearby driveway. This is not unusual.

Many times, the driver pulls into the driveway hoping we will not stop them or, in the event it actually is their driveway, they think they may not receive a citation since they have made it home. Neither one of these outcomes is very common. We approached the driver, identified ourselves, and asked for the young man's driver's license and proof of insurance. The driver immediately handed over his license and was attempting to locate his insurance when the porch light of the residence came on. This also is not unusual and is understandable. When folks see blue lights in their yard, it should pique their interest.

I was watching the porch when a man emerged from the house and headed our way at a fast pace. Being interested in what is happening is one thing; to come running toward the officer conducting the stop is another. I immediately ordered the man to stop. He responded, "That's my son," while pointing at the car. I again gave the loud verbal command for the man to STOP. The authoritative tone slowed the man's pace but he was still approaching. I again gave the loud verbal command for the man to stop. While I could see he did not have anything in his hands, I still did not want to have to go hands on with the man. While I understand a father's concern for his son, there was nothing happening that warranted an overaggressive response. The driver was still seated in the driver's seat and both officers were outside of the car. The man stopped about ten feet from me and demanded to know what was going on. I told him the driver had been stopped for speeding. Without asking the young man whether or not he had been speeding, the man immediately played what I assume he felt was his trump card. He said, "I'll have you to know that I got Terry Wilson elected as sheriff. Do I need to call him?" As you might imagine, that type statement doesn't sit very well. Unfortunately, I did not give a well-thought-out response, rather one right off the cuff. I said, "Go call him!"

Seeing his trump card hadn't sent us running, the man mellowed his tone and decided he might do better making requests rather than shouting demands and threats. I advised him we had conducted a simple traffic stop and the driver had chosen to pull into the driveway and was now complying with our requests. I mentioned his young son had not seen the need to escalate things and neither had we and I felt it would be in everyone's best interest to keep things calm. The man contemplated the situation and decided to calm down.

The last thing a driver who has committed a violation needs is a third party to exacerbate the situation. The side of the road isn't the place for cases to be decided. If you feel the officer is wrong, you will have an opportunity to present your case in court and/or to the sheriff at a later date. Due to the teenager's respectful attitude, he was issued a warning. If his dad had been driving, it might not have gone that way.

We are currently living during a time when many people hold law enforcement in low regard. This is unfortunate. The people in these stories evidently thought they would contact someone who would change what was being done. Many people think that way without even considering what is being done and why. In the first story, a young man had assaulted an elderly cancer patient. Should that simply be allowed? In the second incident, the young driver was driving at double the posted speed limit. Should law enforcement turn a blind eye to that? It is a sad situation when people immediately assume law enforcement is in the wrong whenever they have contact with the public. We, the public, are going to have to decide whether we want law enforcement or not. If we do, we must support it. If the public does not want law enforcement to exist, woe be unto us. Neither your momma nor your daddy will probably be able to help you.

Don't Shoot Me, Jack!

HAVING HUNTED ALL MY LIFE and spent my entire career enforcing game and fish laws and regulations, I sometimes forget that not everyone is familiar with some of the illegal activities that take place. Even some folks in our rural county were startled to learn that there were people shining lights and shooting deer at night around their homes. It happens more than they think.

I always considered myself fortunate in that the majority of night hunting in the counties where I worked was done from vehicles. Having the violators contained in a vehicle normally made for a safer situation. That is unless they decided to take us on a high-speed chase or jump from the vehicle, rifle in hand, and run into the woods. That's another story.

Unfortunately, conservation enforcement officers (CEOs) working often had to deal with walking night hunters. While this occurred all over, it was prevalent in the big crop fields in the southern part of the state. A night hunter on foot armed with a high-powered rifle and a light strapped to their head was a dangerous thing. Attempting to get into position to apprehend such a person was even more dangerous.

Much of a CEO's job was dangerous since we were always dealing with armed subjects. CEO Hershel Patterson, one of my first partners, told me when he hired on with the department, 10

185

percent of the officers working had been shot! He also related to me how his partner had been shot and killed by a walking night hunter in south Alabama. Those comments tend to get the attention of a twenty-four-year-old, green-as-a-gourd wildlife biologist embarking on a career in wildlife law enforcement.

It was my good fortune to work on several occasions with a colorful officer named Johnny Rearden. I would use his real name but the statute of limitations on some things may not have passed. Johnny had worked all over the state as a uniformed officer and all over the country as a covert officer. Believe me when I tell you he had some stories to tell. One of the most memorable tales was about the night he pursued a well-known walking night hunter named Monty O'Toole.

Johnny had received information that O'Toole was hunting some bean fields in his assigned county and had made up his mind to catch him. Saturday night found Johnny at a good vantage point, watching for the telltale flash of a light indicating a walking night hunter was working the field. This was long before cell towers punctured the night with their blinking lights. It was a dark night and Johnny immediately saw the light as it flashed across the field. He quickly made his way toward the outlaw, careful not to make any noise.

Keep in mind the officer is quickly making his way toward a known violator armed with a high-powered rifle and looking for something to shoot. And to think I often had people tell me you couldn't give them our job!

As the officer got close, he could make out the silhouette of the man as he eased through the field. Thinking he was in a good position, Johnny identified himself as a state game warden and told the man to drop the gun. The subject immediately turned toward Johnny and activated his headlight. The officer hit the ground and drew his .357 revolver. The violator had not seen him but was desperately searching with his light in an effort to spot the officer. In addition, he was telling him he had messed up and it was all over for him. Johnny said he aimed his pistol at the light and prayed the man would not see him and attempt to make good on the promise to kill him that he kept repeating.

After a couple of minutes of the man continuously looking and saying he was going to kill him a game warden, Johnny realized he was going to have to do something creative to come out on top in this situation. He decided on a plan he knew was risky; however, he didn't see many options.

When the man turned his head away Johnny yelled, "Jack!" Of course, this revealed the area where he was and the night hunter immediately turned toward him and began scanning with his light. While the outlaw continued to yell he was about to kill a game warden, Johnny was crab crawling through the beans trying to quietly get out of the area the man was searching. Once this was accomplished, he again yelled out, "Shoot him in the head, Jack!" The predator again turned toward the voice and continued his pursuit. Johnny again changed his location. Realizing he had to get closer to the outlaw and that every sound got the man's attention, Johnny picked up a couple of dirt clods and yelled, "Shoot now, Jack!" and hefted the dirt clods over the man's head so they hit the ground behind him. Although the man initially turned toward the voice, upon hearing the clods hit the ground he turned away from the officer. Johnny was now directly behind the man and moving toward him. Hearing a commotion in front of and behind him, the man decided the game warden might not be alone after all.

The man stood still and silent for a moment and then said, "Don't shoot me, Jack!" Hearing someone approaching from behind, the man spun around just in time for Johnny to hit him between the eyes with his revolver, knocking the man to his knees. The officer secured the rifle and arrested the man for hunting at night.

Unfortunately, as was often the case, the judge in the county was sympathetic to "fellers just trying to get a little meat" and fined the violator forty-seven dollars. That was hard to swallow. A reflection off his stainless-steel revolver or badge would have signed the officer's death warrant and yet his efforts to protect the state's wildlife were worth so little in district court. Unfortunately, this was very often the situation many officers worked under. It took a strong dedication to the protection of wildlife for officers to stick with it. It is obvious to me we only survived by the grace of God.

Boom Box

BEGINNING IN OCTOBER and continuing through February, the conservation enforcement officer's phone gets a pretty good workout. The calls run the gamut, including everything from someone who thinks they saw someone hunting on their property to the caller who wants to report they saw a deer that appeared to be chasing another one. Believe it or not, we received our share of that type of calls. I remember when a fellow called to report there were hawks flying around his house. When I asked what the problem was, he gruffly replied, "I have small kids!" While it probably wasn't the best response, I asked, "Well, how small are they?" I explained I did not think the hawks represented a threat to him or his children. He advised me he was going to call someone else who hopefully knew what they were talking about. As he was hanging up, I told him I hoped that worked out for him. I would have like to have reminded him not to dress the kids in fur coats but I'm sure that would have been unproductive. I digress.

One of the most common calls received was from someone who had heard a shot at night. This gets our attention; however, you must remember there are species that can be legally hunted at night and you have people who target practice at night. Yes, it happens. However, the calls we received usually weren't related

189

to someone chasing a raccoon; they normally involved someone shooting at a deer from the roadway. These folks are known as night hunters and chasing them accounted for much of our work time.

Attempting to catch a scoundrel who will shoot a deer at night while shining a light in its eyes can be a cold, long, and lonely ordeal. Many nights I have sat in the middle of nowhere on a "hot" night hunting spot only to have the entire night pass without spotting one single vehicle. Believe you me, that makes for a long night. However, that's what it takes to catch night hunters.

Retired Conservation Enforcement Officer (CEO) Jeff Brown was assigned to Tallapoosa County in east central Alabama. Jeff came to us after having been a police officer in an east Alabama city. He was a good guy and after he was deprogrammed from the fast-paced city life, he became a really good CEO. Despite the fact we were in adjacent counties, I unfortunately did not have the opportunity to actually work with Jeff very often. The workload in Coosa County demanded I stay close to home; however, our paths crossed on a fairly regular basis. I enjoyed working with Jeff when possible and he was a great source of good stories.

Jeff related a story concerning night hunting I found quite humorous. It seems he had been receiving numerous night hunting complaints in one particular area and got with another officer to work a detail. They arrived at around 8:00 p.m. and settled into a good observation post. Take it from me, that time passes very slowly when there is absolutely no activity taking place. Finally, at about 2:00 a.m., Jeff heard the sound of a drumbeat coming from the road.

It is interesting how far you can hear on a cold, clear night in the country. I have heard shots that turned out to be over two miles away. Being able to pinpoint the location of a shot was a skill that was developed over many years and required a good sense of direction and a good knowledge of the road system. I have pinpointed shots with great accuracy and I have mistaken the location of a shot by as much as a mile. One of the most memorable misplacements was when CEO Hershel Patterson and I were working within one-quarter mile of my home. Now one would think I would know that area better than anywhere else and I would have thought that as well. However, on this night a shot rang out and we both placed it on Coosa County Road 18, which was directly behind us but about four miles by road. We decided to go and investigate and took off down the state highway toward the location. As we hurried down the road, we noticed a vehicle behind us obviously trying to flag us down. Although in a hurry to get to the location of the shot, we pulled over for the individual. The man, my neighbor, jumped out of his vehicle and said someone had just shot in front of his house and we had just ridden right past the location. Neither one of us could believe we had missed the location so far. Worse yet, we had obviously passed the shooter on the road in our effort to reach the wrong area. That was embarrassing to say the least!

I remember another night when my supervisor Rick Claybrook and I were working night hunting on Coosa County Road 40, a perpetual night hunting hotspot. We were standing outside our vehicle when a shot rang out. Immediately, I pointed to the south and Rick pointed to the north! Shot placement was far from an exact science!

With great listening conditions on this night, Jeff wasn't too perplexed that he didn't see any lights, although the music was getting louder. It wouldn't be the first time a night hunter had driven around without any lights on. Of course, most night hunters didn't have loud music playing. Jeff eased toward the road, looking for the vehicle. Though there were still no lights, the music was now very loud and plain. Curiosity got the best of the officer so he turned on his flashlight, which illuminated a fellow riding a bicycle with a boom box on his shoulder!

When somebody on a bicycle rides by you in the middle of nowhere at two o'clock in the morning with a stereo on their shoulder, it's time to pack up and head for home! And that's exactly what he did. You can't make this stuff up!

The Guy I Was Waiting For

MANY TIMES, I have said to work nighttime deer hunting you need to be where the deer are. More properly stated, you need to be where the violators "think" the deer will be. While conventional wisdom would make one believe that night hunters would only ply their craft in the middle of nowhere, where the chance of detection would be low, those who believe that would be wrong. Sure, there are some violators who prefer to do their violating off the beaten path; however, my experience has proven that many are opportunists and will shoot a deer wherever they find it. As a matter of fact, even a deer standing alongside the US highway that split Coosa County in half would likely get shot if the right person came along. That also held true if the deer was standing in a subdivision, a cemetery, a soccer field, or someone's front yard. It was often simply a crime of opportunity.

The sad truth is many folks have no qualms about unleashing a deadly projectile into the darkness with no idea or regard for what it might impact. This posed a serious threat to people, livestock, and property. Many folks do not think about that when they hear about someone shooting a deer at night. For these reasons, we often worked in and around civilization. Believe me when I tell you if a deer was stupid enough to stand alongside the road, someone would likely be stupid enough to shoot it!

Night hunting was often influenced by people's personal observations and by word of mouth. Hunters and others like to talk and during the deer season there isn't a much better conversation piece than where someone has seen a nice buck. Not only do hunters do a lot of talking, hunters and outlaws do a lot of listening. When possible, the game warden is listening also. It doesn't take long for word to get around about where a good buck was spotted, and if it was alongside the road, it didn't take long for the area to be visited by window shoppers both day and night. In game warden vernacular, a window shopper is someone who prefers to shoot from the window of their vehicle versus actually going into the woods and taking a stand. Unfortunately, these road warriors (another name for them) are found in abundance.

One season I had heard several folks talking about seeing a couple of bucks standing alongside of US Highway 231 just below the Diamond Mountain Hunting Club clubhouse in the Hanover community. The area is known by locals as Diamond Graphite. Many folks don't know that Coosa County is one of the few areas in the United States that has a belt of high-quality graphite traversing the entire county. In the 1920s, graphite mines were prevalent across the county. One was known as the Diamond Graphite Mine. Although there is little trace of the mine today, the area is still commonly referred to as Diamond Graphite. I don't know if it's just a southern thing or not, but around here, once an area has a name, that's its name forever. That makes me think of an intersection in the east part of the county. Anyone giving you directions in that area will tell you to turn at the big oak. That is well and good for those who have been here a long time. However, seeing how the tree has been gone for about ten years, it doesn't work so well for newcomers. But that doesn't mean we are going to quit using it!

During the deer season, I regularly passed through the Diamond Graphite area and it wasn't long until I spotted the two young bucks standing in the right-of-way of the road. On the east side of the highway, the right-of-way extended about one hundred feet from the road. The open area had some green grass, which made it popular with the deer. I worked the area a couple of times but it was apparent my schedule was not aligned with that of the deer in the area. While I have caught many night hunters when there were no deer present, the presence of deer was always helpful.

Seeing how the highway was the major artery into the county, I knew there would be several potential violators passing through the area before daylight and I decided that would be a good time to set up in the area. I was correct in that there were several vehicles that passed through the area; however, the deer once again failed to cooperate. While I wasn't sure, I feared the two bucks might have already met their demise. However, that did not mean that folks would not still be looking for them.

I knew that having a deer at the location would really be a benefit; therefore, the next time I decided to work the area, I decided to be sure there would be a deer there. The only way I knew to do that was to bring one with me. The only problem with that was our policy and guidelines stated we were not to use the stuffed wonder on a major roadway. This was understandable in that the presence of a deer alongside the road sometimes tended to disrupt the flow of traffic.

I definitely did not want to violate the policy and it just so happened I was in luck. Due to having the same type of night hunting problems along major roadways in other areas of the state, several district supervisors had decided that many of the "major" roadways where we were having problems were not necessarily "major" roadways after midnight. This decision allowed use of decoys in the wee hours of the morning. I decided to take advantage of this loophole and use the deer along the highway. Conservation Enforcement Officer Shannon Calfee and I decided we would deploy the deer around four in the morning and see if we had any takers.

As was always the case, finding a good place to sit and observe the decoy and the traffic was difficult. Eventually, I decided I would have to set up at the hunting club clubhouse and Shannon would be about a quarter of a mile below me. I knew sitting up at the hunting club might be problematic, but there really wasn't another place.

We decided we would try the location on a Saturday morning. We knew there would likely be a high volume of traffic, which could be good or bad. Working the decoy was often a situation of too many or too few. While nobody wanted to sit for hours and not have a vehicle come by, you also did not want so much traffic that an oncoming vehicle would scare off a good prospect. I knew this location had the potential for too much traffic; however, it was where the complaints of folks shooting at night were coming from.

Another drawback to working the deer in the high-volume area was that the word would quickly spread through the hunting and outlaw community that we were using the deer. This wasn't all bad in that it tended to cause people to pause before taking a shot and that no doubt saved the lives of several deer.

Yet another possible problem was setting up at the hunting club, which I felt certain would result in club members questioning what I was doing there. This wasn't really a problem since I was glad for them to know I was addressing their complaints. However, I knew the conversations would distract me from what I was doing.

With all this in mind, I placed the decoy about 250 yards south of the clubhouse and pulled in beside the clubhouse to begin my vigil. Shannon took up a position about a quarter of a mile below me in a pasture on the opposite side of the road. I had advised him he would need to get pretty far back in the pasture to keep from being spotted.

Things started slowly but traffic quickly picked up. Things were going as usual. One vehicle would blow the horn at the deer while the next would blow by at sixty miles per hour. Obviously, not everyone traveling the road would be looking for a deer to shoot, but I was confident some would be.

At about 4:30 a.m., hunters started pulling into the hunting club. The hunters were coming from the north and therefore had not seen the decoy. Their reaction to having the game warden sitting at their clubhouse was somewhat comical. While some were eager to engage me, others seemed to be a little discombobulated by my presence. More than one member mentioned the young bucks they had been seeing just down the road.

Shannon and I had discussed how long we thought we could continue the detail. We decided we had better end the operation at 5:00 a.m. Hopefully, that would be before the traffic got too heavy. We were closing in on the end of the operation when another hunter pulled into the clubhouse parking lot. The fellow walked over to me and commented that if I would stay there, I might catch somebody shooting at one the young bucks that had been hanging around just below the clubhouse. I told him I hoped so. I had barely got that sentence out of my mouth when the one I was waiting for arrived. A pickup slowed to a stop and the driver blasted the mounted deer. The club member looked at me with one of the most astonished looks I had ever seen. I cranked my truck and tore out of the parking area.

I called Shannon and told him "they" had shot and to come on. Seeing my lights advancing upon him, the driver/shooter simply pulled to the side of the highway. I pulled in behind the truck and radioed the county sheriff's office and told them I was stopping a vehicle and gave them the tag number. While watching the driver, I again called Shannon and advised him to come to my location. I received no answer. I approached the truck in the usual manner and told the driver, the sole occupant, to raise his hands over his head. I asked if he had any weapons other than his rifle, which he had placed in the passenger seat. He said he did not. I advised him to hand me his rifle, stock first, and he did. I kept looking for Shannon to come flying up; however, he was nowhere to be seen. I carried the rifle back to my vehicle and once again called Shannon on the radio. No answer.

I returned to the truck and asked the shooter for his driver's license. He fished it out while telling me how sorry he was and that he had never done anything like that before. While that may very well have been the truth, it definitely wasn't the first time I had heard such an exclamation. I again returned to the truck and again tried Shannon on the radio. No answer. By this time, I had nearly convinced myself that the late nights and early morning we had been working had taken their toll on Shannon and he was sound asleep.

I retrieved my ticket book and wrote the violator tickets for hunting at night, hunting from the public road, and hunting by the aid of a vehicle. As I was preparing to return to the violator, I saw Shannon barreling toward my location. When he exited his truck, his frustration was blatantly obvious. He accompanied me back to the truck. I explained to the man by signing his tickets he was not admitting his guilt but was signing his own bond. I gave him the court date and told him he would have to appear. I then told him that I would be holding his gun as evidence and it would be up to the judge as to whether or not he would get it back. That was normally the part the violators hated the most and this time was no exception. Of course, when you are sitting on the side of a US highway, directly across from a fake deer that you have just shot at five o'clock in the morning, there isn't really a lot you can say! The man signed the tickets and went on his way.

Shannon and I retrieved the deer and headed down the highway. I had told him to follow me to the forestry office, which was only about a mile down the road. We pulled into the parking lot and exited our trucks. Shannon was shaking his head. I just looked at him and he knew I wanted to hear the story. I knew he had not been asleep or he would not have known to come to my location. He started his explanation with, "You're not going to believe this."

I responded, "Try me."

He reminded me I had told him to go back far enough in the pasture that no one would be able to see him. He said that had meant he had to pull down into a dip in the field. He explained he did not think that would be a problem; however, he had been mistaken. When he received my call, he quickly realized his truck would not climb the hill. Even when he engaged his four-wheel drive, the truck continued to spin on the wet ground. Seeing that he was hopelessly spinning, he attempted to back up. He then realized he had better get out and look at the situation before he became hopelessly stuck. Shannon said it did not help that while this was happening, I was calling him on the radio. After surveying the situation, he said he decided his only chance of getting out of the field was to back up as far as he could and then accelerate up the hill in front of him. After several attempts, the plan worked and he finally got over the hill. I told him if we ever tried the deer there again, he probably should find a new spot to sit. He quickly agreed with that.

The next month the shooter appeared in court. Interestingly, he was accompanied by a friend of mine, a local forester. My friend approached me and explained the fellow was actually a member of his hunting club. He said the man was very distraught over the incident. He went on to say that the fellow had hoped to be able to retain his hunting privileges. I told him that a conviction for hunting at night carried a mandatory three-year revocation of hunting privileges and the judge normally adhered closely to that. He stated the fellow desperately wanted to avoid that since he had a severe heart condition and he was not expected to live three more years! I advised him we would see what happened.

I knew my friend didn't know the district judge like I did. He had no tolerance for night hunters and I felt it was certain things would not go well for the man. The case was called and the defendant, Shannon, and I approached the bench. The judge advised the man of the charges and asked how he pled. The fellow informed the judge he would like to plead guilty but with exten-uating circumstances. That did not sit well with the judge. The judge had us raise our hands and swear to tell the truth. He looked at me and asked what happened. I gave the short version of the story, saying the deer was set up on the side of the public road and the defendant stopped his vehicle in the road and shot from his truck at five in the morning. The judge looked at the defendant and asked if he had any questions for me and he replied he did not. The judge then asked, in a not-too-happy tone, "So what are your extenuating circumstances?"

The defendant told the judge he was guilty of everything he was charged with. He said he had never done anything like this before and was embarrassed by his actions. I could tell the judge was about to lose his composure. "Get to the point," was his gruff command. The man said he would like to request that his hunting privileges not be revoked seeing how he had a severe heart condition and his doctors had told him he likely had less than two years to live. He explained that he loved to hunt and respectfully asked that the judge not take that opportunity from him in his last years of life. I was thinking to myself, this guy is about to be sorely disappointed.

The judge stared at the man and then looked at the paperwork before him. While I had expected a quick denial of the request, now I wasn't so sure. After maybe a minute the judge was ready to rule. He informed the man that he was being found guilty of all the charges and would be required to pay fines and court costs in each case. He then said, "Your hunting privileges will not be revoked." And that was it. I'm sure my jaw was pretty slack.

The judge scribbled on the file, handed it to me and said, "Take him to see the clerk." That meant he needed to go and pay the fines and costs right then. I told the man to follow me and we left the courtroom. I was still shaking my head when we entered the clerk's office. I informed the clerk that the man needed to pay his fines and costs. As I was handing the file to the clerk, I looked at the order and noticed that while the man had scored a major victory in keeping his hunting privileges, it had come at a price. The judge had ordered the man to pay double the minimum fine in two of the cases.

I had no problem with the judge's decision and would only hope someone would give me some consideration if I were in a similar circumstance. You know we are all probably pretty good at coming up with an excuse for our behavior. I appreciated that this defendant did not try to deny what he had done but in effect asked for mercy. Of course, it is hard to ask for mercy when you are blatantly in the wrong. That is the situation we are all in. We all have sinned and come short of the glory of God. The Bible says none are without sin, no not one. I have had people tell me several times that they were going to get serious with the Lord but they just needed to get their life straightened out before they did it. My friend, that isn't how that works.

Those who are without sin don't need a savior. Of course, there's no one who falls in that category. We all need a savior. Salvation is there for the asking. Jesus says we need to admit we are a sinner and repent of our sin. We must believe Jesus is God's son He sent to save us and confess our faith in Him. You can do that right now. Today is the day of salvation.

I did not keep up with the defendant in this case. I don't know if he lived two more days, two more years, or if he is still alive today. However, I do know if Jesus doesn't return, everyone will die someday. As I write these words, I am saddened by the recent death of a dear friend from my church. She and her husband often served as surrogate grandparents for my two sons. We lived over two hundred miles from their actual grandparents and did not get to visit often. V. B. and Annie Lee played that role well and I thank them for it. They are now together again and I know I will see them again one day. Blessed assurance, Jesus is mine, oh what a foretaste of glory divine. Rest in peace my dear friends.

Just Checking My Camera

DURING THE DEER SEASON, a game warden makes at least a mental note of every area where he sees a vehicle he thinks might indicate someone may be hunting nearby. These are normally good areas to check for bait and officers spend a lot of time doing just that. Of course, there is that occasional vehicle parked alongside the road in a remote area that causes the officer to spend a considerable amount of time surveying the area only to eventually figure out it's where a local landowner meets his ride to work. You can't always be right.

While checking an area where we had noticed some activity, Conservation Enforcement Officer Jerry Fincher and I were easing along a woods road that led into a wildlife opening when we spotted a trail camera strapped to a tree. Actually, we didn't really spot the camera first. First, we spotted a large pile of bright yellow corn on the ground and then spied the camera that was aimed at it.

Being careful to stay out of view of the camera, we made our way to a nearby shooting house positioned approximately fifty yards from the corn pile. Evidence inside the shooting house, a large amount of trash, revealed it had been being used regularly. Beside the shooting house was a large garbage can about half full of corn. I reasoned since the corn supply was right next to the entrance of the shooting house and there was loose corn around the door, that would eliminate the possibility of anyone in the shooting house using the defense they did not know there was any corn in the area. I should say it would keep it from being an actual defense, not that someone would not try it as a defense. We quickly left the area with plans to return.

The next day, Jerry decided to look for another less visible access to the property. Obviously, if we parked on the side of the road, we would quickly get busted. Even among nonhunters, the news of the game warden poking around in the area gets around pretty quickly. Therefore, we spent a lot of time trying to find good places to hide a vehicle. This often resulted in a long walk across multiple properties. Such was the case in this area. Jerry parked far away and stealthily made his way to the property. As he approached the shooting house, he could see the windows were closed, a good indication no one was inside. A good indication, not a guarantee! Just as he was thinking it was another long walk for nothing, he caught movement ahead of him toward the bait. As he watched, a fellow with a rifle slung over his shoulder and wearing no hunter orange was walking toward the bait pile. Jerry walked out and met the man and asked to see his hunting license. The man replied he wasn't hunting; he was just checking his camera. Jerry asked why the man had brought his rifle if he was just checking the camera. "I always bring it with me" was his reply. Jerry asked if he had any hunter orange with him and he said he did not. He again reminded Jerry he wasn't hunting. When asked if he possessed a hunting license, the fellow again reminded the forgetful game warden he didn't need any of those things since he was not hunting.

Contrary to what most people would probably think, being able to explain to a judge what someone hunting looks like can be difficult. Just because you see someone out in the woods wearing camouflage is not a slam dunk that they are hunting. A lot of folks don't wear camo while hunting and many people enjoy the many attributes nature has to offer other than hunting. As a matter of fact, you might be shocked to know the percentage of people in the United States who hunt is very low, at about 4–5 percent. This is disturbing seeing how the license fees paid by hunters and shooters are the backbone of wildlife conservation in the United States.

Jerry did his best to explain to the nonhunting camera-checking individual that someone carrying a loaded rifle over their shoulder in an area where an attractant had been placed and where there was other hunting apparatus would make a reasonably prudent individual deduce the person was hunting. The fellow quickly advised the officer a person making that assumption would be wrong. Despite the man's denials, the officer relied on the old adage that says if it looks like duck, walks like a duck, and quacks like a duck, it's a duck! He issued citations for hunting without a license, hunting by the aid of bait, and hunting without wearing hunter orange.

The next month, a reasonable and prudent district court judge advised the fellow if he wanted to check his camera he should leave his rifle at home or it would cost him another $650!

We can deny the truth all we want, but it is still the truth. Don't be deceived, God is not mocked. You reap what you sow.

How about That Light

WHILE WE OFTEN GET a "gut feeling" that leads to a conclusion, people are convicted on evidence. Sometimes gathering evidence is like pulling teeth and sometimes the guilt is written on their face or, as in this case, strapped to their head.

Many people are under the misconception the majority of wildlife law violators are kids. I have found that to be far from the truth. I guess that may depend on your definition of a kid. It may be people who never grew up, but they aren't really kids. However, every once in a while, it was kids. I do not know of any officer who enjoyed apprehending juveniles. There were a few reasons for this. The first was dealing with a juvenile violator brought a whole host of problems. Unlike adults, they could not be arrested, allowed to sign a bond, and sent on their way. Depending on the juvenile officer in the county, sometimes you had to call the parents, sometimes you were instructed to take them to the jail and wait for a parent, and sometimes they had to be hauled sixty miles to our nearest juvenile facility. It didn't help that the juvenile officer normally worked 8:00 a.m. to 4:00 p.m. Monday through Friday. I can assure you we didn't catch many juveniles night hunting in the middle of the day. Unfortunately, most apprehensions seemed to occur on the weekend when locating a juvenile officer was like looking for an open checkout line at Walmart. You normally eventually found one but it took a while. I never contacted a juvenile officer who was in a good mood!

Eventually, the parents were contacted and a meeting with the juvenile officer would be set. A few months later there would be a court date where the kid got slapped on the wrist and let go. It took more of our time to handle a juvenile case than it did an adult; however, we normally got very little to show for it. While I was not keen on making cases against juveniles, some things could not be handled with a warning. Anyone, no matter their age, who is firing a high-powered rifle into the dark of night needs to be stopped. A bullet leaving a muzzle at three thousand feet per second doesn't know whether it was fired by someone sixty-four or twelve and the outcome can be the same either way. Therefore, juveniles caught night hunting were charged, although it was often an effort in futility.

In late December 2012, I responded to a request from Conservation Enforcement Officer (CEO) Jerry Fincher in Talladega County to assist him with a night hunting detail. I always said Jerry was a good student since I had been his unofficial training officer. Ironically, my wife, Melanie, had been his training teacher during his years teaching school prior to him getting hired as a game warden. He always referred to her as his mother figure. I enjoyed working with him and we made several good cases together.

Jerry explained to me he had received a complaint the previous night of a deer being shot near Fayetteville in south Talladega County and wanted to work the area. In addition, he had received numerous complaints of someone in a light-colored Chevrolet Tahoe hunting in the area. We made plans to meet at his house at 8:30 p.m.

Talladega is a huge county. While it is most well known for the Talladega Superspeedway, it is also a popular hunting, fishing, and recreation destination. Encompassed in the 753 square miles that compose the county are two large lakes on the Coosa River, a large segment of the Talladega National Forest, and a 3,200-acre golf course and resort. As you can imagine, there was no shortage of activities that needed conservation law enforcement attention.

At approximately 9:00 p.m., we set up surveillance on a fallow field on Shelvin Rock Road in the southwest part of the county. The field was just off of the Fayetteville Highway and approximately one-quarter mile from where the night hunting had been reported the previous evening. Having caught multiple night hunters in the same place, I always told Jerry if the hunting was good, the folks would go back again and again.

You never knew how a night would go. I have sat for hours and hours without having a single vehicle come past my location and I have literally been in position for one minute when a night hunter arrived. You just never knew which way it would go.

A good observation point was a valuable thing. In order to watch the fallow field that ran alongside the road, we backed in behind a vacant house. Before you think someone wouldn't shoot near a house, let me tell you that is not at all the case. Not only will night hunters shoot close to one, they will shoot through one! I know of it happening several times.

On this night, we had been in position less than thirty minutes when a vehicle slowly passed our location. As we watched, the driver turned the vehicle, an SUV, perpendicular to the roadway, allowing the headlights to shine in the fallow field. This was a very common method of hunting from the road at night. Violators would often employ this technique because it was sort of borderline whether or not they were in violation. Obviously, the lights of any vehicle driving along the road at night may illuminate the side of the road and even a close by field edge. A masterful driver can maneuver their headlights to view more of the field while still not leaving the roadway or blatantly turning sideways. Whether or not they are "shining" the field is sometimes a judgment call and is often argued in court. It can be a fine line and a tough call. I felt confident this driver had already crossed the line by turning his vehicle sideways in the road. However, if I had not been sure before, the driver removed all doubt when he entered the fallow field and maneuvered the vehicle so the headlights illuminated the majority of the area.

One of the many skills needed to be a good CEO was patience. Although this driver was overtly shining the field and if he had a gun he was definitely in violation, you did not want to jump the gun on stopping him. While you could, and normally did, win a conviction without them having fired a shot, once they did pull the trigger, their conviction was as close as you could get to a slam dunk.

The driver returned to the road and proceeded in the same direction he was going originally. I looked at Jerry and said, "Let's go get 'em." We left our observation point and followed the vehicle. Once we were close to the vehicle, I activated our blue lights.

The driver pulled the vehicle, a gray Chevrolet Tahoe, to the right side of the road. We exited our vehicle and Jerry gave a loud verbal command for everyone in the vehicle to put their hands out the windows. I was on the passenger's side of the truck and I repeated the order for everyone to put their hands out the window. Two hands appeared out of the front passenger window; however, the passenger either had really short arms or the hands were coming from the back seat. Unfortunately, the rear windows had very dark tint. I hated that! The front seat passenger did not place his hands out the window so I again loudly stated, "Let me see your hands." I moved parallel with the vehicle so I could shine my flashlight into the passenger side window. My light illuminated the face of the front seat passenger, who had still not complied with the command. This reluctance of someone to show their hands is disturbing to a law enforcement officer. If a subject is going to kill you, it will likely be with something in their hands. I again gave the LOUD verbal command for the passenger to get his hands up. He raised his hands and I moved to the passenger door.

I heard Jerry tell the driver to open his door and step out and he complied. I told the front and rear seat passengers to keep their hands up. Looking in the vehicle, I saw what appeared to be a 30-30 lever-action rifle lying on a camo bag in the driver's side rear floorboard. I noticed the hammer was cocked on the rifle. I knew this was often indicative of a hastily unloaded lever-action firearm. A lever-action gun is somewhat dangerous in that each time the lever is activated, it cocks the hammer on the gun. I have seen holes shot in vehicles by violators who were hurriedly trying to unload the gun. I told the back-seat passenger not to touch the gun and he replied, "I haven't." I noted that was an interesting response. I told Jerry the gun was in the back floorboard with the hammer back and the muzzle pointing toward the door. He retrieved the weapon. I asked if there were any other weapons in the vehicle and both passengers said there was not.

I opened the front passenger's door and noticed there were four loose 30-30 cartridges in the floor. Two of them were perched on top of a small camo bag. Based on my experience, I knew this suggested the gun had been hurriedly unloaded. I now knew why the front seat passenger had not placed his hands out the window, as he was busy unloading the gun. I said to CEO Fincher the passenger had unloaded the gun but there were only four shells in the floor. Since I knew the gun, a Winchester 30-30, could hold seven cartridges, I wanted to let Jerry know it might still be loaded.

When I said the passenger had unloaded the gun, the passenger immediately began to protest saying he had not unloaded the gun and they were not hunting. He said the driver had hunted earlier in the day and the gun and shells were his. He went on to say the driver was just giving him a ride home. This type of denial was not at all uncommon and often worked in our favor. When the culprits were forced to make up a story on the spot, it often unraveled pretty rapidly. I asked where they were coming from and he replied Fayetteville. I asked where he lived and he said Sylacauga. Now that I had him concentrating on his cover story, I again, in probably a little more accusatory tone, stated, "You unloaded that gun." He immediately denied unloading the gun and again stated they were not hunting. I shot back with a question I felt sure would tell the tale. I asked, "If you aren't hunting, why are you wearing that light on your head?" I guess to say he looked like a deer caught in the headlights would be an appropriate phrase. He simply stared at me with his mouth open in stunned silence. The fact the young man was wearing a head light, which is common among night hunters, was something hard to explain. I could see the realization in his eyes and heard the *pffft* in his pants!

I told the front seat passenger to exit the truck and move to the hood. I had him place his hands on the hood and patted him down for weapons. He asked me if they were in trouble and I answered in the affirmative. Realizing that was not a typical night hunter question, I asked him his age and he replied he was seventeen. This was not evident as he was approximately six feet two inches tall and well over two hundred pounds.

CEO Fincher gave me a rights form and I explained the rights to the young man. Unfortunately, the form was not a juvenile form so I explained multiple times he did not have to answer any questions or make a statement without a parent or counsel

211

present. This was one of the aggravating parts of dealing with juveniles. I again explained he could have his parents present before making any statement and he made it clear to me he would rather his parents didn't know anything about this. He advised he understood his rights and was willing to give a statement. I asked him what happened and he said he had caught a ride back to Sylacauga with the driver. I asked why they were on Shelvin Rock Road and he said they were just killing time. When I asked why they had shined the field alongside the road, he said to see if they would see a deer, but they weren't going to shoot it. He reverted back to his original story that he was only getting a ride and they weren't hunting. I again asked why he was wearing a light on his head and he did not respond. I told him I believed he was night hunting and they shined the field looking for a deer to shoot and when we stopped them, he couldn't put his hands out of the window because he was unloading the gun. Staring at the ground, he nodded his head in the affirmative.

I asked him to again read the form and reiterated he did not have to give a statement without a parent or counsel present. He read and signed the form and wrote a brief statement. I placed him back in the truck and asked the rear seat passenger to get out. I asked his age and he replied he was sixteen years old. I advised him of his rights and explained he did not have to answer any questions or make a statement without a parent or counsel present. He said he understood and did not want to speak with me. I told him that was fine and I would put that on the rights form. I requested his name and his parents' name and contact information. As I was taking down that information, he said he had changed his mind and would give a statement. I again advised him he did not have to tell me anything. He said he understood but he knew he shouldn't have been out doing this and wanted to give a statement. He told me the driver had picked them up to go riding around looking for deer. They had gone down to Coosa County and around Fayetteville and then came here. He said they shined the field looking for a deer to shoot and the front seat passenger had the gun and unloaded it when we pulled them over. He wrote everything in his statement.

While my second suspect was writing his statement, I was listening to Officer Fincher as he talked with the driver of the vehicle. I almost laughed out loud when Jerry asked if the young man had ever done this before and he replied, "Yeah, a lot." Jerry asked if he had killed many deer and he replied, "None. I just can't hit them." With the paperwork complete, we advised the youths to tell their parents what had occurred and that they would be contacted by the juvenile officer.

The juveniles were charged with four charges each: hunting at night, hunting from a public road, hunting by the aid of a vehicle, and hunting without a permit. After a couple of continuances, their court date rolled around. Two of the juveniles were represented by a high-powered attorney, which I knew probably wouldn't go well for us. I was right. While each defendant was found to be in need of supervision (guilty), they barely received a slap on the wrist. This was another annoying part of dealing with juveniles. While I wasn't looking to hang anybody, I did feel they should have at least known they had done something wrong. That wasn't the case. As a matter of fact, it was all I could do to keep from throwing up when another lawyer in the courtroom came over to the defendant who had been wearing the light and told him to remember nobody had to know about any of this when he was applying to colleges. He patted the boy on the back and said he couldn't wait to see him on the football field this fall.

I thought to myself it's no wonder that one of the biggest struggles facing every college and pro football team is trying to keep their players out of jail and on the field. While others may not believe there is a correlation, you'll be hard pressed to convince me that coddling the juvenile violator doesn't generate the adult violator.

Of course, the next season, I got a call from Jerry stating our juveniles were back at it. It's just a matter of time. I checked their birthdates and noted for the two that were turning eighteen, the results would likely be different the next time.

Everyone will have an "oh no" moment like the boy in this story. There may be many of them and some have bad consequences. There is an ultimate "oh no." It's when you realize there is a God in heaven—a jealous and vengeful God that holds the keys to heaven and hell. He holds the keys—you choose the door. Don't wait too late to let that realization set in. Today is the day of salvation. Tomorrow isn't guaranteed. Choose wisely.

Just Step around Her

As I WRITE THIS, there has been much emphasis placed on judges. The battles over putting judges on the Supreme Court have been out of control. Unfortunately, the debate is about the candidates' political leaning and views on hot-topic items. I wish they would look for a judge that had some good common sense. I have been fortunate to bring cases before many good judges. I have been unfortunate to bring cases before a few bad judges. Of course, my view is biased.

Obviously, having been a law enforcement officer for thirty-five years, I believe the majority of people brought before the judge should be found guilty. That does not mean that I think officers never make a mistake. Obviously, there are innocent people who are arrested; however, I do not believe that number is anywhere near what the media would have us to believe. I have caught many people red-handed breaking the law and had them plead their innocence to anyone who would listen. That makes it difficult to believe anyone.

Many times, I have listened to a court case and was thankful I was not the one who had to decide the case. Being a judge is no doubt stressful. I feel certain that is even more true when the judge is hearing a felony case that may carry a punishment as severe as life in prison or even the death penalty. Thankfully, I rarely dealt with that.

Something I have said many times was that students should attend court to see what goes on and they should attend two months in a row. If they would do that, they would likely see the same people are in court each month. Hopefully, it would be unpleasant enough they would decide they didn't want to come back.

It is true that many of the same people are in court each month. I remember many years ago there was a local fellow who would be in court each month charged with public intoxication. Others would be there on various charges. You have likely heard the phrase "the usual suspects." There is some truth to that.

I know our local district judges got tired of seeing the same people month after month. In addition, I'm sure they were extremely tired of hearing the same old worn-out excuses. I've written before about how the folks in traffic court would line up and come before the judge. The judge would tell them they were charged with driving seventy-eight miles per hour in a fifty-five-mile-per-hour zone and asked how did they plead. The driver would plead not guilty. The judge would ask why they pled not guilty and they would answer because they were not going that fast. He would ask how fast they were going and they would reply maybe seventy miles per hour. The judge would then say the court finds you guilty on your admission of speeding. He would assign their fine and court costs and tell them to go and pay the clerk. The next person would step up and they would often repeat the entire procedure. So many times, I wanted to just step over and ask them if they had not just heard what happened with the person ahead of them. However, I knew the judge would not appreciate that.

The first district judge I ever brought a case before was definitely a one-of-a-kind judge. Thankfully, he was a strong supporter of conservation and we enjoyed a good relationship. I have often commented to folks that had our courtroom been wired for video, Judge Judy would have never made it on TV! Our judge would have been a major hit. He was full of witty sayings and was well known as a hard-nosed, by-the-book judge. Although he was elected in our county, the judicial circuit encompassed multiple counties; therefore, he sometimes was called on to occupy the bench in other surrounding counties.

A retired conservation enforcement officer in a nearby county shared a story concerning an eventful day when the judge was hearing cases in his district court. According to the officer, one of the defendants on the docket was notorious for writing bad checks. During a recess, the court clerk approached the officer and told him she was fed up with this woman being in court every month and their regular judge not doing anything about it. Knowing the officer had a good relationship with the judge, she asked if he would bring the substitute judge up to speed on the situation and ask if he could maybe get the check bouncer's attention. As the judge was returning to the bench, the officer relayed the information and request.

The defendant's name was called and she approached the bench. The judge read the charge and asked, "How do you plead?"

"Guilty," she answered, rather nonchalantly.

The judge asked, "Have you ever been convicted of this before?" and she again rather passively answered with a lackadaisical "Yeah." The judge was ready to rule and said, "The court accepts your plea and orders you to pay restitution for the check and a one-hundred-dollar fine and court costs."

Having been there before, the woman was taking everything in stride—until the judge added, "And you need to have that paid by the time you finish serving your thirty days in jail!"

According to the officer, a confused look appeared on the woman's face and she simply fell straight back and hit the floor with a thud. Of course, the district attorney and others rushed over and rendered assistance to the woman. They had her to sit up and someone got her a glass of water. Seeing that the woman was okay, keeping with his normal demeanor, the judge looked at the bailiff and told him, "She's in the custody of the sheriff." He then looked up and announced to the courtroom, "Next case."

The bewildered clerk called the next name on the docket and the judge instructed the next defendant to "just step around her and come on up!" The officer said all the other defendants on the docket lined up to try and make a deal with the district attorney instead of having to appear before the judge. Yep—he was one of a kind.

You can't make this stuff up!

You Try It!

BASED ON THOUSANDS of arrests, I'm going to say violating wildlife laws and regulations is just more fun when shared with a friend. I say that based on the thousands of times I have caught folks breaking said laws and regulations when there were two or more folks involved. It just stands to reason that someone wanting to shoot a deer from their vehicle will have more success if they have two sets of eyes searching the roadsides. I remember one day when it really didn't pay to have an accomplice.

I have often written that the presence of nearby houses was very often not a deterrent to game law violators. It really did not matter whose house it was and yes, this included the game warden's house! Conservation Enforcement Officer (CEO) Hershel Patterson lived in the Weogufka community on Coosa County Road 41. Almost straight across from his driveway was County Road 181, a dirt road about two miles long that connected County Roads 41 and 56. The property on both sides of the road was owned by one family. The north side of the road was wooded and the south side was primarily cattle pastures and hayfields. There was not a house on the road, only a barn. As you may have guessed, it was a great place to shoot a deer or turkey from the road for those folks who were inclined to avail themselves of that type of opportunity.

As you might imagine, folks shooting into pastures with cattle was not something the landowner appreciated. Of course, this type of activity also put anyone on the property at risk. After a couple of incidents, it was decided it would be a good idea to try to curtail the activity by deploying one of our favorite tools, Bionic Bambi, our deer decoy.

Setting up the decoy is often not as simple as it sounds. There were always several factors to consider. We had a set of guidelines that had to be adhered to. While apprehending violators was our goal, it had to be done safely. Any time you were offering someone an opportunity to fire their weapon, you had the responsibility of making it as safe as possible. A major requirement was there had to be a backstop behind the decoy. This meant you could not simply stick the deer out in the middle of a field. As I mentioned earlier, there were cattle on this property, which meant you had to coordinate with the landowner to make sure where the cows would be. In addition, you had to make sure there would not be people on the property while the decoy was being used. These were just a few of the prerequisites for using the stuffed deer.

This episode took place many years ago when we were allowed to have civilians ride with us and assist us. Today, only certified police officers may accompany us. Hershel ended up being off on the day I had decided to use the deer so I enlisted the assistance of the son-in-law of a good friend of mine.

I'm sure you have heard me complain about the scarcity of a good spot where you could use the decoy in the daytime and have an observation post where you could watch the deer and conceal your truck. This being the case, it is often necessary to have someone to hide in the woods and operate the decoy and have a chase vehicle stationed down the road in each direction. I explained to my young helper that his job would be to remain hidden in the woods, operate the decoy, and report to me by radio what was happening. It was made abundantly clear he was not to come out of his hiding spot until I was on the scene and told him to come out. That last point was important. I did not want him to come out until everything was handled. That way he would not be put in danger and the violators would not know there was anyone other than me involved. Although they should be able to figure things out, it was good to keep them guessing.

We had located what I thought was a good natural-looking spot for the deer. It was just in the edge of the hayfield and situated in such a way that anyone coming from either direction would be shooting into a hill in the woods. The deer was about a hundred yards off the road, which was a good minimum distance for using the decoy in the daytime.

I explained to my helper I would let him out at the road and he needed to get into his hiding spot while I drove into the field and set the deer up. I normally would not drive into a field for fear that an observant road hunter might see my tracks. However, in this situation, the landowner regularly drove out through the field to the point where it was not unusual to see tracks there. I got the deer set up and had my helper activate the remote control, which caused its head and tail to move. With everything working well, I hurriedly drove down the road to my hiding spot. Getting caught trying to set the deer up was the worst but was always a possibility when you were working along the public road.

Since the leaves are off in the winter, you usually have to use terrain to make sure you are hidden from view by those who might be looking for a deer to shoot. I had to go pretty deep into the woods to be sure I wouldn't be seen. Soon everything was in place. I called my helper, making sure the radio was working and everything was good. I reminded him that less was better when it came to moving the deer.

You never knew how long the vigil might be. I have had

occasions where we barely got out of the road when someone pulled up and shot and cases where we sat for hours and had not one vehicle pass our location. On this day, the wait wasn't very long. Unfortunately, I could not see the road from where I was hiding. However, I could hear a vehicle crunching on the gravel as it passed my location. I radioed my assistant and told him we had one coming. The play-by-play that came next was fun to listen to.

The excitement in his voice was very evident when my helper said, "I see them." He had never done anything like this before and saying he was pumped up was an understatement. I was not sure whether or not "them" meant there was more than one person in the truck or if it was just the way he referred to the vehicle. Either way, I hoped we were in business.

"They're stopping" was the next excited statement that came through the radio. "Be patient" was my reply. "He's getting out of the truck." Before I could respond, he added, "He's got a rifle." I advised him to stay calm. Almost simultaneously with the *py-wow*, my helper yelled in the mic, "He shot!" I responded that I was on the way. I flew out of my woods road hiding spot and headed to their location. Although I wasn't very far down the road, I knew it would probably take me thirty seconds to get on the scene. While that doesn't sound like a long time, when someone is shooting at a fake deer and you are trying to get to them before they realize it, it can seem like forever.

I hit the dirt county road and pushed the accelerator to the floor. Over the roar of the engine and the crunching of gravel, I heard my helper on the radio saying the other one was getting out of the truck. I wasn't sure what that might mean. Several things ran through my mind. Did the deer fall over and they were going to get it? I did not think that would be the case since I had not ever had anyone shoot the deer and knock it down. I wasn't sure what might be happening but I assured my assistant I would be there shortly. As soon as I said that, I heard a second shot ring out. By this time, I was just around the curve from the scene. As I rounded the curve, I could see the two men standing in the road on the passenger side of their vehicle. As I come sliding up, one of the men tossed the gun into the front seat of the truck.

I jumped out of my truck and gave the loud verbal command for the men to raise their hands over their head. Both immediately raised their hands. I told them to step back from the truck and I moved to the vehicle and retrieved the rifle. Keeping my eyes on both men, I carried the rifle back and placed it in my truck. I asked if they had any other weapons and they replied they did not. I asked for their driver's licenses. While it was very common for road hunters to only have one gun, I checked the truck for any other weapons. I found none.

I looked in the field and saw that the deer was still standing where I had placed it. I collected the licenses and noticed both men had Sylacauga addresses. Sylacauga was the nearest town to the north. It was a small city of maybe twenty thousand people. I call it small, although our entire county had fewer than eleven thousand people!

With the scene secured, I asked the men what was going on. Of course, this was sort of a rhetorical question. However, you never knew what type response you might get. It could be an admission or a total denial. Let me tell you, you would probably not believe the number of folks who would shoot the deer and then swear up and down they had not shot at it. It was both comical and aggravating.

One of the fellows took the lead and said they had spotted the deer in the field and stupidly tried to shoot it. I looked at the other guy with my "What about you?" look and he shrugged his shoulders and then told his part of the story. Once again, I was about to bite a hole in my lip to keep from laughing. The fellow said, "Well, David shot at it twice and missed it and he turned to me and said, 'I can't hit it, you try it.' So, I got out and I shot at it just as you was coming around the curve." He quickly added that he didn't want to shoot it but he did. Yep, I was biting a hole in my lip! When I regained my composure, I asked the pair if they had a permit to hunt the property and they replied they did not.

I retrieved my ticket book and wrote both men for hunting from the public road, hunting without a permit, and hunting by aid of a vehicle. I explained the bonds and they signed them and were on their way.

I turned and looked at my helper and motioned for him to come out of hiding. I don't know that I have ever seen anyone anymore excited. He went through the whole episode, explaining how the driver had got out with the rifle and walked around to the passenger side of the truck and shot. He said he didn't even move the head or tail of the deer and the guy shot again. Then the guy looked at the guy in the passenger seat and said, "I can't hit it, you try it," and the passenger got out and shot at it. Although I had just heard that exact story from the shooters, it was more fun to hear it from someone who was having a hard time believing that had just occurred right in front of them.

I told him I thought that was probably enough fun for the day and we got in the truck and went to pick up the deer. I must admit I was somewhat surprised that the guy had told the truth when he said he couldn't hit the deer, as it did not have any new holes in it! We disassembled the small buck and loaded it up and headed for home.

The court cases had been set for the next month in Coosa County District Court. The pair appeared and pled guilty to the charges. In a rare move for our judge, he allowed the men to make a partial payment and gave them a month to pay the remainder of the fines and costs. The judge rarely allowed anyone to set up a payment plan. As a matter of fact, he was well known for his response to defendants who asked if they could pay their fines and court costs over time. He would tell them this wasn't Sears and Roebuck and he didn't want their repeat business. He would then ask another patented question, "Are you going to pay it or sit it out?" That meant you can pay it now or sit it out in jail.

For whatever reason, he allowed a partial payment. Of course, I was about to learn why the judge almost never did this. The next month the defendants were on the review docket and when their records were reviewed, the fellow who had been the driver had failed to pay the remainder of his fines and costs. The judge promptly issued a failure-to-pay warrant for the man.

The next day, I went by the clerk's office and picked up a copy of the warrant. After a couple of trips to the residence were unsuccessful, I decided to try to reach the man by telephone. I finally contacted the fellow and told him I had a warrant for his arrest for his unpaid fines. He gave me a line I had heard many times before concerning how he had been out of work and just did not have the money. I advised him the next court date was two weeks away and if the fines were not paid by that time he would be picked up and put in jail to begin serving his ninety days. I also reminded him that his warrants were in the system and if he were to get stopped or checked out for any reason he would be going to jail. He assured me he would try to get the fines paid.

The court date rolled around and prior to court, I went to the clerk's office to see if the man had satisfied his debt. He had not. I told the clerk I still had the warrant and would try to pick him up after court. As I turned to leave the office, I saw a somewhat familiar face coming through the door. You guessed it. It was the defendant whom I had the warrant for. He told the clerk he was there to pay his fines. I returned the warrant to the clerk and the cases were closed.

At the beginning of this story, I made the comment that in this instance it really didn't pay to have an accomplice. Thinking about it, I guess I could say it paid double to have an accomplice!

What about you? Ddo you have an obligation that needs to be satisfied? We all do. We all will decide where we will spend eternity. As a matter of fact, you've already decided that. Just like the fellow in this story, we are given some time to handle things. However, unlike him, we do not know when that window of grace will end. His time ran out and a warrant was issued for him, meaning he could be picked up at any time. If you haven't made the decision to spend eternity in heaven by choosing Jesus as your Lord and Savior, then you have made the decision to spend eternity separated from God. The fact that you are able to read this now means you still have time to evaluate your choice. This is a limited-time offer. Don't wait. Choose Jesus. It pays.

And Your Pants, Too!

IT HAS BEEN MY PLEASURE to assist in the training of new officers in our department. My hope is I can provide them the benefit of my thirty-five years of experience and give them a step up. One of the things I always ask them to remember is that all officers are investigators. I also tell them the investigation begins as soon as you observe someone in the field or receive a call. Several times, working with Game & Fish and with the sheriff's office, I have observed a suspect attempting to get rid of some evidence. Whether it's a hunter on a wildlife management area trying to unload the weapon in their vehicle or someone dropping some weed or throwing a beer into the woods, observing their actions is often the factor that determines whether or not the person will receive a citation or possibly be taken into custody. In addition to someone trying to get rid of evidence, on several occasions I have observed suspects attempting to hide a handgun or long gun. As conservation enforcement officers (CEOs), we expect everyone in hunting season to possess a firearm. I have learned over time it is a good idea to expect the same with fishermen and basically anyone in the outdoors. It is imperative that you keep your eyes open.

Unfortunately, I have found that many CEOs don't really consider themselves investigators since the vast majority of our cases are made "on view." That means the offense took place in our presence. That allows us to arrest individuals without a warrant and often without asking any questions or taking any statements. While that is a lot easier than having to work through an investigation, it sets an officer up for failure when a situation requires an investigation. One thing I have told trainees is not to let the first statement they ever take be on a critical case. I encourage them to take a statement even when most of the pertinent facts are already known. There is an art to taking a statement and the only way I know to perfect it is to take a lot of statements.

As I'm sure you can imagine, there isn't a lot of investigation involved in determining whether or not someone has a fishing license or whether or not they are wearing any hunter orange. However, many cases just aren't that simple. Many times, going the extra mile and/or collecting a little more evidence has made the difference between winning or losing a case.

I think my ideas about investigation were nurtured by one of my mentors, CEO Byron Smith. After earning a degree in criminal justice from Auburn University, Byron was hired as a police officer with the Birmingham Police Department. While working in that capacity, he was afforded the opportunity to attend evidence technician school. He said he was open to any training he felt might help him become a more rounded officer. The evidence-gathering training served him well and he continued to utilize those skills after he became a CEO. Byron had been a CEO for six years before I was hired. Seven years as a Birmingham police officer and six years as a CEO in counties with a high volume of violations meant he was a well-seasoned veteran by the time I came on the scene. It was my good fortune that he spent some time with me helping me get up to speed. It made quite a difference.

I remember listening to him relaying the facts of cases to me and expounding on the evidence collected and why. I realized he regularly gave the extra effort needed to secure a conviction. I was impressed and wanted to emulate that and was able to do that in many situations. Something he had passed on to me was if a case was worth making, it was worth doing right. I did my best to follow that philosophy.

Byron told me about a case in which he pulled out all the stops. It was the epitome of going the extra mile. Working in Elmore County, it wasn't at all unusual to receive a call from an irate landowner who had encountered some outlaws on their property. Elmore was a county that was quickly transitioning from rural to urban. Being adjacent to Montgomery, it was a close place to live without being in the "city." However, there were still a lot of woods and farmlands, which resulted in a good population of wildlife and many human/wildlife interactions. Some of those interactions were of the illegal variety and that's where Byron often found himself.

Like all CEOs, Byron's telephone got a good workout during the deer season. Late one afternoon, Byron happened to be at home when the phone rang. The old gentleman on the line quickly told Byron he needed some help. Byron asked for the details and the man told him he had heard someone shoot and he thought it was in his pasture. He had driven to the site and observed two men loading a deer in the bed of their truck. When they saw him, they jumped in the truck and took off. In an effort to get the license plate number, the landowner drove up behind the truck. This prompted the passenger in the truck being pursued to climb out the window and throw full beer cans at the landowner's truck, with several smashing on the windshield. Thankfully, the landowner was able to get the tag number and gave it to the officer.

Knowing the evidence would probably quickly be discarded, Byron ran the tag number through the sheriff's office and immediately headed to the address the dispatcher provided him. There he found the truck matching the landowner's description parked in the driveway. Walking past the truck, he noted the bed was covered with blood and deer hair, but no deer. He quickly took a sample of the blood and secured it in his truck. He went up on the porch and knocked on the door. The homeowner opened the door and upon seeing the game warden standing on his porch he looked as if he had smelled something that smelled bad. His salutation for the officer was, "What do you want?" Byron told him he needed to talk with him about the deer he had shot and about the assault on the landowner. The fellow told him he didn't know what he was talking about and he could get off of his porch. The officer told him that was fine and added that he would be having the man's truck towed. That tidbit of information definitely got the man's attention and he quickly informed Byron he wasn't going to take his truck anywhere. Byron told him the tow truck was en route to get it. At that, the fellow slammed the door and went back in the house.

In a couple of minutes, a pickup truck came flying down the road and pulled in the driveway. The driver pulled his truck behind the homeowner's truck, obviously in an effort to deny access to it. The fellow got out of his truck and approached the officer using a gait that demonstrated he meant business. He informed the officer he was the homeowner's father and he knew the law and he would not be towing the truck. Byron informed the man the truck contained evidence of a crime and he would be towing it and if his truck was in the way he would gladly have his truck towed as well. In addition, he would arrest him for interfering in his investigation. Although the father "knew the law," after kicking the dirt a few times, he decided he had somewhere else he needed to be and got in his truck and left.

Hearing yelling from inside the house, Byron stepped up on the porch. He listened as the woman yelled, "Why did you shoot the deer anyway?" and the man yelled back, "Because it was in the road!" He then added, "I didn't shoot it, Bobby did." Byron would learn Bobby was the defendant's brother.

Byron knocked on the door again and the agitated man jerked the door open and yelled, "What do you want now?" Byron calmly said he would like to speak with the man's wife. "My wife?" he yelled. The wife came to the door and Byron informed her he had just heard their exchange and asked whether she was going to be okay staying there that night. She quickly told him she would be fine and if her husband tried to start something with her, she would shoot him in a place that would definitely hurt.

Byron again summoned the man to the door and told him he would like to see his rifle. This request had a specific reason behind it. He had heard what the man had said to his wife about his brother. Byron felt his reaction to his request might very well solidify that. The guy at first balked at giving the officer the gun. When Byron added he was going to test the gun and make sure it was the gun used to shoot the deer, the fellow's demeanor changed and he said the officer could test the gun if he wanted to because he had not shot anything. Byron told the fellow that on second thought he didn't think he would need the gun. Then he said, "By the way, I need your pants." "My pants?" was the belligerent reply. Byron informed him the pants appeared to have blood on them and he would need to take them as evidence. At that point, the man assumed an offensive posture and asked, "Are you going to take them off of me?" "If I have to," was Byron's quick response. He stripped the pants off and gave them to the officer and then slammed the door.

The tow truck came and collected the truck and Byron left and went to the scene of the crime. He quickly found the blood in the county road where the deer had been loaded into the truck. He took a sample of the blood.

That evening, Byron contacted his partner and asked if he could meet him at the crime scene the next morning and requested that he bring a leaf rake. Early the next day the pair began raking the side of the roadway. They had raked about a hundred yards when they hit pay dirt. They found a spent .270 rifle cartridge.

Based on the evidence he had gathered, Byron convinced the district judge to issue a search warrant for the brother's house in an effort to locate the gun that was used. Further investigation had revealed that the brothers were members of a local hunting club. Since Byron had been unsuccessful in finding the carcass of the deer, he decided to check out the club. When he arrived, he focused his attention on the skinning rack area. There was blood there that appeared somewhat fresh; however, it had now been nearly twenty-four hours since the deer he was seeking had been shot. He went ahead and got a sample of the blood. He prepared the samples and sent them to the forensics lab.

There is only one place in the world that is a dedicated crime laboratory for crimes against wildlife. In 1988, the US Fish and Wildlife Service opened the Clark R. Bavin National Fish and Wildlife Forensic Laboratory in Ashland, Oregon. Their website states their mission is working with others to conserve, protect, and enhance fish, wildlife, and plants and their habitats for the continuing benefit of the American people. One of the primary listed missions of the lab is to identify and compare physical evidence in an attempt to link suspect, victim, and crime scene. As you can see, this type of incident was exactly what the lab was created for.

The next morning at 5:30 a.m., Byron was parked outside the home of the brother whose gun he felt had been used to kill the deer. You can imagine the look on the man's face when he exited the house and spotted the game warden truck in his driveway. As the man approached, Byron exited the truck and met him. He explained to the man that what was about to happen could be easy or hard. He told him he had a search warrant for his home and he was looking for his .270 rifle. He informed the man he knew he had a wife and kids in the house and it would be up to him how things went.

The man turned and went back into the house. Knowing this could be a dangerous situation, the officer stayed behind cover as he watched the house. About three minutes later, the man stepped out on the porch carrying the rifle by the barrel. Byron took the rifle. He worked the bolt and found the gun was still loaded with cartridges that matched the casing he had found alongside of the road. He realized he was lucky that the violator had ejected the spent casing at the scene since that normally didn't happen. He informed the man the gun would be tested and he would be back in touch with him. The man turned and walked back into the house without saying a word.

The gun was test fired and the casings were a perfect match with the casing he had found along the road. Many people do not understand that every gun has its own fingerprint. Although the blood samples would not be back for a while, Byron felt like he had enough evidence to go ahead and obtain warrants for the two brothers. After conferring with the district attorney, it was decided that throwing the full beer cans at the landowner's windshield constituted reckless endangerment. That charge would be added to the conservation violations. The brothers were arrested without incident.

When the results from the forensic lab returned, they could not have been better. The blood taken from the county road, pickup truck, skinning rack, and the truck driver's pants all matched perfectly. The results were not that all of the blood was in fact deer blood. It was that all of the blood was from the same female deer. Talk about a slam dunk! As they say, it was all over but the crying.

The case came to court and you can guess the evidence was overwhelming. The judge was not at all pleased that the violators had put everyone at risk by throwing the full beer cans at the windshield of the landowner's truck as he drove down the road. The men were convicted on all charges. Furthermore, there was the matter of the truck that was used in the incident, which had been in impound since the incident. Impound fees are high. That, combined with the fines and costs with all the cases, brought the total costs to the defendants to nearly $10,000!

The judge made the comment to Byron that he had definitely gone the extra mile in this case. Byron told her he felt the wildlife of the state of Alabama and the landowners and citizens of Elmore County deserved his best effort. I appreciate Byron putting forth that type of effort and for instilling in me the desire to do the same.

Man-Made Road

WORKING IN THE WOODS for over thirty-five years, it was easy to forget that a lot of people know very little about nature and the outdoors. Of course, it should have been easy to remember that, considering I was reminded of it on what seemed like a daily basis. Several times I used something a good 4-H friend, Ann Gallus, had told me to illustrate the point that everyone didn't understand everything we often thought they did. She said while working in a veterinarian's office, she received a call from a lady who stated she had a dog she needed to get "fixed" and wanted to know what it would cost. My friend asked, "Does it need to be spayed or neutered?"

The lady replied, "Which one's cheaper?"

Obviously, some folks either didn't understand how things worked or just didn't give it much thought. A fellow who owned a timber company told me an interesting story about how his grown niece accompanied him to the woods to check on some logging activity. On the way, the man drove through an area where he had harvested some timber the year before. He said he had graded the road and grassed the entire area, making it very aesthetically pleasing. His niece was overwhelmed by the beautifully landscaped grassed roadway and commented how beautiful it was. He replied he also thought they had done a good job of building the road.

Shocked, the young lady asked, "You built this road?" He replied he had and she shook her head and said, "Well, it sure doesn't look like a man-made road!"

You can't make this stuff up!

That's Not What I Wanted
(You've Caught the Wrong Person)

DURING THE COURSE of a career in wildlife law enforcement, an officer will develop many relationships. While relationships are essential, they are often a difficult thing for a law enforcement officer. This is true for many reasons. One of the most difficult aspects of having a relationship is, as an officer, you are suspicious of everyone. This is a behavior you learn when you realize there are few people you can really trust. Officers are often guarded in relationships because you realize at any time you may have to arrest the very person you have developed a relationship with. I've had many people say to me, "I bet you would arrest your own mother." I've responded, "Yes, if I caught my mother in a flagrant violation, she would be arrested." This was easy to say since I knew I would not catch her in a violation, but if I did, she would expect me to do my job and arrest her! Unlike many people today, my mother believed people should take responsibility for their actions.

Many people are all for law and order until it's their name or, worse yet, their child's name being written on a bond! It is amazing how the transformation often takes place. Many times, a hunter or landowner has contacted me with a complaint they

237

definitely wanted something done about. Someone is shooting deer at night over here or someone is shooting from the road and I want it stopped. Some of the situations turn out great when you work the complaint, catch the violator, and the complainant is elated. Other times you work the complaint, apprehend the violator, and the complainant is irate! You may ask why the complainant would be upset when you apprehended the culprit. Well, because you caught the wrong culprit! Allow me to give a few examples.

"Can you not do anything about the people hunting from the road down here?" This was the angry question posed to game warden Hershel Patterson. The landowner was fairly irate when he stated he was hearing shots all the time and he knew they were coming from vehicles on the highway. Hershel told the man he would look into it. "Well, you need to," the man replied in a nasty tone. Hershel immediately got in his vehicle and headed for the location the man was complaining about. This wasn't in the middle of nowhere. It was along one of the two major US highways that traversed the county.

Many folks have an erroneous preconceived notion concerning where illegal hunting takes place. Common sense would tell you people hunting illegally would do so in remote areas out of the watchful eye of the public and the game warden. That's what common sense would tell you. I will tell you wildlife outlaws hunt where the game they are pursuing is spotted. Of course, they would like to practice their nefarious activities out of the view of landowners and sportsmen who might report them; however, that does not outweigh their desire to kill something illegally. Therefore, if the deer were standing alongside the US highway, that's where we needed to be working.

Literally minutes after receiving the call, Hershel arrived in the area and pulled to the side of the road to monitor activity.

Almost immediately, he heard a shot from just over the hill. He knew if it hadn't come from a vehicle, it was at least on the highway right-of-way. At that time, the Alabama road hunting law said it was illegal to hunt or discharge any firearm within one hundred yards of or across any public road, public highway, or railroad or the rights-of-way of any public road, public highway, or railroad. (This law was later revised and really messed up!) Hershel jumped in the car and headed toward the shot. As he topped the hill, sure enough there sat a vehicle in the road and closer examination revealed the driver had his rifle barrel protruding from the truck's window. Hershel stopped the vehicle and wrote the violator a ticket for hunting from the public road.

Talk about quick service. Within thirty minutes of his call to the game warden, the warden arrives and apprehends a violator doing exactly what the man had complained about in the exact location he had described. Who could ask for a more prompt response and desired outcome? One would think the complainant would be elated. Would you believe just the opposite was the case? As a matter of fact, the caller was now irate with Hershel for making the arrest. Although he had known these folks for years and had quickly and successfully answered their complaint, the complainant and his wife didn't speak to him for the next two years. Just because he had apprehended their adult son shooting from the road and had the audacity to write him a ticket! There is no pleasing some people.

Conservation Enforcement Sergeant Keith Mann had the unenviable task of working in Macon County, Alabama. Macon was actually a great county to work in if you liked being worked to death. In the infamous black belt region of the state, the area drew hunters from across the country and unfortunately not all of them understood the game laws and many of those who did understand them were still prone to violate them. Upon receiving a complaint of night hunting from an area landowner, Keith checked the area and determined the best area to work was right in front of the complainant's home. Now I know that may not sound logical. Why on earth in a rural county like Macon would you ever work close to someone's house? Surely no one would shoot near a house when the deer were thick along the roads in the uninhabited areas of the county. Well, although it may not sound plausible, I learned early on, as Keith did, people hunt wherever they see the deer and if that means in someone's yard, then so be it. Many times in my career I have had deer killed literally in the yard of people's homes and I know of many houses that have been shot into by night hunters! (You may want to read "They Shot My House" in my book *It's Not Easy Wearing Green.*)

Keith returned to work the area and set his deer decoy in a field across the road and hid behind the landowner's house. As I have often explained, the most difficult aspect of working the decoy was finding a decent vantage point to work it from. Places to set up the stuffed deer were a dime a dozen but good places to sit and observe were often as scarce as an empty checkout line at Walmart. Several times I have sat in driveways, beside homes, in barns, almost anywhere to get a vantage point of where the activity is taking place.

Keith set the deer up just prior to dark and got into position. Approximately twenty minutes after dark, the officer heard and then observed a vehicle coming from behind him off of the complainant's property. The driver eased past him, past the house, and pulled out onto the roadway. The vehicle came to a stop with the decoy illuminated by its headlights. Seconds passed and just as Keith thought "Surely this guy isn't going to shoot," *py-yow*, a shot split the night. Keith covered the short distance to the vehicle and activated his blue lights. He cautiously approached and quickly apprehended the violator. He prepared bonds for hunting at night and hunting from a public road. He explained the charges to the subject and allowed him to sign his bonds and be on his way. Certain the landowner had heard the shot, the officer decided to return to the complainant's house to give a report on the incident. The landowner came to the door and listened as the officer explained he had just caught someone shooting in the field across the road. He braced for the reply when he revealed the fact that the violator was in fact the landowner's son-in-law. Faced with this news, the landowner thought on it for a minute and replied, "Well, I guess he's going to need to find a new place to hunt, isn't he?"

CEO Earl Brown told me about receiving a night hunting complaint from a landowner that was more than a little upset. He said the woman told him in no uncertain terms there was way too much nighttime shooting taking place around her property and she wanted it stopped. He advised her he would see what he could do. Evidently, to insure he put forth his best effort, the woman told him if something was not done, she would definitely be contacting his supervisor. It was aggravating to receive that type of threat, but it was not necessarily uncommon.

Although the complainant wasn't very eloquent, we always liked getting information concerning what was going on. When you were trying to cover over four hundred thousand acres, someone helping you narrow the playing field was appreciated, even if they were somewhat snotty about it.

The next weekend, Earl was set up watching the complainant's property when lo and behold a jacked-up pickup came slow rolling down the road and shining with a spotlight. After the driver passed his location, Earl pulled out in the road behind the vehicle and immediately, the chase was on. Seeing how I can count on one hand the number of straight stretches of road in the county, any chase on the backroads could be hair raising. Fortunately, the majority of our chases were normally pretty short. This one was not.

Earl told me he knew pretty quickly that the truck he was chasing was not a stock vehicle. Prior to becoming a game warden, Earl was a master mechanic. With his vast knowledge of engines, his low-bid state truck outperformed any of the others in our fleet. That combined with his thorough familiarity with the county roads normally gave him the advantage in chase situations. However, he was having quite a time trying to keep up with the fleeing violator. Before long, the pursuit crossed over into neighboring Elmore County and they were quickly approaching an intersection known as Kim's Corner. Kim's Corner is where the county road terminates at US Highway 231. Earl said he knew at their current rate of speed the driver would in all likelihood fail to successfully negotiate the turn and would end up in the cow pasture across the highway.

When he saw the headlights of the truck going around and round, he knew his premonition was correct. He drove through the gaping hole in the fence and pulled up beside the smoking truck. After retrieving the man's rifle, he generously helped him out of his truck and into a set of handcuffs.

Talking with the violator revealed some interesting information. The smoke coming from under the hood was making the fellow increasingly nervous. He finally told the officer they might should get a fire extinguisher, seeing how his truck was rigged with nitrous oxide and he wasn't sure what might happen if it caught on fire. That explained the exceptionally high speeds they had reached. They checked out the truck and found the smoke was actually coming from a seized brake caliper.

With everything calmed down, Earl decided not to take the man to jail but to write him tickets for hunting at night, hunting from a public road, hunting from the aid of a vehicle, hunting without a permit, and attempting to elude. However, once he had obtained the man's driver's license, he realized there might be a problem with the permit charge. Seeing that the man's last name was the same as the name of the complainant, Earl asked if he knew the woman. "That's my mother," was his sour reply.

Amazingly, Earl's supervisor did receive a call from the complainant. Don't get ahead of me. It was not a thank-you call. The woman was irate that the game warden would put her son's life in jeopardy by chasing him down the road at such high speeds, not to mention the damage done to his vehicle! There is just no pleasing some people!

I once received a call from a fellow who told me he had a tremendous problem with people hunting his property without a permit. The property was adjacent to the Coosa Wildlife Management Area (WMA), which was my responsibility for nearly eighteen years. The caller inferred the trespassers were probably coming from the WMA and he wanted something done about it. Although I had never been on it, I was familiar with the location of the property and knew it was actually owned by a church group of some kind and there would probably be multiple people hunting the property.

I explained to the man the only way we could work a hunting-without-a-permit situation was for everyone who could legally hunt the property to have written permission in their possession. Alabama law requires that any person who hunts, traps, captures, injures, kills, or destroys any wild game on the lands of another without the written permission of or accompanied by the landowner or person in possession or control of the lands shall be guilty of a misdemeanor. In addition, all land in Alabama is posted by law and there are no posted signs required. It is the responsibility of the hunter to know whose property they are on and to have the proper paperwork in their possession. At the time of this incident the minimum fine was $250 (today it's $1,000) plus court costs and up to thirty days in jail. This being the case, I wanted to make sure the man understood the law. He stated only he and his brother could give permission to hunt the property and everyone who could hunt it would have a written permit from them in their possession. I told him it sounded like a situation we could work with and we would try to assist him with the problem.

The next morning, I traveled to the area and lo and behold there was a vehicle parked on the property alongside of the county road. Checking the boot tracks around the vehicle, I determined there appeared to have been one person who had walked the road into the property. I headed down the road, determined to find the intruder and nip this problem in the bud.

After searching the hundred acres for almost two hours, my determination to find the individual was beginning to wear quite thin. Any time you enter a property looking for a violator, you always run the risk the violator will spot you before you see them. Having been on this relatively small property for two hours, I was beginning to fear that might have occurred. I decided the only way to find this guy was to find a good vantage point and apprehend him as he headed to his vehicle. I located such a place and set up my surveillance.

After waiting another thirty minutes, I finally observed the orange-clad subject walking the road in my direction. I had already determined how close I would allow him to approach before making my presence known. Even in the light of day, you never wanted to startle someone carrying a loaded firearm. When he was close enough, I stepped from my hiding spot and announced I was the state game warden and needed to see his license and permit. I took his firearm and checked it while he searched for the requested documents. I found the rifle was loaded with ball ammunition, which wasn't legal for deer hunting. After some searching, the fellow realized he also did not have a license or permit for the property. I advised him he was under arrest and we would handle the paperwork at the vehicle. As we started toward the truck, the fellow commented he had permission to hunt the property. I told him the law required written permission and it must be in his possession. He countered his uncle was a friend of the guys who had the hunting rights on the property and he had permission to hunt the property. I informed the young man the fellows he was speaking of had told me anyone hunting the property would have a written permit from them and, if not, they wanted them arrested. I filled out the bonds for hunting without a permit, hunting without a license, and possession of illegal ammunition. The man signed the bonds, promising to appear in court, and went on his way. I was pretty pleased with having solved this illegal hunting problem on my first day on the property. I thought sure the landowners would be pleased as well. I'd been wrong before.

Approximately an hour later, I received a radio call from Montgomery requesting I call a fellow concerning an arrest earlier that morning. I took the number and advised I would call him when I could. This was before we had cell phones and it would be in the afternoon before I could return the call. I went on to the WMA and worked for a few hours before heading for home. While en route to the house, I again received a call from Montgomery, stating I needed to contact the individual concerning the incident this morning. I told them I was en route to the phone and would give him a call. Although I knew better, I thought it was possible they were really excited I had answered their complaint so quickly and so effectively. It was possible.

I returned home and called the number I had been given. The man answered the phone and I identified myself and asked what I could do for him. "There has been a mistake" was his reply. "What's that?" I asked. "Did you give Ernie Stewart a ticket this morning?"

he asked with a quiver in his voice. "Three of them," I replied. "Well, you are going to have to tear them up because he can legally hunt there." It was obvious to me someone's feathers had been ruffled and mine were beginning to fluff up pretty good. He went on to say his brother was the one who had called me the previous night about people hunting without a permit but he had no right to call me about that. I immediately realized there definitely was going to be a problem but as far as I was concerned, the problem wasn't mine. Although this fellow felt he could tell me what to do, he had another thing coming. After I again listened to how I needed to dismiss the charges against the defendant, I took the opportunity to explain the fellow had not only been charged with hunting without a permit but with other offenses as well and I reminded him it was me and not him or his brother that would be bringing these charges. This infuriated the man, who said the fellow did not need a license since his uncle was actually a member of the group that owned the property and you didn't have to have a license to hunt on your own property. I told him I felt it was quite a stretch to say this guy was hunting on his own property and even if he was, he still was hunting with illegal ammunition. The man countered with the "fact" I should have never been on the property in the first place and therefore the subject shouldn't have been cited for anything. By this time, it was all I could do to hold my composure and I advised the man I would see them in court and ended the call.

I had finally pretty much calmed down that evening when the phone rang. I answered the phone and it was the man who had originally called me. He explained he had a real mess on his hands. I told him it had sounded that way to me when I had spoken with his brother earlier in the day. He humbly asked if I would consider dismissing the tickets against the young man I had arrested. I asked if there was anything he had not understood when I explained the requirement of written permission in their possession. He stated he had understood but the fellow I had caught was a relative of a friend and the friend had permission. I took the opportunity to refresh his memory concerning the fact this was the very reason I had told him *everyone* would have to have a permit in their possession. Dejected, he stated it would probably be best if I didn't work the property anymore and I assured him he did not need to worry about that.

I still hold the warrants on the fellow, who, instead of coming to court, moved out of state. Once again, there's just no pleasing some people!

In each of these incidents, folks did not get the outcome they desired. Did you ever really think you wanted something but later learned it really wasn't what you wanted?

Country music star Garth Brooks had a major hit with a song that said, "Sometimes I thank God for unanswered prayers." I think the truth be told we could all truthfully sing that song. When you thank God for unanswered prayers, that is after the fact. I believe a lot of disappointment could be avoided if we would consult Him on the front end. We are really good at getting the cart before the horse.

One day, and we don't know when, we will no longer have the ability to consult the Lord. The folks in these stories did not get what they wanted. What do you want? My earnest desire is to spend eternity in heaven. I've taken the necessary steps to accomplish that. If you haven't, you may want to, today. Admit you're a sinner. Believe that Jesus Christ is God's Son and confess Jesus is Lord. Romans 10:9 says that if you will confess with your mouth Jesus is Lord and believe in your heart that God raised him from the dead, you will be saved. Now that is something everybody should want!

If I Move, He Will Kill Me

DURING MY CAREER, I had the opportunity to work with numerous officers who I would describe as quite interesting. One of the more interesting characters I ever worked with was a fellow I'll call Johnny Rearden. Although he served as an officer in a nearby county, Johnny was our chief undercover officer. He would later become the leader of our departmental covert unit. Now I had some interesting cases during my career; however, Johnny, had unbelievable cases on what seemed to be a weekly basis.

For the first several years I worked, night hunting was rampant despite the fact we worked most nights and caught a lot of violators. Working with the two local conservation enforcement officers (CEOs), at best we could cover three small areas of the 652 square miles that made up our county. Therefore, once or twice during the deer season a special law enforcement detail would be set up to try to apprehend some of the violators. Multiple officers would be brought in and we would do our best to saturate an area of the county. On one such detail, I was paired with Johnny and it would turn out to be a very memorable event.

Our details were loosely organized at best. We would normally meet at the jail, see how many units we had, and decide where to put the additional CEOs. These decisions were often difficult. The problem wasn't a lack of places to work; it was too few people to cover all the complaint areas. We would put a unit, normally one officer working alone, in what we considered the best spots and let the loose ends drag. This night it was decided Johnny and I would work a deer decoy on the Concord Road in the south end of the county. The Concord Road was approximately three miles long and had a couple of houses on the south end and nothing but Concord Baptist Church, woods, and deer for the remainder of the road. During this time, this type of isolated location was an ideal night hunting area. Later, things would change and night hunting would become common in well-populated areas and along major highways.

With the assigned areas distributed, we were off. We found a likely looking spot and hid our truck and ventured across the road and set up Johnny's decoy. This was in the days when the decoy could be used pretty much anywhere the officer decided it might work. Things are much different today.

Things had been pretty quiet when a pickup slowly moved down the road toward our vantage point. The vehicle slowed to a stop with its headlights illuminating what we hoped they would mistake for a live deer. We held our breath in anticipation. The wait wasn't long, as a rifle blast shattered the stillness. We jumped in the truck and pulled out into the road behind the vehicle and the chase was on. With Johnny behind the wheel, I had a radio microphone in each hand trying to obtain some assistance to help stop the fast-fleeing duo. At the end of Concord Road, the driver took a left onto Coosa County Road 14. As we followed at a high rate of speed, we watched as the passenger threw a spotlight and numerous firearms out of the window. I continued to talk with other Game & Fish units on one radio and attempted to reach the county sheriff's office (SO) on the other radio. At the same time, I was advising Johnny about what the road ahead held in store.

If you've ever read any game warden's stories, you have likely heard them lament about having only low-bid equipment. The groaning was often justified. It is true that we were forced, often by state law, to accept the lowest bid for equipment such as vehicles. I could go on into great detail; however, suffice it to say that the vehicle we were driving was often inferior to the vehicle we were chasing. I must include here that most game wardens I knew were really good drivers. As a matter of fact, I had an instructor at the Alabama Police Academy tell me we, Game & Fish employees, were the best drivers he had ever worked with. I feel that often made up for what we lacked in vehicle performance.

The violator's pickup was beginning to put some distance between us when I told Johnny to try something that, looking back, was obviously prompted by adrenaline and the desire to catch the culprits. I informed Johnny there was a curve coming up ahead; however, instead of staying with the road, I wanted him to hold steady and we would go straight across the grass and cut the curve off. "Do what?" was his response. I quickly explained the curve was sort of a hairpin shape and it was common for kids to cut across the grass and come back up on the road on the other side. There was no ditch and I had done it before. Of course, I didn't really consider the fact we were now running about eighty miles per hour and I had tried it at about thirty.

Trusting in my assessment, Johnny dove off the side of the road and held the wheel straight. Within seconds we were back on the road and once again immediately behind the subjects. Soon Johnny spotted a Stop Ahead sign and asked what was coming up. I told him not to worry about it, we could make it. "What road is it?" he asked with more urgency in his voice. I replied it was US Highway 231 but it wouldn't be busy this time of night. Fortunately, my prediction was right. The subjects barely slowed down as they turned south down the highway. We were right behind them when the driver applied the brakes and took a side road to the right. Almost immediately, he evidently changed his mind and turned back toward the highway. This was the break we were looking for and we were able to cut off their escape by sliding our truck in front of their vehicle.

In a flash, we were out of the truck. Our positioning was definitely not ideal; however, in our work it seemed we often ended up in front of the vehicle we were stopping. I guess this is why my instructor at the police academy told me people working with Game & Fish were just asking to be killed!

Because of the angle we were at, I ran down the driver's side of and around the rear of the assailant's pickup en route to the passenger's door. Running by, I noticed a deer lying in the bed of the truck. I yanked on the passenger's door handle, only to find it locked. I was shining my Maglite in the passenger's face and shouting for him to open the door. He opened the door and looked at me as innocently as you please and said, "What's going on?" I must admit, this behavior stunned me for a second or two. The fact we had just pursued this pair at high speeds for four to five minutes, the passenger had thrown their guns and a spotlight out the window, and they had a dead deer in the bed of their truck at 11:00 p.m. had me a little worked up. Yet this individual acted as if we had just met on the street! I snapped back to reality and snatched the subject out of the truck, placed him over the side of the truck bed, and handcuffed him. We advised the subjects of their rights and sat them down in the road. Other units arrived in minutes and we advised we needed someone to go back and get the decoy and gather up the light and guns that had been thrown out, some of which were sticking in the ground like arrows. The subjects were transported to the county jail.

The pair was pretty tight lipped during the five-minute trip to the jail. Once there, we learned our subjects were brothers from

Louisiana. The eldest, Virgil, still lived in Louisiana; however, he was visiting his brother, Jim, who now lived in Montgomery. Beyond that, they weren't saying anything. Although I had already advised them of their rights, I again reminded them they did not have to say anything. I added they could make it easy or hard; it was up to them. Neither subject opened their mouth.

Seeing they wanted to play hardball, I decided I would throw them a curve. Seated in the tiny intake/dispatch room, I asked the jailer/dispatcher if she could prepare some bonds for the subjects. She replied she could and asked what I needed. During this time, our small county jail was manned by one person. Barbara Joe served as the jailer/dispatcher, booking officer, clerk, and any other position that was needed! Although I knew she probably would not appreciate it, I had an idea about how to possibly get the attention of the two wayward brothers. I told her I needed two sets of bonds for hunting at night, taking deer at night, hunting from the public road, hunting by aid of the vehicle, hunting without a permit, attempting to elude, failure to yield to a blue light, running a stop sign, and reckless driving. Of course, I did not intend to charge the pair with all of the charges but they didn't know that. Neither did the jailer, who had a somewhat dumbfounded look on her face. I gave her a knowing wink and she stated she would get to work on the bonds. I moved the younger man to the interrogation room. Within minutes, the dispatcher summoned me and said the older brother wanted to talk to me. I hoped this meant my ruse had freed up his tongue a little bit. I told the younger subject to sit tight and I went back up front.

I approached the older fellow and he looked at me and said, "I want to help myself." I told him that was fine and I would be glad to take his statement. I reminded him the first thing we had done after getting them stopped was advise him of his rights. "No," he said. I said, "Yes sir, I did read you your rights," and he said, "No, first he said if I moved he would kill me!" Evidently, while Johnny was "removing" him from the truck, he let him know, in a not-so-subtle way, he did not need to make any moves. I had noticed his removal from the vehicle had been very rapid and I remember thinking it may have been easier if Johnny would have removed him through the door instead of the window!

I suggested we start with when he had seen the deer alongside the road. He began to give me some sketchy details about the night's activities. He said they had spotted the deer and his brother had shot at it, although he did not want him to. I asked about the spike buck in the bed of their truck and he explained his brother had shot that one also. I asked, seeing how his brother had already shot the spike, didn't he think he might be going to shoot the next deer, the one in the headlights of his truck, when he had stopped on the side of the road? He didn't respond. I finished with the statement and told him and the jailer he would be charged with hunting at night, hunting from a public road, and hunting by the aid of the vehicle and we would drop the other charges. Although he wasn't happy, he did appear to be pleased some of the charges would be dropped.

I returned to the younger brother and told him I had taken his brother's statement. Not surprisingly, he decided he also wanted to make a statement. I had taken enough statements from multiple suspects that I wasn't surprised when his version of the events was somewhat different from the one I had heard earlier. In actuality, the statement was almost exactly the same. Right down to the point where his brother had done all of the shooting! I asked for him to explain how his brother, who was driving, had shot the decoy when it was on the passenger side of the truck and the shot had come from the passenger side of the vehicle. He stated he had ducked down and his brother had fired the shot over his head. To that I replied, "And you can hear me now?" I finished taking his statement and explained the jailer would prepare his bonds and, once signed, he would be free to go. I went back and explained to the elder brother we would be holding the truck and guns as evidence and he might or might not get them back. This appeared to get his attention.

The next month the cases came to court. The brothers were found guilty on all charges. They received fines and costs totaling $4,200 and had their guns confiscated. The truck, which had been held at the SO since their arrests, was ordered to be released to the owner. After he had announced the sentence, I reminded the judge the charges also carried a three-year revocation of all hunting privileges. He included it in the order and commented he felt it was a moot point based on the amount of the fine. He was proved wrong, however, when the older brother turned to me and asked, "You mean I can't hunt here anymore?"

I replied, "No sir, you can't hunt here anymore."

The subject looked very disappointed as he hung his head and walked to the clerk's office, where he forked out $4,200.

The fact that this man wanted to return and hunt again after paying $4,200 in fines and court costs and losing several guns is indicative of how strong the desire to hunt is in some people. I met a lot of people who ate and slept with hunting on their mind. Fortunately, the majority of them wanted to do it legally and ethically. I once had a fellow tell me he could not enjoy hunting if he had to do it looking over his shoulder. I appreciated that. I don't know whether or not he was enjoying it a couple of years later when my partner caught him hunting over bait! A lot of folks talked a good game.

Go, Go, Go

WE WORKED A TREMENDOUS AMOUNT during the deer season. I have written many stories where I have talked about working every weekend of the nearly four-month-long deer season. We often worked seven days a week, day and night. During the deer season, working seventy hours in a week was not unusual. You get the point: we worked a lot. In effect, we were never off. If something illegal was happening, we hoped we would receive a call about it.

While this lifestyle took its toll on a body, it also was hard on our families. I'll admit I did not realize just how hard it was on them for a long time. I was blessed by God to have a wonderful wife who has always supported me. There were many times when she carried a heavy load of caring for two children and working a teaching job that also carried a lot of nights and weekends with it. I praise the Lord for her every day.

On a rare evening off, Melanie and I had gone to visit and have supper with game warden Earl Brown and his wife. We had just finished with supper when the phone rang. Earl answered the call. I could tell by his questioning of the caller that it was a night hunting complaint. Earl hung up the phone and said, "We need to go to Kellyton." As I was saying, getting a complaint at any time wasn't unusual. The problem with me responding to this call was that we had taken my personal truck to Earl's house and therefore my wife would have to drive it home and she was very inexperienced at driving a vehicle with a manual transmission. I'm sure there is probably someone reading these words that is asking the question, "What is a manual transmission?" Well, believe it or not, not all vehicles have automatic transmissions. Even today, there are vehicles in which you must manually change the gears. The vehicle is equipped with a clutch, which must be engaged in order for you to change the gears. It isn't that difficult once you learn to do it; however, it can be a steep learning curve if you aren't familiar with it.

Melanie had been trying to learn to drive my truck so I asked if she thought she could drive it home and she said she thought she could. I told her once she got going there wouldn't be but a couple of stops and she shouldn't have a problem. After I gave her a quick pep talk, Earl and I jumped in his truck and headed to the call.

We headed to the suspect area and were unable to locate any evidence of anything having been shot. That wasn't unusual. It wasn't that the violation had not occurred, it was that someone telling you where they had heard a shot was generally not a precise location. Trying to pinpoint the sound of a shot close enough that you could locate where the offense had occurred was difficult.

Seeing how this was before cell phones, I told Melanie to call the jail and let them know she had made it home okay. I received the call from the dispatcher letting me know she had made it home. I did not know whether his laughing had anything to do with what he was telling me or if something else was going on. I would soon find out.

We stayed in the area where the shooting was reported for a while but soon gave it up. Since we were both supposed to be off and already had too much time in for the week as it was, Earl dropped me off at the house and told me he would give me a call if he got another complaint. The way things had been going, I figured that would probably happen.

When I came through the door, the look on Melanie's face told me in no uncertain terms she had not enjoyed her trip home. She then told me the whole story and what a story it was.

She said driving the truck on the county road and even the US highway had not been a problem and had given her a little confidence. However, as she approached the town of Rockford, she said she had decided she did not want to go through the four-way stop in the center of town. She said she remembered that the Majik Mart, which was the only convenience store in town and was located on the northwest corner of the four-way stop, was the hang out for local youth and she did not want to have an audience as she tried to take off from the stop sign. Therefore, she decided she would turn off of the main highway and come through town. There were no vehicles coming so she did not have to come to a stop to make the left turn off of the highway. The right turn onto the street we lived on was also not a problem. However, things were about to change.

In her desire to bypass the four-way stop, she had now ended up on a side street that also had a stop sign. And this stop sign was on a hill, which was a difficult thing to navigate in a standard shift vehicle. She quickly made the decision that she would simply roll through the stop sign. That would normally not be a problem in our sleepy little town, but of course you know the saying about best laid plans.

As she approached the intersection, she could see the lights of an approaching vehicle. She mashed the clutch and brake, bringing the truck to a stop. The vehicle passed by and she revved the engine and let out on the clutch only to have the truck jerk and go dead. This wasn't the first time she had experienced this but it definitely wasn't what she wanted to have happen. Another try yielded the same result. Let me tell you from experience that when you are learning to drive a stick shift vehicle, frustration often sets in quickly. After a third failed attempt, she was contemplating whether or not there was another alternative route she might could take. Her thought process was then interrupted by someone hollering, "Hey! Hey Lady!"

Since she was preoccupied with the dilemma at hand, she had failed to think about the fact that she was sitting in the road adjacent to the county jail. Since the town of Rockford was the county seat, it was the location of the sheriff's office and county jail. The jail building was only about sixty feet off of the road. The jail was surrounded by a chain-link fence topped with concertina wire. The fence was only about four feet from the roadway. To make matters worse for Melanie, the jail cells were upstairs with windows that looked out onto the street.

She again heard someone yell, "Hey Lady!" Although she didn't see anyone, she cracked the window a little bit and answered, "What?" "You're letting out on the clutch too fast. You need to let it roll back to the flat ground" was the reply.

Not knowing anything else to do, she let the vehicle roll backward toward the post office. As she looked to her left, she realized a couple of jail trustees had come out into the fenced-in area. She assumed and hoped it was trustees, seeing how they were outside of the jail. One of the men told her he would watch for traffic and tell her when she could try and cross the highway. While that sounded like it would be helpful, what happened next was a bit troubling. The inmate went around to the front of the jail and out the front gate and was now standing beside the road. Although these guys seemed to be all about helping her, she felt her anxiety mounting.

258

Go, Go, Go

Good to his word, the man watched the road and gave her the all clear, motioning for her to come on through. She once again popped the clutch and killed the engine. The prisoner then told her he would be happy to drive the truck for her. That was all the motivation she needed to accomplish her task. She told him she could do it and to let her know when the coast was clear. As the man was giving her the motion to come on across, she again heard yelling coming from the jail. As she looked over, she noticed all of the windows on all the cells were open and the prisoners were chanting, "Go, go, go." She gave it plenty of gas and shot across the highway. She said she yelled "Thank you" out the window and could hear the prisoners cheering. The two blocks from there to our house didn't cause any problems.

Once in the house and somewhat calmed down, she dutifully called the jail dispatcher and asked him to call and tell me she had made it home. She said she could tell it was all he could do not to laugh. We laugh about it today. That night, not so much! So much for not having an audience.

My wife put up with a lot during my career and loved me through it all. I can't thank her enough.

I'm Glad I Didn't Shoot It

THE MAN WAS VERY HAPPY he had stopped short of committing a violation in our presence. He repeatedly stated he was so glad he had not shot with us sitting in the road behind him. Yes sir, he was sure glad about that. However, he obviously wasn't as familiar with the law or the definition of hunting as he thought. He was about to receive some education and it would erase the smile from his face.

As I have stated in several stories, for the first seventeen years of my career, I worked almost every weekend of the nearly three-month-long Alabama deer season. As an area biologist and conservation enforcement officer (CEO) assigned to a wildlife management area (WMA), I spent every Friday and Saturday either on the Coosa, Barbour, Hollins, or Lowndes County WMA. The days were long. They normally began around 4:00 a.m. and often lasted until midnight or later. As one would guess, there was a lot that went on during a deer hunt on a WMA. It began with the issuing of permits to the hundreds, and sometimes thousands, of hunters that showed up to hunt the property. Every hunter was required to present their license at the check station to receive a permit. With the permits distributed, we would normally eat some breakfast and then the biologists with enforcement authority would head out onto the area to check hunters.

Many times, we would go to what we suspected would be a busy intersection and set up a roadblock. Alabama state law 9-11-303 states, "The Commissioner of Conservation and Natural Resources and his designated agents or employees are authorized to search without warrant any automobile, wagon, truck or other vehicle or any hunting sack or hunting coat within any wildlife management area and to confiscate any protected bird, animal or fish found killed or held in violation of the game laws or the regulations of the Commissioner of Conservation and Natural Resources; provided, that this section shall not be operative against persons traveling on state and federal highways within any wildlife management areas." This authority allowed us to stop and search any vehicle on the management area. However, we did not thoroughly search every vehicle. Many times, we would perform a cursory search, primarily to insure there were no loaded firearms in the vehicle, no illegal ammunition, no illegally taken wildlife, or any other blatantly obvious violations. The roadblocks were normally fairly productive.

When not working a roadblock, we often would slowly ride through the WMA, stopping vehicles as we came upon them. This usually resulted in several head-on stops, which were not ideal. In a head-on stop, an officer is very vulnerable during their approach to the suspect's vehicle. I have fortunately survived thousands of such stops. Occasionally, we would come up behind a vehicle and conduct a more traditional stop. Sometimes it wasn't traditional at all.

After observing thousands of people, you learned to pretty quickly assess folks. While issuing permits at the WMA, you theoretically saw everyone who would be hunting on the WMA. Many of these people hunted the area on a regular basis and others would be first-time participants. Several folks would have multiple questions. We did our best to answer their questions and gave them a permit that had a list of the rules printed on the back. Often folks would in effect tell on themselves simply by the questions they would ask. When someone would look up from reading the rules and in an astonished tone ask, "You can't hunt with buckshot out here?" it was generally a safe bet they possessed some buckshot. It wasn't rocket science.

One morning on the Hollins WMA I watched as three fellows exited their car and made their way to the check station window. The driver of the vehicle asked for a management area permit. I told him I would need to see his hunting license and management area license. He dug into his wallet and produced the licenses and I gave him a permit. As the second fellow came up and requested a permit, the third man turned and went back and got in the vehicle. I immediately thought it odd that three guys would come up in the same vehicle and two of them come and acquire a permit to hunt and the other one not. The two guys with permits returned to the car and the trio left. I immediately told my counterpart, Wildlife Officer Gene Carver, what had occurred and that I felt we should keep a lookout for the vehicle since I felt certain all three men would be hunting and one of them would not have any licenses or permit. He agreed. I noted the fellows left the check station in a small gray car and headed toward County Road 511.

As Gene and I were headed toward his truck in an effort to follow the suspects, someone pulled in with a large buck to be checked in. Although we had a biologist aide at the check station, we decided we would stay and assist him with taking the biological information from the deer.

We assisted the hunter in getting the big deer onto the platform scales. The field-dressed buck weighed in at 155 pounds, which meant the live weight would be just over 200 pounds. While a lot of people claimed to kill bucks that weighed over 200 pounds, it was actually pretty rare. We checked the deer's teeth and estimated that he was four and a half years old. The deer sported a nice eight-point rack and it turned out to be one of the largest deer harvested on the area that season. After completing the WMA kill sheet, we helped the excited hunter load the deer back in his truck and he was on his way.

We got in Gene's truck and headed out on the area to check some hunters. We made our way to County Road 511 and drove toward the town of Sylacauga. We soon came up on Rocky Mount Road, which led into the WMA. As we were easing along the road, we rounded a curve and there stopped in the road in front of us was the small gray car containing the three men I had noticed earlier at the check station. As we rolled toward the vehicle, we simultaneously said, "He's got his gun out the window." The driver had a scoped high-powered rifle pointed up into the woods on the left side of the road. We both waited for a shot; however, the man saw us approaching in his mirror and pulled the gun back inside the car. Gene activated his blue light and we exited our vehicle.

We had everyone put their hands up and we retrieved two rifles from the front seat passengers and one from the fellow in the rear seat. We unloaded the guns and placed them in our truck and returned to the car. Gene told the driver to step out. The man hopped out of the vehicle and spontaneously exclaimed, "I'm glad I didn't shoot."

"Shoot what?" was Gene's reply.

The man pointed into the woods and said, "Yeah, there was a big buck up on that hill and I was going to bust his ass." The man again stated he was really glad we pulled up before he got a shot off. I was thinking his gladness was about to turn to sadness.

Gene asked to see the man's driver's license and he fished it out and handed it over. The license revealed the man's name was

Freddie Joe Garrison and he was from the nearby town of Sylacauga. Gene asked if the fellow possessed a hunting permit for the property where the deer had been standing. The man responded by asking if it was management area land. Gene informed him it was not. The man said he did not have a permit for the property. Gene told the man that someone pointing a loaded rifle at a deer from a vehicle sitting in the public road and stating that they were trying to shoot it was in violation of several state laws. The fellow again stated he was glad he had not pulled the trigger. Obviously, the man wasn't comprehending what the officer was saying. Possibly because he did not want to.

As Gene was talking with the driver, I talked with the two passengers. Although they were on a joint venture, I did not think they had done anything they could be cited for. However, that did not mean they wouldn't have pertinent info concerning the incident. I began by asking if I could see each man's hunting license. If you recall, I had my doubts whether the backseat passenger had any license, seeing how he had not obtained a WMA permit when the others did earlier. While the front seat passenger dug in his wallet for his license, the fellow in the back gave me a forlorn look and said he didn't have one. I did not feel the time was right to tell him he really didn't need a license to ride around in a car, although I felt they were, in effect, "hunting." Instead, I decided to hopefully use his angst to learn the truth about his counterpart. I asked him to tell me what had occurred immediately prior to us arriving on the scene. He did not hesitate and stated they had been driving slowly, looking for deer, and Freddie had spotted a big buck. He said Freddie was going to kill that son of a buck and was lining up the shot when we came up behind them. I looked at the front seat passenger and asked him if that was the way it went and he reluctantly nodded his head yes.

I returned to Gene and Freddie just as Gene was explaining the laws concerning hunting from a public road, hunting by the aid of a vehicle, and hunting without a permit were "hunting" violations and a shot did not have to be fired for there to be a violation. Now the guy had an uncomfortable look on his face. When Gene said, "You are under arrest," the look went from uncomfortable to miserable.

Freddie then claimed a defense we had heard a few times when he said this wasn't what it looked like. Thinking fast, Freddie said he was just using his scope to try and see how big the deer was but he was not going to shoot it.

Gene countered that by asking, "Did you not just tell me three times that you would have shot the deer if we had not pulled up on you?"

While the man was trying to come up with an answer for that, I thought it was a good time to interject that his passengers had said he was driving around looking for a deer to shoot. That tidbit of information took the wind out of Freddie's sails. Gene handled the paperwork. Since Freddie Joe was the driver and the attempted shooter, the other two individuals were not charged with anything. Freddie Joe was not a happy camper.

The next month the dejected man appeared in Clay County District Court before Judge George Simpson. Judge Simpson was a strong judicial conservationist. The judge asked Gene what had occurred and Gene advised him we had pulled up behind the suspect, who was stopped in the public road with his loaded rifle pointed out the window of the car onto property he did not have a permit to hunt. He continued that when he approached the car, the man had told him he had spotted a big buck on the property and would have shot it if he had not seen us pulling up behind him. The judge asked the defendant if he had any questions for the officer and he replied that he did not. The judge asked him if

265

he had told the officer that he was going to shoot the deer. The man stammered around and finally said he was just looking at the deer. The judge again asked if he had stated to the officer that he was going to shoot the deer if we had not pulled up. The man finally mumbled a weak "Yes." Freddie was found guilty and received a hefty fine from the judge.

The next deer season, we were once again in Clay County court. When I say we, that included me, Gene, Clay County CEO Glaze and, you guessed it, Freddie Joe. It seemed Freddie had once again got crossways with the law when CEO Glaze had found him to be on a property where he did not have permission to hunt. Freddie was wearing a hopeless look as the case was called and the judge asked him how he pled. He pled guilty. The judge followed his normal routine and asked the officer if he had anything to add and he stated he didn't. However, Gene did have a comment he wanted to share with the judge.

"Your Honor," Gene said.

"Yes, Officer Carver," the judge said.

"I wanted to inform the court that we apprehended Mr. Garrison last season and we had a difficult time getting him to pay his fine."

At that, Mr. Garrison loudly protested, saying, "Judge, he can't say that!"

The judge responded even more loudly when he assured the defendant that he would decide who could and could not speak in his court and right now the officer was speaking and if he knew what was good for him, he wouldn't be! The tone used by the judge left no room for misunderstanding. Gene advised the court he had no further comment. The judge turned his attention to Freddie Joe. He did not ask why he had failed to pay his fine; he did ask why he had seen fit to disobey the order he had handed down in the previous case. I think it was the judge's tone and intense glare that left Freddie Joe speechless and, truth be known, he probably caused him to pee his pants a little bit.

The judge informed the man he would accept his guilty plea and assessed a $500 fine plus court costs and thirty days in jail. The judge allowed that to sink in for a minute and then said he would suspend the jail time if the man wanted to pay his fine and costs today. The defendant quickly told the judge he would have the money by the end of the day. The judge told him if he didn't, he needed to report to the county jail and start serving his time. The fine was paid.

Who Are You—Really?

IF YOU SPEND MUCH TIME in or around a sheriff's office (SO) in a rural county, you will no doubt witness some "interesting" things. In a small county, the SO is often the hub of a lot of what goes on in the county. There is usually a steady stream of folks coming through the door. Some are needing to talk with a deputy, some are wanting to apply for a pistol permit, and others are demanding to speak with THE sheriff. Of course, many are there asking questions that have nothing to do with the sheriff's office. No doubt the SO is a place of service.

As I sat talking with the sheriff, I heard the unmistakable rumble of a Harley-Davidson motorcycle as it rolled into the parking lot. As I watched through the window, the "biker" parked the bike next to the sheriff's Tahoe and dismounted. The rider was a white male who appeared to be around fifty years old. He sported tattoos from his wrists to his shoulders on both arms and a scruffy beard. As he removed his helmet, I was wondering what business he might have pending here. I was not at all prepared for what happened next.

As he stood at the rear of his bike, he reached up and began to roll the tattoos off of his arm! Up until this moment, I was not aware there was such a thing as a tattoo sleeve. He removed the sleeve from the other arm also and placed them in his helmet and entered the SO and requested an application for a pistol permit.

I have often heard it said if you hear a new word, you will likely hear it again within twenty-four hours. I'm not sure that is true, but I have experienced it several times. Evidently it holds true for observing new items as well, seeing how the next day I had a biker pass me on the road and he was wearing a tattoo sleeve! It got me to thinking, "Why do people do that?"

On the face of it, I assume these folks are trying to project an image they would like to embody without totally committing to it. I think most people identify the person wearing the leather vest and sporting the tats while riding a motorcycle as a biker. To me the term *biker* carries with it the connotation of a tough individual whom you probably do not want to mess with. While many of today's "bikers" are blue- and white-collar guys and gals who simply enjoy the open air and rumble under their seat, I feel certain they don't mind the "tough" reputation that goes with it.

I can tell you from experience there is a wide array of bikers out there today. Although central Alabama isn't a haven for gangs of bikers, I have had the opportunity to interact with a few. I vividly recall making a traffic stop on a motorcycle while working with the Coosa County Sheriff's Office. It was misting rain as my radar indicated the biker was running eighty-two in a sixty-five-miles-per-hour zone. I pursued the rider and activated my blue lights and he pulled to the side of the highway. I immediately noticed the Outlaws/Oklahoma insignia on his vest. I kept my eye on the man as I exited the car and approached him. In a very matter-of-fact posture, he stepped off the bike and assumed what I must describe as a fighting stance. While this definitely attracted my attention, I didn't let on. I identified myself as a deputy with the Coosa County Sheriff's Office and asked if he was in a hurry this evening. His curt reply was, "I was just trying to get out of the rain." I replied I could understand that and told him the reason for the stop was he was traveling at eighty-two miles per hour and I asked to see his driver's license. He quickly pulled the license from his pocket and thrust it toward me. I advised I would be back with him shortly and returned to the car.

I had noticed during our encounter that my partner, Deputy Josh Jones, had not exited the car, which was highly unusual. When I returned, I found Josh in the passenger seat with his pistol in his hand. He told me he had me covered if anything happened. I asked why he didn't get out and come up there with me and he quickly replied because some idiot had pulled the car so close to the guardrail he couldn't get his door open! He then asked if I had noticed how the guy had gotten off the bike and the way he was standing. I told him that had not failed to get my attention.

When the man's license came back clean, Josh looked at me and said, "Verbal warning." I agreed and returned to the biker. I had noticed earlier and now looked again at the patches on his vest. One read "1%er" and the other said, "God forgives, Outlaws don't." Although I had made my assessment of the man on my initial encounter, his fighting stance and curt replies were still demanding my attention. However, I did not get the gut feeling he represented anymore threat than what was normal. I advised him I was giving him a verbal warning for speeding and asked if he would try to keep his speed down and handed his license back. I asked where he was coming from and he replied he had been to a funeral in Florida and was returning to Oklahoma. I found it interesting that the only "luggage" he possessed was contained in a Walmart bag on his seat. He asked how far it was to the next town with a hotel and I told him it was about ten miles. I advised him to be careful and he remounted the bike and headed off.

Not being familiar with one percenters, I went home and did a little research. It seems the one percenters are a bunch dedicated to the biker lifestyle and they don't normally have much use for law enforcement. My research led me to believe these guys were the real deal and I would be shocked to no end to find one of them wearing a tattoo sleeve! They are the real article.

This brings me back to the guy wearing the tattoo sleeves. While I understand there are valid reasons someone can't have real tattoos, I must admit I placed this guy in a "biker wannabe" category. I believe he was trying to make himself out to be something he really wasn't. Yes, he was acting just like so many of us!

Who are we, really? Are we the real article or are we pretenders? I'm not talking about how we dress or act in an effort to influence others, I'm talking about who we really are. The Bible says the Lord doesn't look at people as we do, judging them by their outward appearance. The Lord looks on the heart. He knows the truth. We may be able to fool others but if we think we are fooling God, then the word *fool* is appropriate.

Today, transparency is a popular word but things are rarely transparent. While we spend a lot of time worrying about our appearance, we need to understand the Bible says the Lord searches every heart and understands the intention of every thought. With that in mind, we should remember the Bible says to be not deceived, God is not mocked. You will reap what you sow.

Have you admitted to yourself who you are? You don't have to tell God, He already knows. He also knows who you can be and who He wants you to be! God isn't swayed by what we look like. God is all about seeing our lives transformed for our sake.

Maybe it's time to roll your sleeves off and get started being who the Lord is calling you to be. He says those who seek Him will find Him. If you haven't found him, start looking!

Matthew 7:7–8 tells us, *Ask and it will be given to you; seek and you will find; knock and the door will be opened to you. For everyone who asks receives; the one who seeks finds; and to the one who knocks, the door will be opened.*

We need to understand it's not who we are, it's whose we are that makes all the difference.

What's in Your Pocket?

IT OFTEN SEEMED the planets lined up or it was a full moon or we had been paying the preacher appropriately; whatever the reason, some days were just better than others. At approximately 6:45 p.m., Gene Carver and I were working a decoy detail at our favorite location, the old skating rink site in Weogufka, Alabama. We had already made several cases during the day and I guess we were getting a little greedy by still being out there. At dark we had moved the fake deer a little closer to the road and had placed reflective tacks in its eyes.

As we observed from across the road, two subjects in a maroon Toyota pickup eased up and shined the decoy with their headlights. For the majority of my career, this was the preferred method utilized by night hunters to illuminate deer. Coosa County was 92 percent forested with few open fields along the road. Therefore, most of our night hunting was what we referred to as "ditch shooting" since the deer were often literally in the ditch.

After shining the deer, the driver proceeded to pull down into the field with the decoy. While this was not common, it wasn't unheard of. It immediately brought to mind another memorable night. Conservation Enforcement Officers Earl Brown and Hershel Patterson and I were using the decoy in the northeast part of the county. We had placed the deer on the side of a hill on the other side of the road ditch. We had not been there very long when a fellow in a pickup stopped with his headlights illuminating the deer. As we watched, he slowly drove into and through the ditch. At that point, he was only about twenty yards from the stuffed deer. We were thinking he was getting awful close to try to take a shot at the deer. We quickly realized that wasn't his intention when he quickly accelerated and ran over our decoy. We all three just looked at each other in disbelief.

With this driver pulling off the road toward the decoy, I could not help but think the same thing was about to happen. Gene and I crossed the road and positioned ourselves behind the truck as the occupants continued to look at the stationary deer. After a minute, the two young men exited the truck and began to approach the decoy. Using their truck as cover, Gene and I moved in on them and shouted, "Game warden! FREEZE, don't move!" We instructed the two young male subjects to raise their hands and they did so. We moved to them and instructed them to place their hands on the hood of their vehicle. While patting down the passenger, I felt a long, cylindrical object in the left cargo pocket of his pants. I thought the item was a shotgun shell. When I shined my flashlight into the cargo pocket, I did not see a shotgun shell but I did see a plastic bag that contained a green leafy substance that I assumed was marijuana. I told the subject to get down on the ground and I handcuffed him. Although the illegal substance was in the man's pocket, it was in plain view. I stood the man up and read both subjects the Miranda warning from the card I kept in my wallet. I asked the subject his age and he replied he was nineteen. I asked what was in the plastic bag in his pocket and he replied it was marijuana. I reached in his pocket and retrieved two bags of marijuana and found what I thought was a shotgun shell was actually a Tylenol bottle. Fortunately, it actually contained Tylenol! I placed the young man under arrest.

What's in Your Pocket?

While I didn't mind making a drug case, it was really a bummer since we now had to transport the individual to jail, which concluded our decoy detail. I loaded the subject into my pickup and headed toward the Coosa County jail. En route I asked if the brass valve also in his pocket was a pipe used to smoke the marijuana and he advised it was. I began to explain the booking process we would go through at the jail and told the young man he needed to be thinking about who he wanted to call. He told me he would call his father, a sergeant with a nearby county sheriff's office. I placed the man in jail and charged him with possession of marijuana, second degree, and possession of drug paraphernalia. Although we would have much rather caught someone else shooting the decoy, we ended the day having apprehended three road hunters and one dope smoker. It was a fruitful day in which Gene and I wrote eleven tickets. Yep, that was a good day.

Corncrib Hijinks

LIKE ANY TYPE of criminal, wildlife law violators will often go to great lengths to violate the law. I have often thought if they would put forth as much effort to do right as they do to do wrong, they would be exceptional hunters. When the outlaw works hard to violate, the officer has to work just as hard to apprehend the violator. Retired game warden Byron Smith provided me with the details of just such a case.

Byron and his partner had located a corn field pretty much in the middle of nowhere. Their initial thought was the field would be manipulated and utilized as a dove field. I feel safe in saying that several years ago there were more tickets written on opening day of dove season than on any other day of the year. While it was and still is legal to manipulate a standing crop and hunt doves over it, many just couldn't leave well enough alone. Maybe it had to do with the definition or understanding of *manipulate*. If you grew a corn crop, you could come in prior to dove season and mow the corn, scattering it everywhere, and hunt there. One of the few caveats to the rule was you could not remove the crop from the field and then bring it back. Many felt that various fields needed to be "sweetened" with some cracked corn, rock salt, or grain to insure the birds came to the field. Several also thought if a corn field had been mown down, how could any game warden know that more corn had been added. If you would like the answer to that, keep reading.

Byron monitored the isolated corn field and was surprised when it was never cut down. A subsequent trip to the patch revealed the corn had been gathered and placed in a corncrib on the edge of the field. Think about it: you have a corn field in the middle of nowhere. There is no farm, no livestock, no house, or barn anywhere close; and you build a corncrib on the side of the field? Why would you want to leave corn in a crib in the middle of nowhere? If you think like a game warden, the obvious answer is someone planned to continuously put corn on this field and likely hunt over it. Helping to confirm this assumption was the presence of a new shooting house that had been placed on the edge of the field opposite from the crib. These type things are what game wardens call clues. During this time, it was illegal to hunt any game species by the aid of bait. Alabama law 9-11-244 states, in part, "No person at any time shall take, catch, kill, or attempt to take, catch, or kill any bird or animal protected by law or rule of the State of Alabama by means, aid, or use, directly or indirectly, of any bait, such as shelled, shucked, or unshucked corn or of wheat or other grain, salt, or any other feed whatsoever that has been so deposited, placed, distributed, or scattered as to constitute for the birds or animals a lure, attraction, or enticement to, on, or over the area where a hunter or hunters are attempting to kill or take them; provided, that the birds or animals may be taken under properly shocked corn and standing crops of corn, wheat, or other grain or feed and grains scattered solely as a result of normal agricultural harvesting."

Byron contacted his partner, telling him about the crib and shooting house, and they decided another trip to the field was in order. As they checked the field, they noticed it was full of corn stalks but very little corn. With a good idea of what was likely to take place, they moved to the crib and went to work. Having witnessed similar scenarios in the past, the officers knew the difficulty of making the case for hunting by the aid of bait was proving corn had been added or returned to the field. The defendant would always claim the corn present was a direct result of the corn being gathered and was merely incidental.

While pictures of the field with identifiable markers showing the presence and/or absence of corn would normally be sufficient, the officers decided to go a step further. They removed every ear of corn from the crib, marked it with blue magic markers, and placed it back into the crib. Marking hundreds of ears of corn took a couple of hours but both officers figured it would be time well spent.

The second Saturday of the gun deer season, the wardens decided it was time to check the corn field shooting house. They stealthily approached and sure enough there was a man in the house. As was often the case, they were able to walk right up to the structure without the fellow knowing anyone was on the place. They called to the man and had him exit the shooting house. They took his high-powered rifle, unloaded it, and placed it back in the house.

They asked the fellow to accompany them while they looked at the field. The game wardens quickly noticed there were numerous ears of corn on the ground. When they commented about the corn on the ground, the hunter quickly pointed out the corn had grown there and it was legal to hunt over it. It was obvious the hunter was somewhat familiar with the baiting law.

The officers took the opportunity to explain how it was legal if the corn had never left the field. The hunter assured the two officers the corn had not left the field. For good measure, the fellow advised the pair he was an attorney and knew the law well. Hearing this revelation, the officers decided to set the hook just a little deeper. They did not ask the attorney if the corn had ever left the field; instead, they simply reiterated the corn could not be removed from the field and then returned later. The attorney again assured them the corn had not left the field.

Each warden picked up an ear of corn and checked for a blue dot on the end. Sure enough, each ear was marked. They invited the attorney to accompany them over to the nearby crib, where they pointed out that every ear in the crib was marked and had been marked two weeks earlier. The counselor, wearing a look between astonishment and aggravation, was arrested for hunting by the aid of bait.

The case came to court and the counselor was promptly found guilty. To add insult to injury, at the conclusion of the case, the judge commented, "Now that's a good one."

No Headlights and Little Sense

IF YOU HAVE READ many of the accounts of my encounters, you understand by now that people will do just about anything. I have witnessed many things that were hard to believe. Many of these had to do with people just being stupid. I'm not sure who coined the phrase "You can't fix stupid," but I think they knew what they were talking about.

If you spend much time sitting in the dark in the middle of the night, you are liable to see some crazy stuff. I observed this firsthand one night in southern Coosa County. In response to numerous complaints of night hunting of deer, Conservation Enforcement Officer Earl Brown, Wildlife Officer Gene Carver, and I were set up on a dim woods road just off of Coosa County Road 14 about three miles west of US Highway 231 near the Richville community.

It was a good evening for working night hunting in that it was clear and cool with no wind. That meant that we would be able to hear a long way. Unfortunately, it was rare that we would set up in the right spot for someone to shoot right in front of us. This was due in part to the fact that our most common type of night hunting was what we referred to as ditch shooting. Ditch shooting was just what it says: the deer were shot while standing in the road ditch. Forestry was the biggest business in rural Coosa County. There were hundreds of thousands of acres of timberland in the county and few areas of open fields. Therefore, the opportunities to see a deer standing in an open field were relatively few compared to the chance of seeing a deer standing in the ditch. The woods were often thickly planted in pine trees, which kept the sunlight from reaching the forest floor. Therefore, there was a paucity of grasses and forbs, which deer liked to feed on in the wooded areas. Unfortunately, in many areas, the only place the sun could hit the ground and produce food was along the sides of the road. This resulted in a lot of deer standing near the road. The ones that did not run into the road and get hit by vehicles were often shot at by folks who could not resist the temptation of the close shot.

As you can imagine, you could normally see a deer in the ditch at night along almost any road in the county. This meant there were plenty of deer being shot illegally, but we almost had to win the lottery to be in the right place at the right time to apprehend these ne'er-do-wells. Since it was hard to be in the exact right spot, we liked a night when we could hear for a good distance. Not that we would always try to run the shooter down, but that we at least could get an idea of what was going on. While we did sometimes try to locate shooters, it was often difficult to make the case. However, being able to hear vehicles and shots gave us a better idea where to try and set up the next night.

Traffic was light and we heard few vehicles and saw even fewer. However, about 9:00 p.m. we heard a vehicle east of our location moving toward us. During this time, we had so much night hunting taking place we always considered everyone traveling the road at night to be a good prospect.

As we listened to the vehicle advancing, our hopes were somewhat diminished due to the fact the vehicle was traveling at a rate of speed we felt was too fast for someone who was hunting. Of course, we all knew the driver could either apply the brakes or turn around and come back if they were to see a deer on the side of the road.

As we continued to listen, we realized the vehicle was getting really close yet we still had not seen any headlights. Soon the vehicle was right on top of us and still no headlights. We all watched in amazement as the vehicle drove past with no lights whatsoever. It was a moonlit night, but this was still extremely unusual. We all looked at each other and quickly decided we needed to check the vehicle out. Gene and I jumped in the truck and took off in pursuit of the blacked-out truck. While we didn't really intend to write them a ticket for running without lights, we did want to see what they had to say.

As we were catching up to the truck, the driver obviously spotted us in the mirror and turned his headlights on. We activated our blue lights and the vehicle quickly pulled to the side of the road. We observed there were three occupants in the truck. I approached on the passenger side as Gene went up to the driver's window. While we did not know whether these folks were armed, any traffic stop has to be handled as if they are. A common technique on a vehicle stop in the middle of nowhere at night is to have the occupants of the vehicle to show us their hands. Gene and I both were giving the occupants that command. I noticed that while the driver and middle passenger had their hands up above their heads, the passenger-side passenger's hands were not nearly as high. I could see both of his hands and could see they were empty; however, his demeanor told me something wasn't quite right. I asked if they had any weapons and the pregnant-pause response told me they did. I gave the loud verbal command for them to keep their hands up and I opened the passenger's door. At this point, I would not have been surprised if a long gun had fallen out of the truck. I had that occur numerous times. The favorite place for a night hunter to carry their gun was between them and the door. A gun carried there was blocked by the passenger's body and could not be seen by an officer looking in the driver's side window. It could also not be seen by looking in the passenger-side window. In addition, it was handy for the shooter trying to get the gun out the window to shoot.

During the deer season, we expected to see a long gun in everyone's vehicle. Not seeing one, I wasn't sure what these folks had or which one had it. I shined my Maglite flashlight into the truck and must admit I was somewhat shocked at what I saw. The reason the passenger had not raised his arms straight up was that he was keeping his elbow against his chest. That way, the long gun that he had between his legs with the barrel under his chin would not fall out! I had never seen anyone carry a gun in that manner. However, I was about to experience something else I had never seen before and fortunately never saw again.

While I wanted to get control of the gun, I was hesitant to reach and grab a gun the barrel of which was positioned under someone's chin. I would soon be very thankful I did not grab the gun. I told the man to slowly move the gun out from under his chin. He reached and gripped the gun by the forearm and moved it from under his chin. As I reached for the gun, I asked the fellow if it was loaded and he affirmed that it was. I took the gun from him and brought it outside the truck. Our normal procedure was to take a gun back to our vehicle and place it inside until we were finished with the stop. That is if they were going to get it back.

The gun was an old Chinese SKS 7.62 x 39 caliber rifle. While Gene watched the trio, I started back to our truck with the gun. We normally would unload the firearm before putting it in our vehicle. This was a safety precaution. In the event the stop went bad in some way, you did not want there to be an unsecured loaded weapon they could get to. As I got to our truck, I stopped in front of our headlights to unload the weapon. That is when I received another shock. The trigger guard, the curved piece of metal that keeps anything from bumping the trigger, was missing. This means the trigger was unguarded and if it brushed against anything it could go off. This unsafe situation coupled with the man holding the barrel under his chin was totally unnerving.

I actually wondered if the fellow had been thinking of shooting himself. I was also wondering what kind of idiot would ride down the road with no lights on and a loaded gun under their chin. We questioned the trio as to what they were doing and they said they were just riding around using the moonlight to see. When we asked why they brought their rifle, we received the age-old response that they just kept the gun in the truck all the time. Of course, that prompted me to ask the passenger if he always rode with it under his chin. That question did not get a response.

While we felt the group had probably brought the gun to shoot a deer if they saw one, we knew we would be hard pressed to charge them with hunting when they did not possess a handheld light and didn't even have their headlights on. While the answers to our questions left a lot to be desired, we knew the only option we had was to write the driver for driving without headlights. If the law had existed, I would have written the passenger a ticket for being stupid! Of course, as I've said before, if we wrote everyone who did something stupid a ticket, we would probably run out of trees. I know I would have to write myself a few as well. To be honest, when I began my career, it was common practice for us to drive at night without our headlights on. However, we never did that with a gun under our chin!

What about you? Have you ever done anything stupid? If you're honest, you probably will admit that you have. Looking back, I can recall things I did that weren't the smartest. Yet, I survived them. How does that happen? I think it's by the grace of God. I know that in law enforcement, a mistake can cost you your life. We all need to remember that's true no matter what you do. As I mentioned at the start of this story, the largest industry in our county was forestry. That meant that tractor trailer trucks hauling logs traveled our roads every day of the week. I had a good friend that used to say that every time you meet a log truck on the road, you were forty-eight inches from death. While I didn't like thinking about that, I must admit that it crossed my mind thousands of times when meeting log trucks.

The bottom line is that whether we do something stupid that costs us our life or if we live to a ripe old age, if the Lord doesn't return first, we will all die. That's a fact. Jesus afforded us the opportunity of eternal life if we accept Him as our savior. I have chosen to accept that gift. Not accepting it, well, that's just stupid!

He's Been to School
on That Stuff

AS A WILDLIFE BIOLOGIST, I was fortunate in that I had the leeway to set my own work schedule. Now before that sounds great, let me assure you there were many times when my schedule was set for me. As I have often stated, I worked almost every weekend of the deer season for my first seventeen years with the Department of Conservation and most weekends until I retired. Although I worked most days, I was not on a set schedule with set off days. This allowed me to manipulate my schedule for my benefit. Of course, working sixty hours a week much of the time, you still didn't have a lot of leeway. However, one thing I was able to do was attend church almost every Sunday. This was important to me. I was so blessed by God, there was no way I could disregard what he had done for me. This included seeing me through each day and allowing His Son to die in my place. Worshipping regularly was the least I could do. Therefore, I didn't like it when I had to work on Sunday; however, sometimes it was unavoidable.

One Sunday morning as I prepared for church, the phone rang. The caller was my new next-door neighbor, a retired air force pilot. It was obvious he was upset. I had to tell him to slow down and tell me what was wrong. He hurriedly explained he was on his property in Talladega County and had just had an armed encounter with a couple of poachers. I asked if they were still there and he said they had left. After he calmed down, he said he had observed a man with a gun on his property and had gone to confront him. He caught the man, who was carrying a high-powered rifle, near the property line and had asked for his name and informed him he was trespassing. He said the man told him he had better mind his own business. A scrappy sixty-eight-year-old, the retired air force fighter pilot told him since he was on his property, it was his business. The poacher then told him all he had to do was say the word and the man behind the landowner would blow his head off. Although he felt the man was bluffing, he turned around and saw a second man with a rifle pointed at him. This unnerved him and he moved to his truck, retrieved his phone, and called the local game warden. Getting an answering machine, he hurriedly left a message. While he was on the phone, the second man was yelling at him and telling him to tell the game warden it was Robert Burgess. I found this interesting but I wasn't totally surprised.

Robert Burgess was a key member of a group locally known as the Fayetteville Renegades. The renegades were a bunch of redneck good ole boys that felt the law didn't apply to them. Their mantra was they would do whatever they wanted to whenever and wherever they wanted to. Many of the locals were afraid of the bunch, which allowed them to run amok. The rumor was the local game warden was also scared of the bunch and rarely messed with them and even let them know if he was going to be in their area. Now you must understand this kind of rumor circulated all the time and was one of those things you just took with a grain of salt. However, it was interesting Mr. Burgess would scream at the landowner to tell the game warden who it was that was illegally hunting on the property.

I asked my neighbor how long ago this had happened and he said they had been gone for probably fifteen minutes. I told him I would come up there if he wanted me to but I figured everything was over for the day. He concurred and we agreed to meet first thing Monday morning.

Being somewhat familiar with the renegades, I had a good idea about the identity of the first man encountered on the property. I met with my neighbor and asked him to tell me everything that had happened, beginning first thing in the morning. He explained he had traveled up to the property to hunt for a while but had ended up working on the road. He was on a high point and could see a long way across the tract. At around 8:00 a.m., he observed a man walking across his property. He got in his truck and went to the location, cutting the man off from his vehicle that was parked just across the property line. He exited his truck and informed the man he was trespassing. The landowner had not seen the second individual until the first man referred to him. I asked if the second man, Mr. Burgess, was on his property and he said he didn't think he was to start with but he eventually came over to him. He said Burgess had said he would blow his head off and they hunted wherever they wanted to. The pair had then walked over and gotten in a small pickup and driven off. Fortunately, the victim had the presence of mind to make a note of the tag number on the vehicle. A license check revealed my suspicion had been correct. The culprit was the leader of the renegade group.

The fact that anyone would treat a landowner that way on his own property infuriated me. This was compounded by the fact that this landowner was sixty-eight years old, about five feet six, and weighed maybe 140 pounds soaking wet. I told him I felt we should pursue charges of hunting without a permit and menacing on the pair but it would be a good idea to talk with the district attorney (DA) and get his thoughts.

Although I occasionally worked in Talladega County, I was not totally familiar with how the DA liked to do things. The DA had the power to decide whether or not charges would be brought against the individuals so it was a good idea to consult him before going any further. We went to Sylacauga and met with District Attorney Robert Rumsey. Robert was considered one of the best DAs in the state.

I explained to Robert what had occurred and who was involved. He was familiar with the renegades, as he had prosecuted some of them on arson charges in the past. I must admit I was somewhat shocked when the DA told the landowner he had better think it through before signing a warrant on these guys because they were rough customers and might retaliate against him. Looking back, I realize what he was saying was true; however, I was surprised he would not be more aggressive in getting after these guys. I was anxious to see how the veteran would respond after hearing the DAs somber warning. I was encouraged when he looked at the DA and said, "I'm sixty-eight years old and I've never let anybody run over me and I'm not going to start now." Robert said he would have the clerk prepare the warrants.

The pair was arrested on the warrants and the court date was set for the next month. As fate would have it, the court date fell when all of the assistant DAs were gone to a conference at the beach. This meant "the" district attorney would be handling the case. He told me this was the first misdemeanor case he had prosecuted in ten years. That statement, coupled with his reluctance to have the victim sign the warrants, left me a little uneasy about how strong of a prosecution we would get.

The cases were called and the defendants pled not guilty and the judge said we would have a trial. I did not know it at the time, but I was about to see a master at work. The DA called the landowner to the stand. He asked him to tell what had happened and he gave the full story. The DA verified this had occurred in Talladega County and dismissed the witness.

The first defendant was called to the stand and sworn in. The DA went through the preliminaries of having him state his name and so forth and started preparing a trap the unsuspecting violator would soon stick his head in. After several benign questions, Robert asked the man if he had enjoyed much success during the deer season. "Some" was his short reply. "Did you have a chance to hunt very much?" The man replied he had gone a few times. Robert then said, "Of course you might not want to tell me how much you've been hunting since you are a convicted felon and aren't supposed to possess a firearm, isn't that right?" The man looked like he had been slapped in the mouth. He didn't utter a word. Robert again asked, "Isn't that true?" and the man reluctantly said, "Yes." The defendant was more than rattled now. Robert went to work tearing up the man's story. Finally, with the man torn to shreds, Robert mercifully said, "No more questions."

The second defendant was called to the stand and sworn in. Robert wasted little time dismembering the man. When Robert asked the defendant why he was on the landowner's property, the man replied he wasn't on that property. He stated he was on the power line and everybody knew that didn't belong to anybody. This was a widely held belief among many people. I have been told many times that anyone can hunt on a power line right-of-way. Obviously, this is totally inaccurate. The reality is, in most cases, a utility holds an easement for their power line, gas line, and so forth to cross someone's private property. That definitely does not give anyone else permission to hunt on the property.

When Robert realized the man was angling toward the right-of-way defense, he immediately asked the man if he was a registered surveyor. The defendant was sort of dumbfounded by the question but soon answered, "No." The DA asked the man if he was familiar with the plat map of the area that revealed who the landowners were. He again replied, "No." Robert turned to the judge and said he was not interested in where the man thought he was.

He again asked the man why he was on the landowner's property with a rifle. The defendant replied he wasn't on that man's property. Robert immediately said, "Your honor, I object. This man is admittedly not a registered surveyor and has stated he has no knowledge of the landowners in the area. Therefore, I don't want him stating where he thought he was." The judge said, "Sustained." Robert asked the man if he had a permit to be on the Smiths' property and the man replied, "I wasn't on his property." Robert again said, "Your honor, I object. Please instruct this witness to answer the question that was asked." The judge looked at the man and told him he needed to answer the prosecutor's question. The man looked at the judge with the most befuddled look I have ever seen. I must admit, it was somewhat confusing to me that Robert would ask him several times where he was and then would object to him answering; however, I soon realized his tactic had totally destroyed the man's thought process. At this point I don't believe the man could have told the court his mother's name!

Robert asked the man if he had possessed a rifle on the day in question. The man said, "Yes." He asked if he was with the other defendant and he again answered in the affirmative. The DA pointed at the landowner and asked the defendant, "Did you encounter that man?" "Yes," he replied. He then slammed the door on the man when he asked, "Did you tell him to tell the game warden your name?" The defendant hung his head and mumbled, "Yes." The DA asked the judge if he could have the defendant answer loud enough that the court could hear it. The judge instructed the now totally defeated man to answer loudly. The man looked at the judge and said, "I did it, Judge." The DA looked at the judge and said, "The prosecution rests, Your Honor." He then looked over at me and winked. I took it that was his way of saying, "That's how you do it."

The judge took a short recess and then returned with his verdict. He found both defendants guilty on each charge and fined each of them $500 plus court costs in both cases. Never before or since have I seen a case where a district attorney so totally chewed up and spit out a pair of defendants.

Wildlife Officer Gene Carver and I were in the courthouse parking lot when we saw one of the defendants approaching. I didn't know what might be on his mind. The man was still looking confused when he asked us if we had ever seen anything like that. He then said, "That feller has been to school on this stuff." I bit my lip to keep from laughing out loud and told him I didn't think this was that guy's first trial. He agreed with that and turned and made his away across the parking lot to his vehicle.

The landowner never had any repercussions from the cases. However, he did sell the property a couple of years later. Robert Rumsey soon retired and became a defense attorney. He later represented several defendants I had arrested. Although I always joked with him that he had gone over to the dark side, we always enjoyed a good relationship. Toward the end of my career, his son, Ryan, became a district judge in Talladega County and heard several of my cases. I met Robert and Ryan at a social function in Sylacauga and Robert, not knowing I already knew Ryan, introduced me and told his son I was one of the good guys. It meant a lot to know he had a good opinion of me. I must admit he was the best district attorney and defense attorney I ever worked with.

And the Evidence Ran Off

THIS STORY IS IN MEMORY of Wildlife and Freshwater Fisheries Enforcement Section Assistant Chief Michael Pollard. Mike was a true friend and confidant. I always enjoyed being around him and he had some great stories. Cancer took Mike from us much too soon. I still miss him and I think of him often.

Mike began his career with Game & Fish as a conservation enforcement officer (CEO) in Chambers County. Chambers County lies in east-central Alabama, bordering Georgia. It is over six hundred square miles in size, fairly rural, and blessed with good wildlife populations. Those attributes add up to a good amount of hunting activity and if you have a lot of hunting activity, it's a good bet that plenty of it will be illegal.

When Mike began working with us, he was partnered with a seasoned officer who was a pretty funny guy. Mike did not start from scratch; he had served as a county deputy prior to starting with us. I remember meeting with Mike one day early in his career and he was totally frustrated that he was not having what he felt was enough success in making cases. The situation was exacerbated by the fact that his partner was making numerous cases. In frustration, Mike told me he could bust his rear end all week and make three cases and his partner could sit at the truck stop and make six! While that sounds like an exaggeration and may have been, it wasn't necessarily untrue. Once an officer is established in a county and has made significant contacts, cases often will flow to them. I tried to ease Mike's mind and tell him things would turn around.

Although most officers have their hands full trying to cover their own county, it is not at all unusual for officers to work across county lines with other officers from time to time. Retired CEO Byron Smith was working in Macon County when Mike had started work with us. He told me about a night patrol with Mike that was pretty interesting. The duo were in Macon County, where night hunting was prevalent. They had heard a shot and were trying to access the area where they thought it had come from. Mike was driving Byron's car. Yes, the vehicle he had been assigned was a 1990 model Caprice Classic. Just what was needed to work the wilds of Macon County—not! They took the car down a woods road they thought would bring them out to where the hunters were. However, after they had pulled down the road, they realized they could not access the property and would have to back out and go around to the next road. Not wanting to be seen by the violators, Byron told Mike to turn off the back-up lights before he put the vehicle in reverse.

Turning off the back-up lights likely needs a little explanation. Years ago, as soon as an officer got a new vehicle, one of the first things that was done was to install a set of switches to control the lights on the vehicle. Normally, there would be a switch installed to turn off the brake lights, a switch to turn off the back-up lights, and a switch to turn on a running light, which most would place on the front bumper or in the grill. These switches and lights were necessary when you did not want a suspected violator to see that you were on the brakes or backing up. During this time, it was not at all unusual for us to drive at night without using any headlights. This method was often employed when following a possible night hunter. Utilizing the small running light on the bumper, you could follow a vehicle without being seen. While this method resulted in numerous arrests, it was also incredibly dangerous. Therefore, midway through my career, the department put a stop to it by adopting a policy that forbade the practice.

As I said, Byron told Mike to flip the switch beneath the dash and turn off the back-up lights before putting the car in reverse. Mike quickly located the switch and flipped it. You can imagine his surprise when the siren began blaring. Obviously, that wasn't the right switch! So much for sneaking up on some night hunters!

Mike shared an interesting case with me. He said he was working in the Buffalo community of Chambers County, where he had received numerous night hunting complaints. He had located a likely looking spot with some green grass under a thin stand of trees. Fortunately, there was a woods road directly across from the area where he could sit in his truck and observe the grassy area and the road in both directions.

Around 10 p.m., Mike slipped into the lookout spot and began his vigil. He said there wasn't a lot of traffic. Around midnight, he noticed a slow-moving pickup coming his way. The vehicle slowed to a stop and the driver lit up the area with a spotlight he held over the cab of the truck. The light settled on a young buck standing in the grass. A shot from the passenger split the night and the deer dropped. Although his first instinct was to crank his vehicle and pull out into the road, he hesitated for just a few seconds. It was just long enough for the driver to turn the trucks headlights off. Not sure what was going to happen, the officer sat tight. As he watched, the two occupants exited the truck carrying a flashlight and headed toward the deer.

The pair quickly dragged the deer to the truck. They dropped the tailgate and lifted the deer into the bed of the truck. As they slammed the tailgate shut, Mike started his vehicle and pulled in behind the truck with his blue light flashing. He approached the truck and retrieved the men's firearm and secured it in his vehicle. He gathered the men's driver's licenses and advised them they were under arrest. He returned to his truck and began writing the tickets.

As he was starting on the second ticket, some motion from the truck caught his attention. He looked up and was startled to see the deer standing in the bed of the truck. As he watched, the young buck jumped out of the truck and ran off into the woods. He said he had never had his evidence run off before!

As I mentioned earlier, a good deer population coupled with a rural landscape was a good recipe for widespread night hunting. Another contributing factor was the fact that the main highway through the county was a well-used route for people traveling to south Alabama to hunt. Of course, saying they were traveling to south Alabama to hunt was a bit of a misnomer. I should say it was a well-used route for folks who wanted to hunt their way through the state.

Like myself, Mike was blessed with a good conservation-minded judge. In my opinion, one of the worst things that can befall a game warden is to be assigned to a county where the district judge doesn't take conservation laws and regulations seriously. Unfortunately, there are many of those counties in Alabama. Think about it. You may have worked for years to catch a perpetual outlaw and finally you were in the right place at the right time and made the apprehension. Some cases literally took years to make! You haul the scoundrel into court only to have the judge slap him on the wrist or even worse let him go with not even a stern talking to. Situations like that make officers reconsider whether or not they need to be out there. If anything ever got my dander up, that was it. Judges like that made me want to hug the neck of the good judges.

Mike related to me a great story about his judge in Chambers County. It seemed that Chambers was much like Coosa County in that as you traveled southward through the eastern side of the state in the 1990s, it was the first county that held a significant number of deer. Unfortunately, that meant it was a hotspot for night hunting by folks traveling to south Alabama to hunt. Highway 431 was a true night hunting thoroughfare.

Mike explained to me how he had received some information about a fellow who was traveling the road on a regular basis, shooting every deer he saw. Mike and other officers were putting forth a lot of effort to catch the culprit; however, it was proving difficult. Hunting season is a battle against the clock for the game warden. There simply were not enough hours in the work week. You could not work hunting all day and all night seven days a week, although sometimes you desperately needed to! However, every once in a while, the Lord would smile on you and you would be in the right place at the right time. Such was the case for Mike and the Highway 431 night stalker.

When you have multiple areas where deer routinely feed alongside the road, it is just a guessing game as to where you need to set up on any given night. Every officer working has likely heard a shot in the night and said to themselves they knew that was where they should have been.

Fortunately, on this night, Mike had set up in the right spot. He observed as the driver, the only occupant of the vehicle, had maneuvered his pickup so the headlights illuminated the young buck standing near the wood line. A shot split the night and the deer immediately dropped. This night there was no hesitation. Before the violator knew what was happening, Mike was pulling the man out of the truck. Finally, this perpetual night hunter had been apprehended.

The court date rolled around and the defendant was in the courtroom. As the judge worked through the long docket, the defendant sat in the courtroom, growing more antsy. Watching the judge adjudicate cases, the night hunter turned to his friend and stated, "I wish that old son of a gun would have a heart attack and die before my case comes up." Unbeknownst to the rogue, a friend of the judge was within earshot. Soon the judge took a short recess. His friend went to him and told him what the lawbreaker had said.

The judge soon returned to the bench and placed the court back in session. He continued to work through the docket, eventually reaching the night hunting cases. The judge called the case and the defendant approached the bench. A nod from the judge's friend let him know he was dealing with the man who did not have his best interest at heart. Have you ever had an instance where you said you wished you had a picture of someone's face? I say that a lot. Well, according to Mike, this was definitely one of those times.

The judge dismissed the formalities of reading the charges or asking the defendant how he would plead. Instead, he looked at the man and snarled, "I understand you were hoping I would have a heart attack and die before you made it up here." Mike said the defendant was dumbfounded. However, the man's face had yet to reach the expression for the ultimate photo. That look came when the judge said, "I ought to come down off this bench and whip your *#&!" Mike said he just thought the guy was dumbfounded previously. He was now in a deep state of disbelief. The man was having a difficult time comprehending that this senior citizen was telling him he should wipe the floor with him. The judge was not finished. He went on to say, "That is what I ought to do, but I'm not going to do that. What I am going to do is hear your case, and if you are found guilty, I will sentence you accordingly!" The judge looked at the officer and asked, "Was this man night hunting?" The officer answered, "He was, Your Honor." Mike said he quickly gave the judge the facts of the case. In a tone that was definitely understandable, the judge asked if the defendant had anything he wanted to say. The dumbfounded violator shook his head no. Without any further testimony, the judge pronounced the man guilty as charged and moved directly to the sentencing phase. Suffice it to say, the fine was the maximum and the man had ample opportunity to experience the ambience of the county jail. Yep, I sure loved a good judge!

While I was humbled to receive many awards and accolades during my career, one thing I truly appreciated was a letter from Mike. The two veteran officers in my county retired within about a year of each other. This left our county without an experienced game warden. While I was a conservation officer, since I was in the wildlife section, my priority was managing the 38,000-acre Coosa Wildlife Management Area and performing wildlife biologist duties in twelve counties. Fortunately, I had worked closely with the game wardens and knew how to fill that role. I put forth a tremendous amount of effort to meet the needs of the people of the county while we were shorthanded. Mike sent me a letter acknowledging that and it truly meant a lot.

Mike told me he couldn't believe it when the deer that was dead suddenly came back to life. That is pretty hard to believe. Obviously, the deer wasn't really dead. However, there is a story about a man who died and came back to life three days later. It's a unique story. His name is Jesus and he was sent to earth so that we could have eternal life. He said if we will admit we are a sinner, believe He came to save us, and confess Him as our savior, we too can spend eternity in heaven. It's a choice that needs to be made now. Mike was planning what he would do in retirement when his cancer was diagnosed. He left us way too soon. Cancer is cruel.

It was my good fortune to have Mike as a friend. I look forward to reminiscing with him when we meet again in heaven. I'm sure there's more good stories we will be able to share.

You Know Who It Is

I ASSUME MOST conservation enforcement officers (CEOs) utilized the deer decoy much like I did and that was to catch people who were shooting from the road both day and night. However, that was not the only cases that were aided by the use of the stuffed wonder. CEO Byron Smith relayed to me a tale about how he used the decoy to apprehend a retired law enforcement officer who had bragged he would never be caught.

In the county where Byron was last assigned, there was a wealthy landowner whose property was known to be home to several large white-tailed bucks. The area was a large property that bordered the Tallapoosa River and even encompassed a large island. It was professionally managed and had a full-time caretaker. Like many large landowners, this landowner was always interested in purchasing any property that bordered his. To that end, he was able to acquire a property that another neighbor had wanted, which aggravated the other landowner to no end. Evidently, the ticked-off landowner, a retired investigator, decided he would get back at the landowner by illegally killing the big deer on his property and leaving them to rot. When this type of revenge takes place, the game warden often gets involved.

Byron had received a couple of calls from the caretaker concerning dead deer; however, by the time he had located them, they were of no use as evidence. However, the caretaker did note that there had been some corn poured out where the deer had been killed. Byron told the caretaker to let him know if he located any corn on the property. As with many outlaws, the fellow who was killing the deer didn't think it was enough just to kill the deer, but he wanted the wealthy landowner to know he was the one doing it. When someone he had told about his deeds asked if he wasn't afraid the game warden would catch him, he commented he would kill the game warden if he tried to apprehend him. Fortunately, the fellow who overheard the statement was a friend of law enforcement and contacted our officer. That kind of statement does get our attention.

A few days later Byron received a call from the caretaker stating he had found some corn on the property. Byron made his way to the property and met the caretaker. Unfortunately, the corn had been there for a while and was of little value. However, two days later, Byron received another call from a very excited caretaker who had found a really fresh pile of corn. Byron again returned to the site and verified the corn was indeed fresh. A quick canvass of the area revealed something much more exciting, at least for the officer. Approximately fifty yards from the pile of corn was a shooting bench. A poacher setting up a shooting bench was unusual. It was obvious the poacher wanted to make a good shot. Of course, that was somewhat ironic in that he was leaving the deer where they fell. So, one might wonder why he was evidently worried about making a good shot. Let me tell you, I learned a long time ago that you can't get inside some of these folks' heads!

Byron theorized the fellow wanted to be sure the landowner knew his deer were being killed. If he just shot deer at random and they ran off and died, the landowner may not have ever known it. However, by dropping the deer in the areas where he

301

felt certain the caretaker would find them, he knew the word would get back to the landowner. Byron thought if he could stand a decoy at the corn pile, the poacher would probably shoot it. However, the poacher was evidently doing his best to shoot the big deer the property was known for and Byron wasn't sure whether or not he would shoot a small buck. Furthermore, he knew the longer the look the violator got at the decoy the higher the odds he would realize it wasn't a live deer. Therefore, he decided to request permission to use a decoy with a larger set of antlers than what the policy allowed.

As I have discussed in several stories, a very common question about using the decoy was whether it constituted entrapment. The answer was no; however, to ensure we were not enticing people to do something they ordinarily wouldn't, we were required to use a small set of antlers on the decoy. I think it stands to reason that if you put a record-book deer on the side of the road, more people would shoot it than if you used a small six point. Of course, some folks would shoot whatever would stand there long enough! I am reminded of the fellow that shot my decoy with the dinky little three-point rack. He told me when he saw it, he could see those antlers on his wall. I thought to myself he must not have much wall space!

Byron made the request to use a larger rack on the decoy and it was quickly denied. The officer returned and met with the landowner and caretaker and advised them his request to use a large rack had been denied. The landowner asked why and he told him he wasn't sure. The landowner left and Byron and the caretaker discussed when they thought the fellow might be hunting the property. The caretaker said he thought the poacher was shooting the deer on Mondays because he knew people were on the property during the weekend. Byron agreed that was probably the case. As he was preparing to leave, he received a radio call from Montgomery telling him his decoy request had been approved. Although he wasn't sure what had occurred, he thought he had a pretty good idea.

Once he reached a phone—this was before everyone had a cell phone—he called the office and inquired as to the change of heart. He was informed that although he had explained the situation initially, they had not understood this was going to be confined to the landowner's property and could not be viewed by the public at large. From that explanation, he felt the landowner was probably the more important part.

Having received the go ahead from the Montgomery office, Byron went to work altering a decoy to make it fit the situation. Monday morning before daylight, Byron met the caretaker and they headed into the property. Since the violator lived adjacent to the property, the best way for Byron to avoid detection was to enter the property by boat. He met the caretaker at the boat launch and they headed for the location. Byron stood the decoy with the large ten-point rack with its front feet in the pile of corn. The deer was broadside to the shooting bench. He advised the caretaker he was prepared to stay all day and would contact him by radio when he needed him to come back and pick him up.

Byron was in full camo and took up a position hidden in the vegetation behind the shooting bench with his Remington 870 shotgun. It was a long wait. At four in the afternoon, the officer heard a familiar sound. He identified it as a chain rattle, the type of noise a chain that has been removed from around a post and dropped makes. Of course, this put him on high alert.

As he strained to hear, he next heard what he identified as someone driving slowly on gravel. Even someone being careful while walking on gravel still can generate enough noise that the trained ear can detect it. That sound quickly vanished and for the next fifteen minutes the officer did not hear anything.

Straining to hear, Byron began to hear a slight rustling in the grass. As he looked toward the sound, he observed a man belly crawling through the grass with a rifle cradled in the crook of his arms. The man was steadily working his way toward the shooting bench.

When he reached the shooting perch, he slowly slid the rifle up and rested it on the bench. He then slowly eased up behind the gun. He immediately spotted the large buck. He got the rifle to his shoulder. The poacher wasn't the only one that had been stealthily moving and Byron was close enough that he heard it when the poacher clicked the gun's safety off. Knowing he had seen enough, Byron gave the verbal command for the man not to move. The poacher replied, "Who is it?" And Byron replied, "You know who it is. It's Byron Smith, the state game warden, the man you said you would kill if he tried to apprehend you." He told the man to place the gun on the bench and to raise his hands. He slowly did so. The officer told the man to lie on his face and he complied. He then asked the man where his handgun was. He replied, "I don't have one." Byron reminded him there was no one else there. The man thought about that statement for a few seconds and said the pistol was in his right rear pocket. Byron dropped his handcuffs on the man's back and told him to put them on. The man replied he couldn't do that and the officer told him he better figure it out in a hurry. The man asked, "Why are you being so hard on me?" and the officer replied, "This is how I treat everyone who tells folks that if I try to arrest them, they will kill me." Getting the point, the outlaw put the cuffs on. Byron removed the handgun from the man's pocket and told the man to maintain his face-down position. Byron contacted the caretaker and asked him to come and pick them up. He arrived shortly thereafter. Byron escorted the violator to the boat. The man told him he would not get in the boat handcuffed because if he fell in the water he would drown. The officer told him he better not fall in the water. The man climbed in the boat. A deputy was contacted and met them at the launch and transported the man to the jail.

I have always found it interesting how some folks act when interacting with law enforcement. For many, it seems they feel any encounter is an opportunity for them to be belligerent. I used to think maybe that was because they knew they were in the wrong and would likely be receiving a ticket so they thought they would at least get the satisfaction of telling the officer just what they thought about them. Through the years this has changed and recently it has taken a significant turn for the worse. Today you have many individuals who believe law enforcement should not even exist. Unfortunately, this sets the stage for bad encounters.

Being belligerent in the field is one thing; however, when that comes into the courtroom, it can get quite interesting. I have been in court with many different judges and I don't remember any of them who would tolerate an individual with an obstinate attitude. I can't remember anyone taking such a stance and it benefiting them. That was about to play out once again.

Courts and judges vary greatly. I have been before judges who wanted to hear the minimum amount of info needed and I've been before judges who wanted you to tell them every detail of what took place. In a case like this one, there were facts that were not necessarily part of the case; however, they still needed to be made known. While the defendant had not been afforded the opportunity to display his disdain for the officer during the arrest, he had done so before and after the fact. He evidently thought the courtroom would be a good place to condemn the officer for his unreasonable actions during the arrest.

The district judge called the case and the officer and defendant approached the bench. The judge asked Byron why he had arrested the man and he laid out the case, including that the defendant had stated he would kill him if he attempted to arrest him. He explained what had occurred on the day of the incident, which led to the man's arrest on charges of hunting without a permit, hunting by the aid of bait, and hunting without wearing hunter orange. When the judge asked the defendant if he had any questions for the officer, his smart-aleck attitude was on display. While he didn't offer a defense, he told the judge that the officer had no call to treat him like he did. The judge countered that anyone who threatens an officer should be treated accordingly. She made it clear she would not tolerate that type of behavior and found the man guilty. Her disdain for the violator was reflected in the fine she levied. She charged the man $3,000 and ordered him to serve six months in jail for hunting without a permit. The bait charge garnered a $500 fine and the no-orange violation cost the defendant another $50. The defendant asked the judge when he would get his gun back. The judge asked Byron if the statute allowed her to take the man's rifle and he told her that unfortunately it did not. She told the defendant that he could get his gun back after he served his six months in jail. She added that the officer would keep the weapon and use it if needed until such time it was to be given back.

Anyone familiar with district court probably understands that this type of ruling is unusual. While I feel certain the ruling was made to get the defendant's attention and to send a message to those who break the law and threaten the officers who attempt to apprehend them, it was unfortunately outside the guidelines of what the law allowed. Therefore, when the defendant appealed the sentence to circuit court, it was reduced. The man actually served only ten days in jail. However, that is ten days more than anyone else who is convicted of hunting without permission normally serves. Evidently ten days behind bars was enough for the former law enforcement officer to decide he would no longer violate game and fish laws and regulations since Byron never received another complaint about him!

Double Team

ONE THING YOU LEARN fairly quickly when working for a game and fish agency is it seems the majority of the hunting public not only think you don't know how to manage fish or wildlife, they think they do know how.

It was interesting to me how most hunters considered themselves to be experts when it came to wildlife management. It really didn't matter whether you were talking about white-tailed deer, wild turkey, or coyotes, most hunters believed they knew a lot more about it than those who were attempting to manage the species. I vividly remember giving a talk to the largest hunting club in the county. The topic was deer management and the newly implemented deer management assistance program, or DMP. DMP began in Alabama in 1986. In a nutshell, it was an effort to better manage the deer population in the state. The primary tool used in the program was antlerless deer tags. Up until that time, we had "managed" our deer herd primarily by killing as many bucks as possible. Our limit was one buck per day of our three-month-long season. It was not at all uncommon for folks to kill eight or ten bucks each year. Killing antlerless deer was taboo. They were only killed by bowhunters or hunters who would stoop so low as to kill a doe during the antlerless season, or "doe days," as they were often referred to. The length of the antlerless season varied across the state, with some areas having a couple of days and some having a whole week! Of course, this type of management had resulted in an extremely out of balance sex ratio and deer in many areas of the state being in very poor condition.

When I arrived on the Coosa Wildlife Management Area in 1987, I learned the average live weight of a 1.5-year-old buck was a whopping seventy-seven pounds. It should have weighed one hundred pounds. This was not an isolated situation. The DMP offered hunters and landowners the opportunity to actually manage the deer herd on their property with the assistance of a wildlife biologist.

Although many areas in the country today have too many deer, that obviously hasn't always been the case. I remember very well growing up in northwest Alabama when anyone spotting a deer anywhere other than on the state wildlife management area was very newsworthy. I often made the nearly one-hundred-mile round trip to the Lauderdale Wildlife Management Area to hunt deer since there were none where I lived. Today, that is not the case. Let me say that when the deer population was low, it was a wise decision not to harvest antlerless deer. Believe me when I tell you that idea was deeply ingrained in many hunters. I learned quickly that it was difficult to change the mindset. Even though "doe days" were few and far between, most hunters had little desire to shoot a doe.

As you might imagine, the DMP wasn't always an easy sell. Many folks believed things were great the way they were. Granted you saw plenty of deer and every once in a while, a buck would somehow survive to three years of age and would produce a decent rack. However, many folks were ready for a change. Unfortunately, most hunting clubs had members who held strong opinions both for and against the antlerless harvest, which made it difficult.

While many folks were against the idea, many others embraced the program. Human nature took hold and many that were not in the program began to feel slighted, which resulted in many more sign-ups. During the height of the DMP program, I was working with eighty deer clubs across twelve counties.

A couple of years into my career, I got a call from my supervisor saying the largest club in our county had expressed interest in the program and I needed to go and explain the process to them. I was not overjoyed. While I didn't mind talking with any group, I felt certain my reception would be rather cool. I met with the group and gave a short presentation describing the DMP and then took a deep breath and opened the floor up for questions. I had anticipated the first question would be how many antlerless deer I thought the club should kill and I didn't think my answer would go over very well. Lo and behold, I was right on both fronts. I prefaced my answer by telling the group that the first year would provide the data that would allow me to analyze the condition of the deer herd and therefore make a better recommendation. I had looked at the data they had kept on their harvest and although it was far from complete, it did indicate they significantly overharvested the buck population while taking only a handful of does each year. The weights of the bucks taken appeared to be about 25 percent below optimum and the majority appeared to likely be 1.5 years old. After pointing out these things, I told the group I didn't think it would hurt their population to kill a hundred does. The corresponding silence was deafening. I filled the void by reminding the folks they were hunting fifteen thousand acres and a hundred deer wasn't a tremendous amount. Of course, they did not agree with that analysis.

Once again, I was about to learn that my six years of college had been for nothing since one of the club's elder members knew exactly what their problem was. Mr. Reed Vance was one of the oldest of the nearly 150 members of the club. He took great exception with my contention the reason for the small body size and antlers of their deer herd was a result of a nonexistent doe harvest. Although their herd possessed classic indicators of overpopulation, some of the older members would not accept that an increased doe harvest and reduced harvest of young bucks was necessary. Mr. Vance addressed the group and totally dismissed everything I had said. He then informed the group that he had raised cows for many years and he knew that the problem with their deer herd was inbreeding. I attempted to tactfully explain that inbreeding was normally not a problem in a wild, free-ranging deer herd; however, he would hear nothing of it. I must admit it was difficult not to tell the group where I thought the inbreeding problem was!

The club did enter the program and did increase their antlerless harvest. A few years later, I again addressed the group. This time they were upset that they weren't seeing as many deer as they had in the past. I explained that was something that was to be expected. I looked at their deer data and saw that the first doe harvested that season had weighed 127 pounds. I asked the group when the last time was they had killed a doe that big. All I heard was crickets. I was encouraged that before I left, several club members did approach me privately and told me they were seeing good results from the program.

Fast forward a few years. "Well, you've got it all fixed up now, don't you?" That wasn't the nicest greeting I had ever received but also wasn't the worst. I had just walked into a local convenience store and encountered Mr. Vance from the hunting club. I wasn't sure what he was referring to but had the suspicion he would let me know very soon. I would not be telling the truth if I did not tell you that I normally took notice of what trucks were in the store parking lot and often just kept driving to avoid a confrontation. Unfortunately, this day I wasn't as observant as I should have been.

The game warden is known by virtually everyone in the county and although I was actually a wildlife biologist, seeing how I had enforcement authority and made arrests throughout the county, everyone considered me a game warden. It was not at all unusual for folks to treat us with disdain or contempt. They often thought of us as a villain or killjoy. In addition, we made a great scapegoat. Whether the problem is small deer, too few rabbits, or a stop sign where a yield would be better, we often received the credit. Yes, we were often blamed for a little of everything!

"What have I fixed for you now," I asked. He quickly responded not only had I got the season opened to kill all the does but I had also outlawed buckshot. The fact neither of these two claims was accurate was obviously totally irrelevant. What he was referring to was the hunting club had decided to participate in the deer management program and my recommendation was to take one hundred does. While that was a tremendous increase, it wasn't a heavy harvest when you considered the club had fifteen thousand acres! However, to someone who thought no does should be killed, recommending the harvest of one hundred surely meant every doe would be killed!

To further infuriate the man, the conservation advisory board had implemented a new dog deer-hunting permit system and a new regulation forbidding deer hunters in stalk hunting areas from using buckshot. It did not prohibit dog clubs from using buckshot. I realized the man had misinterpreted what the new regulation said when he nearly screamed, "People my age need to be able to shoot buckshot!" I responded, "You still can." However, it was as if I hadn't said a word. It was obvious he didn't want to be confused with the facts.

Much like umpire bashing, warden bashing is often a spectator sport where bystanders feel obligated to put their two cents' worth in. This was the case on the day I walked into the store and was confronted by the angry dog deer hunter. As if I didn't have my hands full, my nemesis was about to receive reinforcement. Another of my "fans" waddled up and, seeing what was going on, thought it would be a good time to pile on. The fellow's name was L. C. Gentry. L. C. was a member of the same hunting club. I was familiar with his family, seeing how his brother had threatened to bushwhack (kill) me. Later I would become more familiar with the group after arresting his son several times.

With his newfound cohort, Mr. Vance started in about how if I had my way, we would kill every deer there was and how we didn't have enough deer to shoot a bunch of does. Having already been through this with him and the other 150 members, I didn't really feel like rehashing it now. At that point, L. C. decided it was time for him to jump in and he did by saying, "Yeah, have you ever tried to have a garden in Coosa County?" I must admit it took me a minute to understand what exactly he was trying to say since it appeared to be just the opposite of what Mr. Vance was saying. "What did you say?" I asked and he said he couldn't have a garden for the deer eating it all. I said, "Whoa, wait just a minute." I looked at Mr. Vance and said, "You are saying we don't have any deer left and he is saying we have so many deer he can't raise a garden. Now it can't be both ways." I looked at L. C. and said, "It sounds like to me you are saying we need to shoot some does."

He thought for a minute and replied, "It's just bucks eating in my garden!" At that, I literally laughed out loud. I turned to Mr. Vance and told him as far as the buckshot was concerned, anyone with a dog hunting permit or on their own property could still use buckshot. Feeling I had thoroughly decimated their arguments and ruined their fun, I turned and left the store. Man, it felt good to win one every once in a while.

Each man in this case was wrong. Mr. Vance was wrong in thinking the club members shouldn't kill any does on their property. While my recommendation to take one hundred does was many more than they had ever taken before, they could have taken two to three times that many. However, taking does was something they had never done before and they were afraid of it.

The permit system was an effort to try to get a handle on renegade dog hunters. The clubs had to provide maps of their property and a list of members. It was relatively painless and actually worked to the betterment of the club. The system was later adopted for use in several counties. It had no effect whatsoever on Mr. Vance's ability to hunt with buckshot.

It was true it was difficult to have a garden in our county due to deer depredation. However, I had not been aware there were areas where only bucks ate in the gardens. Mr. Gentry had been caught trying to add to my grief and had made himself look foolish.

The other man in the episode, myself, was also in the wrong when he took pride in belittling and embarrassing the others. Sure, they brought it on themselves; however, I took a little too much pleasure in dishing it out.

What did I learn from this? One should be quick to listen and slow to speak. Don't be afraid of something new; just because we've never done it like that before doesn't mean it's wrong. After thirty-five years of wildlife management and law enforcement, I realize I don't know everything. However, I have seen and heard a lot. I know that!

And His Pants Fell Down

HIGHWAY 259 in far east Coosa County was a consistent producer of night hunting complaints and many arrests. This was due in part to the fact the road was sparsely populated. Of course, the primary reason was there were always deer standing alongside the road. While we often used the decoy in various places along the roadway, we would often simply find some deer alongside the road and sit up close by. That was the technique I was employing one cold winter night when I witnessed an "interesting" event.

One reason the decoy was so beneficial was it often allowed you to witness the violation taking place. Making a case for night hunting when you did not actually observe it required a lot more effort. While the decoy afforded several advantages, there was a problem associated with it. If you were working alone, which wasn't wise but often necessary, you ran the risk of having your decoy stolen while you were running down the vehicle of the person who had shot it. While I fortunately never had that happen, it occurred in other counties. Therefore, when working alone, we often did not use the decoy.

Let me explain that a violation occurring in your presence did not mean that you had to see the incident, you could also hear it. We were often fortunate in that we could testify that there were no other vehicles on the road when we heard a shot and we stopped a vehicle. This became much more difficult when the hunting moved from the rural areas to the main highways.

I learned early on that the older officers were normally very reluctant to move toward a shot. Their philosophy was you should always let the violator come to you. They felt that by moving you were more likely to be spotted by the violator and it was much harder to prove they had shot and so forth. While I understood their thinking, I often found it very difficult to sit tight after hearing a nearby shot. This was especially true when I knew the area well and felt certain I knew where the shot had come from.

When you were working alone and heard a shot that you tried to run down, when you encountered a vehicle you would often have to establish some probable cause before you could legally initiate a stop. This probable cause would sometimes be challenged in court. This meant you had to be able to articulate to the court why you had the authority to stop the vehicle. If I could state that based on my observation and hearing, they were the only vehicle on the road in the area, that was normally sufficient. To be able to truthfully state that meant you had to have an intimate knowledge of the road system and what was happening at the time. Many times, I would stop a vehicle from which I believed a shot had just been fired and the driver would swear up and down they had just met another vehicle on the road and that must be where the shot came from. This was another reason why it was imperative that if there were multiple people in the vehicle, you immediately separated them. With them separated, it was extremely difficult for each of them to give you the same story. When one would tell me they had just met a vehicle, I would ask them to describe it. Then if another occupant said they had met a vehicle, I would get their description. They rarely ever matched. Their conflicting stories made my position stronger. However, in most cases, I knew there was not another vehicle on the roadway. I knew this because theirs was the only vehicle I had heard, no vehicle had passed my location, and there were no other roads that another vehicle could have come off of. Although I normally already knew all of that, when you got their stories and then pointed out how different they were, you often would end up with a confession. Believe me, a written confession was a great asset. However, more than once I have had someone give me a confession and come to court and plead not guilty! Go figure.

It was after 10 p.m. and the traffic had slowed to a trickle. All was quiet until it wasn't. A shot from a high-powered rifle split the calm night. It was south of my location and close. At that point, I faced the decision I faced many times. Sit tight or go and try to find it. I quickly analyzed the situation. Since the vehicle had not passed by me, it was most likely headed toward me. Of course, if they had shot a deer, they could load it up and go back the way they had come and I would never see them. Fortunately, as I was deciding I needed to move toward the shot, my decision was made for me when I saw headlights coming my way. Interestingly, I did not hear a vehicle. Even when the small car passed my location, I still could barely hear it.

I pulled out behind the vehicle and activated my blue lights. The driver immediately pulled two tires off the side of the road and stopped. I knew I had I did not have a lot to go on. The car had two occupants. As I shined my flashlight in the vehicle, I gave the command for them to put their hands up. When I got to where I could see inside the small car, I observed a high-powered rifle between the driver's seat and the console and another long gun in the rear seat of the car. I also was able to see that the driver appeared to be a man probably thirty-five years old and the passenger was a kid maybe ten or twelve years old. I told the man to leave the gun where it was and get out of the car.

The man got out and I told him to place his hands on the top of

317

the car. I asked if he had any weapons on him and he stated he did not. Of course, having been lied to by several folks who claimed not to have a weapon but did, I was still going to pat the man down. Just as I was reaching to do that, the man's pants fell down to his ankles. Of course, he immediately started to grab his pants; however, I immediately told him to keep his hands on the roof. As fate would have it, just at that time another vehicle came rolling by. Although I wasn't thinking about it at the time, later I couldn't help but laugh as I wondered what the people thought seeing the man draped over the top of his car with his pants down around his ankles!

At this point it was obvious he did not possess any other weapons and I told him he could secure his pants. I then employed a technique I had learned over time. I did not ask him what had occurred, I simply began explaining that he was under arrest for hunting at night. As I reached in the car and retrieved the rifle from the front seat, for both of our safety, I asked if the gun was still loaded. He advised it was. I told him to step around behind his vehicle while I unloaded the gun and placed it in my vehicle.

I decided I would go ahead and read the man his rights and proceed as if everything was a done deal and hope he would just give it up. I walked back to him and asked his name. He said he was Johnny McGee and that he had screwed up. I was sure glad to hear him say that. I did not say anything, I just gave him my "Tell me about it" look. It worked like a charm.

"I can't believe I did that and my brother is going to kill me" was his first spontaneous exclamation. I learned early on if folks would talk, let them talk. "Who all has to know about this?" That was a question I would be asked many times in my career. The guy went on to say that I might know his brother, who was somewhat of a hunting celebrity. He gave me his name and I was vaguely familiar with him. He continued saying that the kid in the car was his brother's son and his brother was going to kill him if he found

318

out he had shot at a deer with the boy in the car. I was fighting to keep the grin off my face, knowing this guy had basically confessed without me asking him anything. The man again asked if his brother had to know about this and I told him that although it would be a matter of public record, it was not my habit to spread it around. I told the man to listen as I read him the Miranda warning. I said for him to tell what all happened.

He explained he and the boy had hunted all day in south Alabama without having any luck and were on their way home. He had spotted a small buck standing beside the road and had foolishly shot at it. He went on to say he missed the deer and the next thing he knew I was behind him with the blue lights flashing. He then again requested that his brother not know about this. I told him that I would get his tickets turned in at the first of the week and he either needed to contact the judge or be in court the next month. As I was returning home, I remembered hearing in a seminar at some time that many wildlife law violators witnessed their first violation by the time they were eleven years old. I couldn't help but think this kid might be on that path.

I never heard whether or not his brother found out about the incident; however, there are at least two reasons that I feel certain he did. First, I have not found twelve-year-old kids to be that good at keeping secrets. Second, during my career when someone desperately did not want anyone to hear about their arrest, I normally heard about it from someone before I even got the tickets turned in. I guess I could say good news travels fast but that likely depends on whose perspective you are viewing it from. Of course, the news of the game warden holding the man on the side of the road with his pants down around his ankles probably spread pretty fast as well.

Jeff Trips the Trap

I HAD NEVER had anything like this occur and hoped it never happened again. I wasn't sure whether to bring attention to my embarrassing situation or just let the loose ends drag.

Giving talks and presentations was a major part of my career, especially in the latter years. I spoke to many diverse groups, including elementary school students, senior citizens, land-owners, and the heads of all the resource agencies in the state. I covered topics ranging from red-cockaded woodpeckers to black panthers (or the lack thereof)!

Around 2006, I was asked to serve on a panel of speakers who would give presentations and field questions from the audience. Although questions from the audience always had the potential for mayhem, when you encouraged them with a panel of "experts" to answer them, you were sometimes asking for trouble. The panel included my good friend Dr. Jim Armstrong, the extension wildlife specialist at Auburn University; local extension agents Shane Harris and Tommy Futral; and Conservation Enforcement Officers Jeff Brown, Michael East, Jerry Fincher, and myself. At the time, I was serving in a partnership with the USDA Natural Resources Conservation Service as the private lands biologist for central Alabama.

320

Jeff Trips the Trap

Our topic was nuisance wildlife. The setting was a church fellowship hall in Willow Point, a ritzy lakeside community on Lake Martin in Tallapoosa County, where some residents had had their fill of Canada geese, white-tailed deer, raccoons, and coyotes. While you would think having a high population of raccoons and coyotes would help limit the population of Canada geese and white-tailed deer, these were the stated problems.

Midway through my career, I received numerous requests from landowners asking if I could acquire them some Canada geese for their lake. My answer was always the same: "No." I would explain that Canada geese are a federally protected species that is illegal for them to possess and furthermore, they really didn't want the birds on their recreational lake. Of course, this prompted the "Why not?" question. I would inform them the birds were often loud and aggressive and they pooped about every eight seconds. Even after receiving that glowing review, several would ask if I was sure I couldn't get them some!

Fast-forward about fifteen years and I received numerous calls from folks asking if there was anything they could do to get rid of these %&#! geese. I often could not resist the urge to ask what the problem was. The most common answer was, "They poop on everything!" You only had to slide down in goose poop on your dock a time or two to develop a deep hatred for the birds. It was very common to receive calls concerning someone who had either shot a goose or killed one with a golf club. I kid you not.

Willow Point was and still is heaven for deer. The grounds are all manicured and adorned with many aesthetic species that deer find very palatable. Although hunting is allowed in much of the area, the deer quickly learn to stay close to the houses. Seeing a deer in your yard is neat. Seeing twenty deer eating flowers on your porch, not so much! That's not to mention the high incidence of deer/car collisions.

Seeing how the community was developed around forty-four-thousand-acre Lake Martin, most areas were great raccoon habitat. Even with good natural habitat, both raccoons and coyotes could not resist the bird food and pet food that were often present. In addition, the coyotes were not above making off with a pet when the opportunity presented itself.

Jim had brought several traps and noisemakers used to deter various species. Prior to any landowners' arrival, we were looking at the display and someone commented on the different sizes of leghold traps used for different species and actually set one of the traps and laid it on the table.

As people began to arrive, Jim said we had better not leave the trap set since someone would surely end up with their finger caught in it. He asked if anyone had a pencil he could use to spring the trap. Jeff spoke up and said he would handle it. We did not immediately realize Jeff was evidently in the midst of a brain fart! However, this became blatantly obvious to even the most casual observer when Jeff retrieved the ink pen from his pocket and placed it on the pan of the trap. The jaws of the trap snapped shut and the pen instantly shattered.

I don't know if everyone has had something happen to them when everything went into super slow motion; however, this was one of those times. As I watched Jeff extend his arm, pen in hand, toward the trap, I could not believe it was happening. However, once I realized what was taking place, my mind was yelling "stop" but nothing was coming out of my mouth. When the pen hit the trap pan, releasing the jaws of the trap, the slow-motion perception was in full swing. The plastic barrel of the pen was no match for the steel jaws of the trap and the ink was released like a Tasmanian devil!

Although it happened in a fraction of a second, I swear I could see the black ink flying through the air and landing on my khaki

322

pants, on Dr. Armstrong's white shirt, and on the light blue carpet covering the floor of the fellowship hall. We all stood in stunned silence for a few seconds, wondering if this had really happened. The black ink covering everything let us know it was all too real and we immediately began the search for cleaning supplies.

We located some cleaner and began working on the carpet. I felt certain the folks that started filling the hall were somewhat confused by all the agency personnel on their hands and knees feverishly scrubbing the floor. After applying some rigorous elbow grease, the floor was in pretty good shape so we turned our attention to trying to clean our clothes. By this time, the ink was set and very difficult to remove.

Unfortunately for me, the ink had not only gotten on my pants, it had landed on the crotch and the thigh of my pants. I went to the bathroom and, after scrubbing with soap and water, I was able to turn the few ink spots into a rather large wet spot and stain. I'll give you one guess as to who the first person was who got to stand in front of the crowd.

I debated whether to let those in attendance in on what had occurred or to just leave it to their imagination. Although I tried to explain to the fifty-seven people in attendance what had happened, I could tell by the looks on their faces and the obvious lack of eye contact their imagination was working overtime! However, the show must go on.

Something I learned through my career was if you were dealing with more than one person, you would likely have a difference of opinion. This was true whether you were talking about how to manage a deer herd, how to prepare a dove field, or, as in this case, what constituted a nuisance animal. While we had anticipated the folks in attendance wanted to hear some advice on how to combat the deer, raccoons, Canada geese, and coyotes that were causing them multiple problems, we had not necessarily anticipated the residents that would show up in defense of the animals. You have probably heard the old saying "one man's trash is another man's treasure." Well, sometimes one person's nuisance animal is another person's beloved species.

We did not expect that, but we should have. When we began to tell the crowd some ways to dissuade the animals from frequenting their yards and homes, we were quickly informed that not everyone wanted to keep the animals away. It was quickly brought to our attention that part of the problem was the residents who were actually putting food out for the various species. We quickly surmised this wasn't going to be an easy fix.

We did our best to answer the questions asked while trying to consider everyone's point of view. That type of diplomacy was often required in our job. Animal damage problems were often difficult to solve even when the folks were working together!

I cannot mention this type story without including an incident that occurred in Elmore County coming to mind. I had received a crop damage complaint, which was not at all unusual in the summer. These calls ranged from deer eating someone's okra to deer destroying large fields of vegetables, beans, and so forth. Unfortunately, later on these complaints changed to wild hogs destroying huge crop fields. This call, however, was a backyard garden call.

I arrived on scene and met the landowner. As we walked to the rear of their home, they were explaining that the deer had been coming into their garden regularly and were eating a little bit of everything. Once I saw the garden, I could understand how deer in the garden would be a problem, seeing how the garden covered about one hundred square feet. It was obvious the deer had made quick work of the few plants in the garden. However, the small garden spot wasn't all I had spotted. As I looked at the deer feeder hanging from the tree about ten yards from the garden spot, I was thinking surely this guy hadn't been feeding the deer here. I walked over to the feeder and, sure enough, there was corn on the ground beneath it. I looked at the landowner and asked, "Are you feeding the deer?"

The fellow replied that he thought that if he put the feeder up, maybe the deer wouldn't eat the plants in the garden.

I asked, "So how's that been working out?"

He shook his head and said, "Not too good."

I tried to tactfully explain that the addition of the corn doubled the incentive for the deer to come and feed and, as he had seen, they did not discriminate between the crops and the corn. I explained I would not be able to issue him a crop damage permit since he was actively attracting the deer to the area and because there was nothing left in his garden for the deer to eat.

You might be surprised to learn that many times I have had gardeners tell me they had planted a small garden patch near the wood line or somewhere else close by in an effort to keep the deer from feeding in their garden. It rarely works.

I realize I have covered a lot of ground in this story. Suffice it to say, don't lure deer to your garden if you don't want them to eat it. It is difficult to keep deer, geese, raccoons, and/or coyotes off your property if your next-door neighbor is feeding them. And finally, and possibly most important, don't use an ink pen to trip a trap! Lessons for life.

Learning Lessons on Highway 259

I'M SURE EVERY conservation enforcement officer (CEO) has their favorite area to work in their efforts to apprehend those who will stoop to shining a light in a deer's eyes and shooting it at night. I know my favorite areas were those where I repeatedly caught violators. It would be my guess that when you explain to folks that people are out at night shining lights in deer's eyes and shooting them, those folks would likely assume this type of illegal activity would be occurring in the middle of nowhere. That assumption would be wrong. Sure, there were those who night hunted far off the beaten path; however, the majority hunted where the deer were and if that happened to be along the state highway, so be it. I learned a lot of "lessons" working with the two veteran officers in the county. I must admit, I was, as people around here often say, "green as a gourd," meaning I had plenty to learn.

It has been my experience that many residents in our rural county have no idea that people are shooting deer at night around their homes. Many people, due to various reasons, simply do not hear shots fired around their homes. On several occasions, I have heard a shot and, in an effort to better pinpoint it, I have called a nearby homeowner and asked if they heard it. These calls have revealed a couple of things. First, many folks don't pay a lot of attention to what is going on around them. Second, many folks are reluctant to report someone shooting outside their home. I must admit that makes little sense to me. A prime example of this was the night I heard a shot from my house. I went to the location where I thought the shot had come from and found several family members outside the house. When I pulled into the driveway, my headlights illuminated a deer lying in the yard. Investigation revealed someone had just shot the deer from the road and that wasn't all. At least one of the buckshot pellets had penetrated the wall of the home, knocking a picture off the wall inside the house! The startling part of this was they had not called and reported the incident to anybody! That incident is chronicled in the story titled "They Shot My House" in my book *It's Not Easy Wearing Green.*

I've got to say I just can't understand someone having their house shot into and not calling and reporting it. However, I think back to a documentary from probably thirty years ago. As I recall, it was entitled *Wildlife Wars.* It told of an undercover night hunting investigation in the northeast United States. The officers involved stated they had shot deer both day and night in people's front yards, backyards, side yards, and under their security lights and not one call was received from the public concerning the activity. I thought that was amazing then. Today, I'm not so easily surprised.

Alabama Highway 259 was basically a cut-through road that ran between Alabama Highway 9 in the Equality community of Coosa County and Alabama Highway 22 in Alexander City in Tallapoosa County. Early in my career, the highway was a night hunting hotspot. As a matter of fact, it was where I had my first night hunting experience catching three night hunters six days after I was hired! It was also where I had a night hunter try to shoot my partner one night. (See "By the Grace of God" in

Parables from Poachers). It was a memorable place. For many years, our first night hunting complaint of the season would come from Highway 259. Therefore, it was deemed a honey hole and I guess that's why CEO Hershel Patterson and I were sitting alongside the road in the dark on a cool November night.

We were sitting pretty close to the road, seeing how it was pretty wet and Hershel's Ford Crown Victoria wasn't a great off-road vehicle. It was good on the road, good in a chase, and pretty comfortable but it had its limitations off the roadway. As we sat with the windows down, we heard the telltale roar of a set of mudder tires on the highway coming in our direction. As we listened to the tires' rhythmic whining on the pavement, we could tell the vehicle was slowing down. While we were listening, I was visualizing the truck rolling to a stop and I was hoping a deer standing alongside of the road was the reason. Almost as soon as the tire noise stopped, a shot split the night. Immediately we could hear the *wah-wah-wah-wah* of the tires as the vehicle accelerated toward us.

Soon we could see the illumination from the headlights. We let the vehicle pass our location and we pulled in behind them. Hershel activated our dash-mounted blue light. Our windows were still down and I noted that as the truck slowed down, it sounded just the same as when we had heard it stopping earlier. The vehicle pulled to the right side of the road. There appeared to be two people in the truck. As we were getting out of the car, Hershel simply said, "Watch their hands." I was still new to this and thankfully he was constantly mentoring me. Hershel went up on the driver's side and I approached on the passenger's side.

As he neared the driver's door, he gave the loud verbal command for the people to put their hands up. Being able to see their hands provided a modicum of security. However, knowing a shot had just been fired from this vehicle, we were still on high

328

alert. Hershel asked the driver where his gun was and he replied he did not have one.

Let's go on a little aside here for a minute. Another lesson I learned early on was to listen to how people answer questions. You must remember many violators think they are smarter than those apprehending them. They erroneously believe by carefully crafting their answers to questions, they achieve some type of plausible deniability. I've often thought if they were that smart, they likely wouldn't be being arrested!

When you ask the driver of a vehicle where the gun is and they reply that they don't have a gun, you must understand they did not say there isn't a gun in the vehicle, they just said they did not have one. I probably need to mention that when an armed law enforcement officer is approaching you and a shot has just come from your vehicle, it is not wise to parse words!

When the fellow said he did not have a gun, Hershel replied that if he didn't have one, he must have thrown it out the window because we had just heard them shoot and there wasn't anyone else on the road. I had been told it was not uncommon for night hunters to throw their gun out the window if they thought they were about to be apprehended. However, in this case, I felt certain we would have seen them throwing the gun out since we were on them really quickly.

Little did I know I was about to learn yet another lesson and I was going to realize that Hershel was somewhat of a prophet. Hershel had opened the driver's door, so I reached up and opened the passenger side door. When the door opened, a shotgun fell out on the ground! I picked up the gun and carried it back to our vehicle.

Another lesson I'd been taught was to ALWAYS unload the gun and place it in our vehicle. If you were to place a loaded firearm on someone's tailgate or the hood of our vehicle, someone could knock you down and grab the gun and shoot you. Before I placed it in our vehicle, I opened the action on the pump shotgun and ejected a spent shell. That was another lesson. Violators often know that we can identify whether or not a spent hull was fired by a particular gun. For that reason, people who shoot from the roadway often utilize guns such as bolt actions or pump actions that do not automatically eject the fired cartridges, thereby not leaving any "evidence" at the scene. Finding the spent hull in the shotgun solidified, in my mind, that these folks were guilty. I placed the gun in the front floorboard of Hershel's car.

Earlier that evening, Hershel had reminded me that night hunters often carried their guns between themselves and the door. A long gun carried in that manner is almost impossible to see by looking in the window since it can be totally hidden by the person's body. While this lesson was fresh on my mind, I had not anticipated it falling out on the ground! I saw this numerous times during my career.

I returned to the truck and watched the two individuals while Hershel searched for any more weapons. Finding none, he told both of the young men to hand over their driver's licenses. Still trying to deny what had happened, they handed us the licenses. We had them sit back in their truck while we wrote citations for hunting at night, hunting from a public road, and hunting by the aid of a vehicle.

We returned to the truck and explained the bonding process. The driver again stated they had not shot anything. I noted he did not say they had not "shot at" anything. Hershel looked at the man and asked, "Have you seen anybody come by while we have been sitting here?" The man answered, "No." Hershel then said, "There wasn't anybody that came by immediately before you got here and your vehicle was the only one on the road and you are the ones that shot." He then told the man he had two options. He could sign the bonds we had prepared or we could load them into our car and take them to jail. They decided to sign the bonds. I learned another good lesson when Hershel told the man that cases were not decided on the side of the road and he could plead his case in court. In a somewhat belligerent tone the driver said, "We'll be there."

I wasn't sure just what to expect in court. Although the fellow had been adamant that they had not been the ones who fired the shot, we knew they were the only folks around. I had noticed the passenger, who in all likelihood had fired the shot, was not nearly as confident as the driver. I was thinking it was going to be interesting hearing him explain having the gun in a position where he could not get in or out of the vehicle without moving it. Looking back, if I had known then what I know now after thirty-five years of experience, I definitely would have pulled the passenger off to the side and taken a statement. Another lesson I learned was with a significant case, it was always good to take a statement from folks if possible, even in the case of an on-view arrest.

About six weeks later, we entered the courtroom and I immediately spotted the two violators. Finally, the judge called the first man's name and told him to approach the bench. Hershel stepped up and told the judge there was a codefendant in this case and the judge said to get him up there. Hershel turned and motioned for the other man to come forward. The judge read off the charges and looked at the defendants and asked, "How do you plead?" Both men pled guilty. So much for an interesting trial! That was another lesson. You never knew what would happen in court!

I eventually realized that while every case was different, they were also all similar. By reading books written by game wardens from across the country, I have learned things are much the same everywhere. When I set out to write my first book, I consulted with Terry Gross, the author of *Wildlife Wars* and several other best-selling game warden books. One of the things he told me was that it was necessary to write these books for the benefit of other officers who might pick up a technique or tip that might prove valuable for them. I really had not thought of the books as being a how-to type thing but hopefully it will help others learn some lessons.

During the past season, I received a call from the sheriff's office dispatcher at 9:30 p.m. stating someone had just shot on Highway 259. I asked exactly where and she gave me the address. I told her I was sitting in the driveway at that address two nights earlier! Some nights were better than others.

Gun Launch at
Shady Grove

IT WAS A FAMILY OUTING. The cool, clear night was just right for a drive through the country. Mom was behind the wheel with the kids in the backseat. Dad was riding shotgun—literally!

I have penned several stories lamenting about how difficult it was to find an area with a good place to utilize the deer decoy with a corresponding place for the officers to hide and observe the violators. That type of place where all of the elements were in close juxtaposition was indeed a rare find. However, I was fortunate to have worked a few of those places and one of the best ones was on Shady Grove Road in Clay County.

Wildlife biologist/Conservation Enforcement Officer (CEO) Gene Carver and CEO Andy Howell introduced me to the area. Gene had often accompanied the former Clay County game warden, Lee Bonner, who had worked the area for years. Gene relayed to me that Andy had received some night hunting complaints in the area and asked if I would be interested in working it with them. He added it was an ideal decoy setup site and I quickly agreed to help.

Clay County was just north of and very similar to Coosa County. It was a very rural county with forestry being the number-one industry. The good habitat coupled with the low number of residents was a combination that resulted in good wildlife populations and when you had that, you had violators.

Arriving at the area, I quickly realized Gene's assessment was dead-on. The area consisted of about three-quarters of a mile of paved county road with a house (the complainant) on one end. There were two open fields adjacent to the road about one-half mile from the house. The timber had been cut along the remainder of the road and the area had grown up in brush. Across the road from the fields were two old logging roads slightly higher than the paved road. There was enough brush for concealment yet it was open enough for us to be able to observe everything. The only thing lacking was a deer standing in the field and a vehicle to come down the road.

Fortunately, we could supply the deer for the field. The deer decoy was and is a tremendous tool for wildlife law enforcement. Many people erroneously assume the decoy is a huge buck no one could resist. The truth of the matter is my first decoy was a small-bodied buck with a dinky three-point rack. We had to retire him when his chest resembled Swiss cheese. Although we referred to him as Timex because he could take a licking and keep on ticking, he soon had so many holes in him that he would barely hold together. We then purchased a new decoy. This one came with a movable head and tail. It had a small six-point rack with about a twelve-inch spread. Very few hunters would consider it a trophy; however, you would not know that based on how many folks shot it!

Although we could supply the deer in the field, the traffic was something else. With only eleven thousand residents, there really wasn't a lot of traffic anywhere in the county. However, the area was a high probability area in that anyone who did travel the road was a dang good prospect!

We hid our trucks in the secluded road and carried the decoy to the field and got it hooked up and situated. After making sure it was functioning properly, we started back toward the truck to perform a road test of the deer. Even in this good spot, a road test was important to make sure the deer appeared natural and wasn't leaning over or his head hadn't got turned around backward or anything. There was nothing like the feeling you got after sitting patiently for hours and then going to retrieve the deer to find it had actually fallen over and had not been visible for no telling how long. I always tried to make periodic inspections of the deer for just this reason. That was one thing that made this such a good spot since the deer could be observed from the comfort of the truck.

We made final adjustments and headed toward the truck. Just as we stepped into the road, headlights appeared to the north. There would be no time for a road test. We hurried toward our trucks as the vehicle neared our setup. The car was moving quickly. Too quickly to be hunting, I thought. However, I also remembered what my mentor, Coosa County CEO Hershel Patterson, would always say whenever I said a vehicle was going too fast to be hunting, "They've got brakes." Hershel was about to be proved correct once again.

We were only twenty yards from the road when the car, a small, compact model, passed by. Within seconds, the brake lights came on and the car did an immediate U-turn in the county road. It hurriedly came back to our location and turned into the open field with the headlights shining on the decoy. Just as soon as the car came to a stop, the passenger blasted the decoy with buckshot from a shotgun. Although we were somewhat stunned at how quickly the events had unfolded, at the sound of the shot, Gene and I took off toward the vehicle on foot. When we reached the road, which only took a few seconds, we identified ourselves and yelled at the occupants of the vehicle to put their hands up.

We each had our flashlights trained on the vehicle when the passenger launched the shotgun! Evidently all of his adrenaline kicked in as he decided to get rid of the weapon. I don't know any other way to explain how someone could throw a long gun that high and that far from a car window! Seriously, I bet the gun went at least twenty feet in the air and landed in the field in front of the car and near the deer, which was still facing the violators. We now knew where that weapon was; however, it was not at all uncommon to find more than one weapon in the vehicle. We yelled for the driver to turn the car off and we cautiously approached. We soon learned there were five occupants in the small vehicle. I took the front-seat passenger from the car and placed him on the hood and handcuffed him while Andy did the same with the driver. Gene covered us and then tended to the three in the back seat.

All officers have at one time or another had to deal with multiple subjects. It was one of my least favorite things to do. It was normally always my preference to keep the subjects in the vehicle. This way they were a lot easier to monitor. When you get multiple subjects out of the vehicle and around you, it is a very uneasy feeling. Multiple subjects definitely increased the danger level of any night hunting situation. Although Gene had kept the three in the car, they were becoming increasingly unruly and vocal. The subjects were apparently extremely upset that the front-seat passengers had been removed from the vehicle and were now face down on the hood being checked for weapons. Although I had made a lot of stops and dealt with multiple subjects numerous times, I could not remember ever dealing with a situation just like this one. Not only were the oral protests growing louder but now one of the subjects in the back seat had literally started kicking and screaming.

With our violators secured, Andy and I moved over to assist Gene. Gene was doing all he could but was obviously no match for the trio. After we had ascertained there were no more weapons in the car, a quick decision was made to uncuff the driver and let her deal with the three in the back seat. You see, some things a mother just does best and these three children wanted their momma. The unruly passengers were ages two, four, and six and evidently did not like having their parents arrested!

We advised the shooter of his rights and questioned him concerning the family outing. He stated he had been required to work all day and did not have a chance to hunt so he had told his wife, "Let's go kill something." You always wanted to include a telling phrase like that in your statement. He stated they had loaded up in the family car and headed for Shady Grove. We wrote the two adults tickets for hunting at night, hunting from a public road, and hunting by aid of a vehicle. After we explained the bond-signing procedure—including the part about how if they went to jail, their children would likely be turned over to the Department of Human Resources—they were allowed to sign their bonds and go on their way.

The cases were set for Clay County District Court with the Honorable Judge George Simpson presiding. I always enjoyed Judge Simpson's court; after he realized what we were up against (that's another story in itself), he was tough on violators. He was very much by the book. If you had a good case, you would get a good verdict and the sentence would get the violator's attention! The judge called the cases and the husband and wife approached the bench. The judge asked if they wanted an attorney and they stated they would proceed without one. He asked how they pled to the charges and they replied, "Guilty." I appreciated what the judge would do at this point in the trial. He would ask the arresting officer if he had any comments about the case and then if he had a recommendation concerning the sentence. This gave the officer the opportunity to let the judge know if the defendant had been a horse's butt or if there were any aggravating circumstances and also allowed the officer to ask for the minimum fine if they felt that was in order.

Gene spent his entire career in Clay County and had become very adept at using this part of the trial to his advantage. He had the knack of saying just the "right" thing to convey his feelings about the case and this day was no exception. Gene stepped toward the judge's bench and stated the subjects were very cooperative and there were no problems during the incident once the children were calmed down. The comment was not lost on the judge, who looked at Gene and asked, "You mean they had children with them?" Before Gene could respond, the husband demonstrated that either he had been in this situation previously or had watched a lot of *Matlock* on TV when he said, "Judge, he can't say that. We pled guilty." The judge quickly gave a brief, yet blatantly clear, law lesson. He told the defendant the officer would answer any question the judge posed to him and he, the defendant, would keep his mouth shut until he was asked a question. The judge looked at Gene with a look that said, "Tell me."

Gene stated the defendants did in fact have their three small children, under six years of age, in the vehicle on the night of the incident. The judge was visibly upset by this information. He stared at the paperwork before him and looked at Gene and asked something I had never before heard a judge ask: "What is the maximum amount I can charge these people?" We quickly added the numbers and gave the judge the total. We also mentioned the charges carried up to thirty days in jail and a three-year revocation of hunting privileges. The judge promptly sentenced the pair to nearly $6,000 in fines and costs and jail time. The husband stated the wife could not go to jail because she was scheduled for surgery the next morning. I knew telling the judge his wife couldn't do what the judge had just ordered wasn't a wise move. However, the judge held his composure. He looked at the man and asked what time her surgery was scheduled for. When the man replied six o'clock, the judge replied, "I'll tell them to let her out at five o'clock!" He followed that by informing the pair they were now in the custody of the sheriff.

Reflecting on that case reminds me of several assumptions made by young officers and the general public that are normally wrong. The people were not in a truck, like most people think they will be. There was a woman involved. This wasn't the only time I had caught women night hunting. They had their small children in the car. Fortunately, I've only witnessed that a few times. Most people would have thought this was just a family out riding around to look at deer. I have encountered many families doing just that. Thankfully, most were not armed with a shotgun. There is no typical profile of a night hunter. As a matter of fact, the next ones we caught there were totally different. Man, that Shady Grove was sure a good decoy place!

This story is filled with life lessons. As you read, the judge was more than a little upset upon learning the couple had their three young children in the car. I think that was because the judge had seen more than his share of folks who had been led astray and ended up in front of him. I think most people emulate their parents in some ways. We all serve as examples to someone. That may be good or bad.

The Bible speaks clearly to this in Matthew, Mark, and Luke, where the Lord says if anyone causes one of these little ones, those who believe in me, to stumble, it would be better for them if a large millstone were hung around their neck and they were thrown into the sea. It doesn't take a Bible scholar to figure out that if you set a bad example for a little one to follow, Jesus takes it seriously. He sees it all.

Epilogue

ONCE AGAIN AS I relive these stories I have to stop and thank the Lord above for allowing me to survive them. There were a lot of good ole boys who shot decoys, hunted over bait, ran from the law, and hunted at night. It was definitely a mixed bag. One of the best aspects of my job was how each day was different. I have been blessed.

As I was doing the final edits on this book, I received a call informing me of the death of another retired conservation officer. A condominium in Florida collapsed and over one hundred people are unaccounted for. A tragic traffic accident took the lives of eight girls from the Tallapoosa County Sheriff's Girls Ranch. They were returning from a trip to the beach. There were a total of seventeen vehicles in the wreck. A father and his nine-month-old daughter were killed. We never think that will happen. I fear we often forget just how fragile life is. We shouldn't. It can be gone in the blink of an eye.

I realize I've lived a charmed life. I appreciate the love and support of my family and friends. My wife supports me in every endeavor and loves me despite my faults, which are many.

I am truly blessed.

I would like to thank retired conservation enforcement officer (CEO) Byron Smith for his friendship, mentorship, and support. I appreciate the many stories he allowed me to use in this book. I thank the other CEOs that contributed and encouraged me in this endeavor. I thank Dr. Jeff Fuller, my pastor, for his support. There are many others and I thank you all.

Most of all I thank the Lord above for sending His Son to die in my place. He died for you as well. Romans 10:9–10 says if you declare with your mouth "Jesus is Lord" and believe in your heart that God raised Him from the dead, you will be saved. Choose Him. Do it today.

God bless.

www.ingramcontent.com/pod-product-compliance
Lightning Source LLC
Chambersburg PA
CBHW072048020426
42334CB00017B/1435